CW00326613

James Boswell, in the costume of a Corsican chief

BLUE GUIDE

CORSICA

Roland Gant

Maps and Plans by Andras Bereznay

A. & C. Black
London

W. W. Norton
New York

First edition 1987

Published by A & C Black (Publishers) Limited
35 Bedford Row, London WC1R 4JH

© Copyright Roland Gant 1987

Published in the United States of America by
WW Norton & Company, Incorporated
500 Fifth Avenue, New York, NY 10110

Published simultaneously in Canada by
Penguin Books Canada Limited,
2801 John Street, Markham, Ontario L3R 1B4

British Library Cataloguing in Publication Data

Gant, Roland
   Corsica.—(Blue guide)
   1. Corsica—Description and travel—
   1981– —Guide-books
   I. Title   II. Series
   914.4′94504838   DC611.C812

   ISBN 0–7136–2844–8

ISBN 0-393-30374-8   USA

PREFACE

What has Corsica to offer visitors that is different from what can be found in other parts of Europe with Mediterranean shores? Taking the sea first, Corsica has a phenomenally varied 1000km coastline, bathing to suit all tastes and ages, underwater fishing and exploration, wind-surfing, sailing and sea angling. Accommodation ranges from modern hotels to well-appointed camping sites with a wide choice in between.

This is the most familiar picture of the attractions of the 'nearest of the faraway islands' and since pearly clichés are formed around grains of truth Corsica is in fact 'a mountain in the sea'. Within a few kilometres of the shore are landscapes of soaring peaks—many snow-covered for most of the year—dramatic gorges, tumbling torrents and forests of gigantic pines. There are almost unlimited possibilities for mountain walking, on the GR 20 long-distance path that runs diagonally through nearly all the island, and on many other well-marked paths, for rock-climbing, pony-trekking, river exploration by canoe and kayak and, in winter, an ever-increasing number of ski centres.

Add to Nature's gifts to Corsica the enduring evidence of Man's presence during more than 4000 years and there is something to attract and interest everyone. Archaeological discovery has increased rapidly during the past 40 years, both at sites first recorded by Prosper Mérimée a century and a half ago and at others, Neolithic, Bronze Age, Greek and Roman, which have been discovered since and are still being excavated. Pisan churches, Genoese fortresses and watch towers, medieval religious paintings, Romanesque and Baroque flourishing in unexpected and unheralded places, and many museums devoted to every aspect of Corsican life—one can observe and relish the richness of Corsican history, and the acute regional variations in the way of life, throughout the whole of the island.

There is also the pleasure of just being in and absorbing the atmosphere of the farmlands, vineyards, olive groves and orchards. All this generous variety is packed, yet never diminishes the sense of wide open space, into an island 180km long by 80km wide at its maximum, with an area of 8800 square km or 3352 square miles, third largest island in the western Mediterranean, and a population of just under 300,000. A few comparisons: Cyprus 9250 square km, pop. 645,000; Jamaica 10,960 square km, pop. 2,080,000; Puerto Rico 8900 square km, pop. 3,435,000. Of roughly the same area: Lincolnshire and Leicestershire, pop. 1,386,100; Connecticut, pop. 3,142,500; Grampian Region of Scotland, pop. 469,168; Delaware is smaller but has a population of 587,600. So wherever you come from you will find room to breathe and move around freely in Corsica.

There is also the attraction of being in a country which, although an integral part of France, has an individual and colourful history of foreign occupation, courageous patriotism, and a strongly developed sense of identity as a people with a language of its own and of being different in history and tradition from the French and Italian mainland, just as Scotland and Wales (the latter includes the language question) are from England. The feeling of being 'separate' does not in any of the three countries imply widespread political separatist feeling or opposition to the parent countries' international outlook and actions. War memorials in all of them all testify to the extent of sacrifice. In World War I Corsica lost 40,000 men, more than any other French département.

Corsican bandits used to figure in the sensational press like Aberdonian skinflints and stagecoach robbers were to Scotland and the western USA. The bandits were not criminals as a rule but men who had taken to the dense *maquis* brushwood (giving French Resistance movements a name later) after some clan killing carried out in the harsh Corsican vendetta tradition. There are no longer bandits but extreme separatists and their actions serve as fuel for sensational headlines in French newspapers. Often their exploits are exaggerated and have little in common with carefully planned (usually foreign-aided) 'terrorism' such as exists in so many countries throughout the world today. Property in Corsica is sometimes damaged, human beings rarely and tourists never. After many visits to Corsica over a number of years and having met people of every shade of political conviction, my advice is not to give a second thought to alarmist newspaper reports. At the same time, observe the courtesy, as one should anywhere, of not trying to involve one's hosts in political discussion.

Corsicans, with centuries of invading foreigners much in mind, were for long less than enthusiastic about the development of tourism in their island but rapidly and within the past few years the importance of the industry to the local economy has been accepted readily and efficiently. My experience of Corsican hospitality has been almost limitless. People such as those unaware that I was writing this book who, on being asked the way or for the key of the church invited me into their houses for a cup of coffee or local wine and cheese, a man who after a casual conversation in a restaurant paid for my dinner on his way out, those who without question included me in planning a convoy of cars to drive across the island to the funeral of (after Napoleon Bonaparte) Corsica's most famous son, the singer Tino Rossi. Proud of their land, Corsicans welcome visitors with warmth, courteous dignity and a 'polite eagerness to share the beauty and blessings of their island with all who choose to seek its special qualities.

Acknowledgments

I wish to thank the following for their help while I was preparing this book. The nature of their help is so varied that space allows only an alphabetical list but my gratitude is unlimited. Antoine Angeleri, Madame Judais-Bolelli and the Association des Amis du Parc Naturel Régional de la Corse, Jacques and Victor Cangioni, Dorothy Carrington, Paul Ciavaldini, Jean Baptiste de Peretti, Cathy Dolphin and Continental Shipping and Travel Co., London, Christiane Dutron and Air France, Nice, Simeon Fonci and the Centre de Secours, Galéria, French Leave, London, French Travel Service, London, Douglas Matthews and the London Library, Abbé Millelini of Bonifacio, Antoine Milanini, Michel Mohrt of the Académie Française, Frank and Polly Muir, Tamara Nicolini, Jean Olhagaray, Jean Pagni, Antoine Piereschi and SNCF Chemins de Fer de la Corse, Daniel Vidoni.

The Etapes Hotelières Corses organisation and the generous owners, directors and staff of the hotels in that group who offered me hospitality. And all those whose names I never knew, for inviting us into their houses for food, drink and information, for delaying a hunting trip to put us on the right path up a mountain at 3.30 am, a restaurant owner who spent an hour helping to repair a car and six young men who left their village café to lift bodily back on to a mountain track the same car on another occasion. Nadia Legrand I thank for encouragement, companionship, photographs and advice, and Tom Neville and Blue Guides for much help and infinite patience.

CONTENTS

III CENTRAL CORSICA

Maps and plans

Maps

Plans

BACKGROUND INFORMATION

Geography

Corsica is the fourth largest island in the Mediterranean, after Sicily, Sardinia and Cyprus. Its area is 8720 sq km (3367 sq miles) and its greatest length, from the tip of Cap Corse in the N to the Straits of Bonifacio in the S is 183km and at its widest point it is 83km. 'A mountain in the sea', Corsica has a wide and attractive variety in its landscapes but the island's backbone is granite mountains of which the highest are Monte Cinto (2710m), Monte Rotondo (2622m), Paglia Orba (2525m), Monte d'Oro (2389m), Monte Renoso (2352m) and Monte Incudine (2128m). A central depression running NW–SE, where there are no peaks over 700m, divides the granite ranges from the schist mountains, much more recent in formation, of eastern Corsica.

Geographical division made virtually two Corsicas through the centuries when roads barely existed and transport was by foot and hoof. The En Deçà-des-Monts was 'this side of the mountains', i.e. the E which was colonised from the Italian mainland, consisting of Cap Corse, Castagniccia, Casinca, the Eastern Plain, the lowlands of the interior and Balagne. L'Au-Delà-des-Monts was 'beyond the mountains' and comprised the jagged and beautiful W coast, the Ajaccio region, the SW and S of the island and the E coast as far N as Solenzara. There are similarities in topography and native character between Corsica and Scotland where the Highland Line marks the great subsidence of the Central Lowlands and separates the Highlands from the Southern Uplands.

In 1974, when Corsica became once again two départements of France, La Haute Corse and La Corse du Sud followed in general the ancient En Deçà and Au Delà partition.

The W coast is irregular with the gulfs to which the rivers flow from the watershed for the most part rocky, studded with sandy coves below the dark red rocks. The E coast has long stretches of sandy shore, fewer rocks except in the N and S. Rivers slowed down by their passage through the alluvial plain formed marshlands close to the sea. Here the anopheles mosquito flourished and the resultant malaria, and repeated invasions by Vandals and Barbary pirates, depopulated the E plain following the departure of the Romans in the mid 5C. Drainage and irrigation systems became derelict and were restored only after the Second World War when the US Army's DDT had banished the mosquito from what Baedeker in 1907 called 'the malarious plain of Aléria'. A virtually uninhabitable and deserted part of the island has been transformed into a thriving agricultural area and tourism develops rapidly along the coast itself. As on the W coast which was developed for tourism much earlier, there are hotels in every category from *pension* to 4 star, camping sites, *villages de vacance*, châlets or 'bungalows', and self-catering *gîtes*. There is a fast-growing tourist development in mountain districts as well.

Climate

The Corsican climate is, not surprisingly, Mediterranean in character but with sharp distinctions according to altitude. Above 1500m is an

Alpine climate and the island has the distinction of being unlike practically anywhere else in that it is hotter in the N than in the S and the E coast is wetter than the W. Corsica gets more rain than southern mainland France and this keeps the island green. Most of the rain falls in the winter, beginning in November; snow is often heavy, with mountain passes blocked for weeks at a time in late winter and early spring. Summer is warm, sometimes very hot, but the evenings are fresh by the sea and cool, often cold, in the mountains.

The prevailing winds are from the SW, W and NW and are called *libeccio* and *mistral*. The *sirocco* blows on the E coast from the SW, the *levante* from the E, the *grecale* from the NE and the *tramontane* from the N. Whatever the temperature there is usually a breeze. The two most exposed points, at the top of Cap Corse in the N and at Bonifacio in the extreme S, are those subjected to the liveliest winds.

In short, the climate of Corsica is pleasant and offers a variety at all times of the year. When the mid-summer beaches are too hot to stay on all day, the cooler mountains are nearby. One can get down from the peaks and the ski-slopes to the shore well within an hour's drive.

Average temperatures at sea level

Month	Min.	Max.
April	8.9	18.5
May	11.7	22.2
June	15.7	28.1
July	17.8	29.4
August	17.8	29.4
September	16.1	27.2
October	12.2	22.2

Average temperatures of the sea

April	13.9
May	16.3
June	19.3
July	22.3
August	23.4
September	22.0
October	19.7

Historical Introduction

Corsica's history is as stormy and eventful as one would expect of an island, which is fertile in many parts, has plentiful water and whose high central mountain system forms a wall to protect the backs of defenders alert to invasion from the sea. Its favoured position made it a staging place on Mediterranean trade lanes and one of great strategic importance. He who held Corsica turned that 'mountain in the sea' into grit under the lids of predatory eyes looking from Europe and North Africa and into a reef on which acquisitive hopes could be wrecked.

There were people in Corsica some 8000 years ago. A human skeleton unearthed at the archaeological site of l'Araguina-Sennola has been dated to c 6570 BC and there is the later but abundant evidence at Filitosa, Cucuruzzu, Torre, Cauria and the numerous other sites (including many still to be discovered and examined) of continuous occupation by men who kept domestic beasts, cultivated cereals, fashioned weapons and defeated rivals or were defeated in turn by newcomers. But the sophisticated and calculated appraisal of

Corsica, its wealth and strategic value, came with the development of boatbuilding and seafaring. When the problems of transport, arrival and departure were solved, rivalry set in and Corsica began to be fought over like a succulent bone.

For the Greeks, who founded Alalia (Aléria) in 540 BC, Corsica was *Kyrnos*. Alalia existed as a Greek town and staging post on the way to the Greek settlement on the mainland at Massilia (Marseille) for 30 years and then the tussle for Corsica, which has marked its history through the centuries, began in earnest. The Greeks were beaten in a naval battle by the Etruscans and abandoned Alalia. Greeks from Syracuse drove out the Etruscans in 453 BC and in 280 BC the Carthaginians moved in. It was the E coast of Corsica that was always invaded, where landings were easier than on the rocky W coast and because of the relative closeness (82km) of the long Italian shore; the Spanish coast is 450km distant; Nice is 180km and Marseille 360km. It was the Greeks who brought contact with the outside world to Corsica. They also brought vines, olive trees and cereals. In 260 BC Carthage was driven from the E plain by the Romans who replaced Alalia with their city of Aléria, not as a mere trading port but, following Roman custom, as a military base for the conquest and subjection of the whole island. Corsican resistance delayed total conquest for a century but from 163 BC Corsica enjoyed nearly six centuries of comparative peace, acquiring Latin speech and Christianity. When the Roman Empire crumbled Corsica fell prey during the 5th and 6C to the Vandals, Ostrogoths and Byzantines in turn, and then in 725 to the Lombards who lingered for only 30 years.

In 755 the King of the Franks, the little but good Pepin le Bref (son of Charles Martel and father of Charlemagne) promised Corsica, when liberated from the Lombards, to the Pope and this was confirmed in 774 by Charlemagne. But the protection of the Papacy did not safeguard the island from Saracen raids during nearly three centuries until in 1077 Pope Gregory VII sent Landolfe, Bishop of Pisa, to assert Papal authority over Corsica and particularly over the Corsican bishops and nobles. There followed the two centuries of Pisan church and cathedral building, including some of the most beautiful buildings in the island (as at Murato and Nebbio). But also during those two centuries there was fighting between the forces of Pisa and Genoa who in 1133 were given by the Pope equal shares in the Corsican bishoprics.

The Genoese took Bonifacio and Calvi, and defeated Pisa in the naval battle of Meloria in 1284. It was at this time that Sinucello della Rocca, who became known as Giudice—the Judge—supported one side and then the other to his own advantage so that he succeeded in making himself master of Corsica. The Genoese, having defeated Pisa, captured Giudice through the treachery of one of his own bastards and kept him in prison until he died, aged almost 100 years.

If the Pisans built churches the Genoese built fortifications—the great bastions of Calvi, Bonifacio and Bastia and a ring of watchtowers around the coasts. Much of this defence work was raised by the Bank of Saint George. Apart from their troubles with the Corsicans, from beyond the island was the threat of the Aragonese whose kings had been invested with the sovereignty of Corsica by Pope Bonifacio VIII in 1297. The threat from the Aragonese did not come entirely from Spain because there were Corsican clan chiefs, the Cinarchesi seigneurs, who sided with Aragon the better to oppose Genoa. For a quarter of a century from 1376 Arrigo della Rocca, with the support of

Aragon, waged endless war against Genoa and often had more of Corsica under his control than had the Genoese.

Genoa reaffirmed supremacy through the Bank of Saint George which played a somewhat similar role to that of the East India Company in British India. And still the Cinarchesi resisted until they exhausted themselves and their resources. The last effective Cinarchesi leader, Rinuccio della Rocca, was assassinated—not by the Genoese who were hunting him and his pathetic little band but by Corsicans made desperate by the never-ending war. Corsica has seldom lacked characters and events of Shakespearean proportions. Rinuccio was one and so was Sampiero Corso. A soldier of fortune, colonel in the French army, leader of a rebellion against Genoa, betrayed and believing his wife was responsible, he strangled her, and then died fighting in an ambush in 1567.

The Genoese republic ruled Corsica directly until 1729 when widespread rebellion broke out, national independence was declared and a constitution adopted by a national assembly at Corte. There was a lull in 1732 but the Corsicans continued their revolt and a measure of how desperately they sought an alternative to Genoa was the crowning of the Westphalian adventurer Theodor von Neuhof King of Corsica in April 1736. He had talked merchants in Tunis into providing money and supplies and persuaded the Corsicans to set a crown upon his head at Alesani. Corsica's summer king left the island in November of the same year, his brief reign marked only by some coins minted as hastily as the titles he bestowed on some of his supporters. Six years later he appeared off the Corsican coast aboard a British warship but nobody was sufficiently interested in his restoration to invite him ashore.

The grip of Genoa weakened and the interest and influence of France increased during the 18C. Corsica's only period of independence was from 1755 to 1769 when Pasquale Paoli was elected General of the Nation, Corte became the capital, the university was founded, and the constitution drafted and adopted. Genoa finally ceded Corsica to France by the Treaty of Versailles (15 May 1768). The French army was opposed by Paoli's troops but their resistance was crushed at the battle of Ponte Nuovo in May 1769. Paoli left for England, returning in triumph to Bastia on 17 July 1790. Most Corsicans thought that the French Revolution would end all their troubles. It did not. Although Paoli was chosen President of the Conseil General of the département of Corsica there were intrigues against him, helped along by the Bonaparte family who were now in the ascendant. When an attempt was made to arrest him, a National Assembly at Corte proclaimed Paoli Father of the Nation and defied the orders from Paris. In the summer of 1793 Paoli and Charles-André Pozzo di Borgo, both of whom had been outlawed by the French Government, appealed to the British and in January 1794 Sir Gilbert Elliot landed in Corsica and discussed a constitution with Paoli. In June the Anglo-Corsican kingdom was announced at the national assembly at Corte and a constitution formulated and adopted. Paoli was head of the provisional government but, to his humiliation, Sir Gilbert was appointed Viceroy in October. The French Republican agents went to work to stir up riots and this kingdom (lasting a little longer than Theodore's) came to an end when Sir Gilbert and his forces left Corsica in early October 1796. French soldiers from Italy landed and occupied Corsica without meeting resistance on 15 October and from henceforth Corsica was French and subject to

French laws, to some of which sections of the population and particularly priests, who objected to the Civil Constitution of the Clergy, did not take kindly. Napoleon did not do anything special for his homeland but Corsica became a single French *département* with the capital Ajaccio, the Décret Imperial signed by that town's most famous son.

Perhaps the Corsicans did more for Napoleon than he did for them. On 4 March 1815 some Bonapartist agents landed secretly and organised a rising in support of the ex-Emperor. They defeated the Royalist garrisons and the island was governed until Waterloo by Arrighi de Casanova, a general created Duc de Padoue by Napoleon. Corsica had provided Napoleon with some 10,000 soldiers including over 40 generals.

Improvements to the island economy, now an integral part of France, continued steadily throughout the 19C although meeting with resistance, as in agriculture, from the general wish not to change farming methods. Communications improved: the E and W, for so long virtually two lands separated by the mountains, were brought in touch by the new roads and the railway begun in 1887. The salvation of the malarial E coast had to wait for the US army in 1943. In 1908 Clemenceau, then Minster of the Interior, announced a long-term plan for further improvements in Corsica, a plan which was a victim of the Great War of 1914–18.

Emigration increased and Corsicans continued to swell the French army, the French police force and civil service, in fact almost every job carrying a pension which helps return to the native isle.

The Italian and German troops soon found the Corsicans more than a match for them. The term *Maquis* came to mean during WWII any resistance organisation but obviously it originated in Corsica where it took one Axis soldier to control two Corsicans, including women and children. Corsica was the first département of France to be liberated, through Corsican efforts aided by the Allies from 1942 onwards, until the Axis departure in late 1943.

Corsica's progress since the end of the WWII has been rapid and impressive. In 1957 plans were made by the French government to revitalise and develop Corsican agriculture and SOMIVAC (*Societé de mise en valeur agricole de la Corse*) was set up. There was a certain amount of opposition from farmers and shepherds to changes in their centuries-old working methods and living habits but persuasion, aided by practical education in how to improve quality and increase yield, extensive help with money, machines, irrigation, selling and transport of produce, triumphed in the end. At the same time as SOMIVAC, another organisation was created for the expansion of tourism which it was obvious could earn a lot of money on an island so blessed with sun, sea, mountains, good harbours, little traffic and a large amount of space. SETCO (*Societé d'équipement touristique de la Corse*) also met with some initial opposition by an island race, proud, independent in mind and outlook, fiercely attached to a traditional way of life, who feared erosion of tradition, language and manners through massive and repeated invasions by 'Continental' aliens bringing decadence and condescension with them. The growth of tourism was not like this and most Corsicans (there are always diehards— Little Corsicans like Little Englanders and US Isolationists) have come to welcome with warmth and dignity most tourists. There are always a few unpleasant tourists who are treated with basic 'correctness' but nothing more.

The material help given to Corsica to develop profitably in these two fields was tangible proof that the island was not a neglected offshore département, a poor appendix of the Provence-Côte d'Azur Region from which it was separated in 1970 and named as a Region in its own right. In 1974 Corsica was divided into two départements, Haute Corse and Corse du Sud. Not only did this division into roughly the traditional En Deça des Monts and Au dela des Monts appeal to the conservative in outlook, but in creating Ajaccio prefecture de la Corse du Sud and Bastia préfecture de la Haute Corse much was done to damp down ancient rivalry. The reopening of the University of Corte in 1981 and the granting to Corsica of its own Regional Assembly in 1982—the first such assembly in the whole of France under the decentralisation laws—underline the importance of Corsica as an integral part of France while at the same time acknowledging the island's history, specific local differences and requirements which can be most sensibly dealt with by authorities on the spot.

The international Press, and particularly the French newspapers, give much space to Corsican nationalist movements and their aspirations and demonstrations. How strong and how violent are these parties? Varying from demands for autonomy to complete independence, the parties have frequently regrouped and changed names. The one likely to impinge on the tourist consciousness is the *Front de Libération Nationale de la Corse*—and that because the letters FLNC are sprayed on walls, bridges and public offices. Sometimes the movement claims responsibility for an explosion but it is usually small and confined to military or other government targets and seemingly organised to avoid anybody getting hurt. Such protests and the changing of place names, mostly substituting 'u' for 'o' and Corsican spelling to replace French or Italian, e.g. Porti Vechju for Porto Vecchio, are closer to similar protests in Wales and Scotland than to those in the Spanish Basque country or Northern Ireland. As happened in Wales, e.g. Conwy for Conway, the spray-canned vernacular is being overtaken by the official road signs which are generally clear to the tourist faced with a different, older spelling on the map.

As for the likelihood of getting hurt, delayed on the road or railway, of being awakened by things that go bump in the night, forget it. The idea of nationalist gunmen behind every tree can be relegated to historical limbo along with mountain bandits and malarial swamps.

Is there any language difficulty? No more than there is in Wales, Provence or Brittany. Just as there are Bretons who are much more at ease in speaking their language than French, so there are older people in isolated parts of Corsica who in the main converse in Corsican. Should you by chance encounter one he or she will always call somebody more at home in French. Everybody speaks French, the language taught in schools, there are Italian speakers in Bastia and Porto Vecchio, and in the larger towns there are people who speak or at least understand English. Corsicans are as proud of their language as the Bretons, Welsh and Gaelic speakers of Scotland and Ireland are of theirs. The minor courtesy of learning a few words and phrases in Corsican brings appreciation of the effort in smiles and sometimes a cup of coffee, a local cake or a glass of wine. Corsicans have an innate and dignified sense of hospitality. Try never to refuse and certainly never try to pay for a gift of any kind although it is in order to give chocolates to children and to offer cigarettes to adults.

The origins of the Corsican language are not clear cut and have attracted many theories, some as far-fetched as the 19C belief that

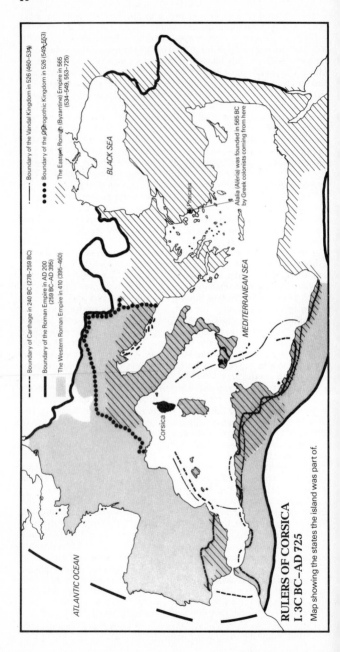

RULERS OF CORSICA

I. 3C BC–AD 725

Map showing the states the island was part of.

- - - - Boundary of Carthage in 240 BC (278–259 BC)
———— Boundary of the Roman Empire in AD 200 (259 BC–AD 395)
The Western Roman Empire in 410 (395–460)
●●●● Boundary of the Vandal Kingdom in 526 (460–534)
Boundary of the Ostrogothic Kingdom in 526 (549–553)
/////// The Eastern Roman (Byzantine) Empire in 565 (534–549, 553–725)

ATLANTIC OCEAN

BLACK SEA

MEDITERRANEAN SEA

Corsica

Phocaea

Alalia (Aléria) was founded in 565 BC by Greek colonists coming from here

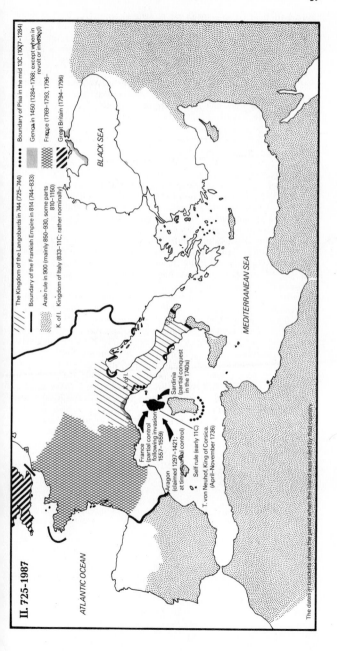

II. 725–1987

Legend:

- The Kingdom of the Langobards in 744 (725–744)
- Boundary of the Frankish Empire in 814 (744–833)
- Arab rule in 900 (mainly 850–930, some parts 810–1150)
- K. of I. Kingdom of Italy (833–11C; rather nominally)
- Boundary of Pisa in the mid 13C (1067–1284)
- Genoa in 1450 (1284–1768; except when in revolt or invaded)
- France (1769–1793, 1796–)
- Great Britain (1794–1796)

ATLANTIC OCEAN

BLACK SEA

MEDITERRANEAN SEA

France (partial control following invasion 1557–1559)

Sardinia (partial conquest in the 1740s)

Aragon (claimed 1297–1421; at times partial control)

Self rule (early 11C)

T. von Neuhof, King of Corsica. (April–November 1736)

The dates in brackets show the period when the island was ruled by that country.

there had been Welsh-speaking American Indians. Leaving aside the myths of the survival in 'the mountain in the sea' of a tongue now vanished, whether Greek, Celtic, Iberian, Ligurian, North African or 'pure Latin', it can be fairly said that Corsican is neither *patois*, nor an Italian dialect.

The language spoken by the first people to inhabit the island has left no traces but there are echoes of the pre-Latin language in some place names. Although the Roman conquest was complete by 111 BC, Seneca, exiled to Corsica around AD 40–49, described the natives as ferocious and their language incomprehensible. Latinisation nevertheless took place slowly and subject to fluctuations of accent, pronunciation and variety of meaning. This formed the basis of the Corsican language which was then subjected to Tuscanisation, particularly in the E of the island, during the time of Pisan occupation. Genoa, who occupied and ruled the island for some 500 years, used Tuscan as its official language and Tuscan was retained by the French for all state and legal documents until the middle of the 19C. Until the early years of the present century Church business was conducted not in French or Latin but in Italian. Osmosis between Corsican and French is minimal because the two languages are used side by side. There is therefore no problem of 'Francorse' such as there is of 'Franglais' in Continental France. Due to a determined campaign by the Scola Corsa, the island's cultural federation, the French Government recognised Corsican as a 'regional language' in 1974.

Corsican has always been the language spoken in the home, at work and in the streets and cafés. Songs have been transmitted orally from generation to generation, such as the *chiama e rispondi*, a dialogue improvised in 16-syllable lines, and the *voceri*, lamentations composed and sung by a woman for the newly dead—often *vendetta* victims— and having much in common with the old authentic American blues. Ancient Corsican hymns are sung by participants and spectators on Saints' Days and other religious processions such as the Catenacciu on Good Friday. Collections of songs were noted and published during the 19C but it is particularly from the middle of the present century that Corsican syntax, spelling and vocabulary have become subjects for enthusiastic and close study and that a vernacular literature has developed and flourished.

Have a good Corsican day

good day good morning	how do you do	bondiornu
good evening	bona sera	
good night	bona notte	
how are you?	cumu state (coomoo stahty)	
how do you say that in Corsican?		cumu si dice in corsu?
		(coomoo see deechay in corsoo?)
good-bye	a vedeci (ah vedaychi)	
farewell	addiu	
yes, no	yé, no	
bread	pane (pahnay)	
Corsican wine/red/white/rosé	vinu corsu/rossu/biancu/russulatu	
a minute	u minutu	
an hour	un'ora	
a day	u diornu (deeornoo)	
tomorrow	dumane (doomanay)	
breakfast	u spuntinu (spoontinoo)	

luncheon	a cullazio
dinner	a cena (a chena)
what is the time?	chi ora e? (key ora eh)

A Chronology of Corsican History

3rd millen-nium BC	Archaeological discoveries (e.g. menhirs, dolmens) record megalithic civilisation in Corsica, Mediterranean Bronze Age.
2nd and 1st millennia BC	End of Bronze Age. Torréen ('tower builders') civilisation in SE of island. Name derived from circular tower monuments of death rites significance. Examples Torre, Cucuruzzu. The *torre* similar to Sardinian *nuraghi.*
c 565 BC	Alalia (now Aléria) founded by Phocaeans (Greeks from W coast Asia Minor) on E coast, later same century taken by Etruscans and Carthaginians.
259–162 BC	Romans conquer E coastal plain, first building Aléria on site of former Alalia, then founding colony of Mariana. Central mountainous region unconquered.
2–4C AD	Growth of Christianity in Corsica. Martyrs include Restitute, Julie, Devote, later canonised.
5–6C	Invasions by Vandals and Ostrogoths. Vandals hold Corsica until defeated by Byzantine force, commanded by Belisarius, in 534.
522	Corsica and Sardinia incorporated in Byzantine Empire.
8–10C	Frequent Saracen invasions.
c 725	Corsica annexed to Kingdom of Lombardy.
774	Charlemagne confirmed gift of Corsica by his father Pepin le Bref to the Papacy in 754. Thenceforth the Pope titular sovereign of the island.
1014	Pisa and Genoa join forces to eject Moors from Corsica.
1077	Pope grants rule of Corsica to Bishop of Pisa.
1133	Pope divides Corsica between Pisa and Genoa.
1264	Sinucello della Rocca, nobleman of Cinarca, gains control of Corsica by favouring Pisa and Genoa turn and turn about and becomes known as Judge, Giudici di Cinarca.
1284	Definitive victory by Genoa over Pisa in naval battle of Meloria.
1296	Pope hands Corsica and Sardinia to Kingdom of Aragon.
1306	Giudici di Cinarca dies in Genoese prison.
1347	Genoa supplants Aragon as ruler of Corsica but hindered by ravages of Black Death which kills two-thirds of population.
1358	Rising under Sambucuccio d'Alando. Creation of Terre des Communes, agreement between Corsican people and landowners. Latter support Aragon against Genoa.
1378	Arrigo della Rocca, Aragon partisan, lands in Corsica. Genoa assigns control of island to a Genoese financial organisation, la Maona.

1404	Arrigo's nephew, Vincentello d'Istria, named Lieutenant in Corsica by Aragon. Gains control of most of island, notable exception Bonifacio. Captured and executed by Genoa 1434.
1453	Genoa assigns Corsica to another financial organisation, the Office or Banque de Saint Georges. The Banque had its private army, rebuilt fortresses, set watchtowers around the coast, founded the present town of Ajaccio and ruled Corsica with iron hand for a century.
1553	Henri II of France, at war with Charles V of Holy Roman Empire, invades Corsica with help of Turkish fleet and support of Corsicans under Sampiero Corso, Corsican patriot and colonel in French army. Calvi and Bastia hold out against France who hand Corsica back to Genoa in 1559.
1564–67	Sampiero Corso raises rebellion against Genoa. Controlled island for a while. Betrayed and assassinated in ambush 1567.
1571	Amnesty accorded by Genoese Governor and publication of *Statuti civili et criminali di Corsica*.
17C	Known as the Century of Misery, Corsicans chafe helplessly at harsh administration by Genoa's officials.
1676	Genoa gives permission for 700 Greeks, in flight from Turks, to settle in Corsica, first at Paomia near Sagone and then at Cargese.
1729	Beginning of armed revolt throughout the island—Corsican War of Independence.
1731	First National Constitution adopted at a National Assembly at Corte.—Genoa asks Austria for help in crushing insurrection; four battalions of Imperial troops land in Corsica.
1736	Theodor von Neuhof, Westphalian adventurer, lands from English ship at Aléria on 11 March with money and munitions provided by Greek and Jewish merchants in Tunis. Crowned King Theodore I of Corsica at Alesani 15 April, achieves nothing, leaves Corsica 11 November.
1739	French suppress, at request of Genoa, revolt led by Gaffori and Giacinto Paoli (Pasquale's father).
1741	French troops withdraw.
1743	Corsicans supported by Sardinia and Britain, planning to occupy and divide the island, during Austrian War of Succession. British warships twice bombarded Bastia in 1745 and 1748.
1747	Successful landing by French.
1753	Genoa plots and succeeds in assassinating Gaffori.
1755	Pasquale Paoli elected General of the Nation on 15 July. His Constitution for Corsica adopted by National Assembly November, University founded at Corsica from 1765, l'Ile Rousse created as rival port to Genoa's Calvi.
1764	France occupies Corsican fortresses in name of her ally Genoa. Paoli refuses to serve France.
1765	James Boswell meets Paoli at Sollacaro in October.
1768	Genoa cedes Corsica to France.

1769	Corsicans, under Paoli, defeated by French forces at Ponte Nuovo, 8 May. Paoli leaves for England. Napoleon Bonaparte born Ajaccio 15 August.
1789	Corsican Constituent Assembly votes 30 November that 'The island of Corsica is hereby declared to be part of the French Empire and its inhabitants subject to the same consitution as all other French...'.
1790	Paoli lands at Bastia in triumph 17 July. At Congress of Orezza in September elected Commander in Chief of the Corsican National Guards. Later appointed President of the départemental Conseil General.
1790	Corsica accorded, as a département of France, same administrative, judiciary and religious organisations.
1793	Failure of expedition against Sardinia. Paoli and Pozzo di Borgo indicted and order for their arrest issued. Corsican National Assembly opposes French Government and proclaims Paoli Father of the Nation. Paolists enter Ajaccio, loot houses of pro-French families, including that of the Bonapartes. Napoleon, serving with French military and naval forces who fail to take the town, gets his mother, sisters and her half-brother Fesch away by sea to Toulon on 11 June. Paoli and Pozzo di Borgo declared outlaws by French Government on 17 July and they appeal to Britain for help.
1794	In January British envoy Sir Gilbert Elliot arrives in Corsica and discusses with Paoli the creation of an Anglo-Corsican kingdom which is proclaimed at National Assembly at Corte in June. Paoli head of government until October when Sir Gilbert appointed Viceroy. British besiege and capture Saint-Florent, Bastia and Calvi where Nelson loses an eye.
1796	At end of September British withdraw from Corsica. Paoli returns to London. In October French forces re-occupy Corsica unopposed. In December Corsica divided into two départemes on advice of Napoleon.
1807	Paoli dies in London, buried in Saint Pancras. On 3 September 1889 his ashes buried in private chapel at his birthplace, Morosaglia. Bust of Paoli in Westminster Abbey.
1811	Corsica declared a single département with Ajaccio as centre of administration for whole island.
1814	Bastia appeals to British for protection against French severity. Troops landed but withdrawn when Napoleon abdicates.
1839–40	Prosper Mérimée visits Corsica as Inspector of Historic Monuments. His discoveries stimulated interest in Corsican archaeology and 'Colomba', his novel set in Corsica, brought to the attention of readers outside the island the Corsican phenomenon of the *vendetta*.
1850	In the mid 19C emigration increases.
c 1860	British discover Corsica (e.g. Edward Lear, Thomasina Campbell).
1887	Work begins on Corsican railway.
1882	Introduction of compulsory education. Schools built.
1914–18	Corsica loses some 40,000 men in the Great War.

1920–40	Mussolini reiterates Italian claims to 'Nizza, Corsica, Tunisia'.
1940–43	Corsica occupied by Italian and German troops—one soldier to two Corsicans, men, women, children.
1943	Italians surrender 8 September. Germans continue to fight the Partisans—the original Maquis. End of 1943 Corsica first French département to be liberated. US troops stationed in Corsica clear E coast of mosquitoes and resultant malaria, opening the way for post-war agricultural development.
1957	Plans for Corsican economic growth in two domains, agriculture and tourism. Formation of SOMIVAC (Société de mise en valeur agricole de la Corse) and SETCO (Société d'equipement touristique de la Corse).
1970	Corsica separated from 'Provence-Côte d'Azur Région' and made a Région in its own right.
1972	Creation of the Parc Naturel Régional de la Corse.
1974	Corsica reverts to being two départements of France, now called Haute Corse and Corse du Sud.
1981	The University of Corsica reopens at Corte.
1982	In accordance with French intention to decentralise government Corsica becomes first region to elect a regional Assembly.

Bibliography

A selection of books in English. There have not been many outstanding books about Corsica in English and most of them are out of print. Three classic works, spaced by chance precisely by a century one from another, are in print. They are the *Journal* of James Boswell (1768), the *Journal* of Edward Lear (1870) and Dorothy Carrington's *Granite Island* (1971).

Boswell, James. *An Account of Corsica: the Journal of a Tour to that Island, and Memoirs of Pascal Paoli* (London, 1768). Contained in *Boswell on the Grand Tour: Italy, Corsica, and France 1765–1766*, edited by Frank Brady and Frederick A. Pottle (Yale Editions of the Private Papers of James Boswell; New York and London, 1955). Boswell showed himself to be much more than a diligent reporter. His heart was in that journey and the visit to Paoli. 'Having resolved to pass some years abroad for my instruction and entertainment, I conceived a design of visiting the island of Corsica...I should find what was to be seen nowhere else, a people actually fighting for liberty'. On his return to England he worked tirelessly for the Corsican cause and when Paoli lived in London in exile Boswell introduced him to Samuel Johnson, feeling like 'an isthmus that joins two great continents'.

Lear, Edward. *Journal of a Landscape Painter in Corsica* (London, 1870). More than anyone else it was Lear who gave the outside world an idea of what Corsica's fortresses, mountains and laricio pines looked like. The impact of the island's landscape is reflected in his dramatic and romantic engravings.

Carrington, Dorothy. *Granite Island: a Portrait of Corsica* (London, 1971. Paperback edition, Penguin, London and New York, 1984). Recipient of the Heinemann Award 1971, the reissue in paperback of this, the best book in English about Corsica, is invaluable as the intelligent visitor's guide to the island, its history and its people. The author has lived in Corsica for more than 30 years and everything she writes about the island is lit with shrewd and loving understanding. *Granite Island* is 'based on the observations of a visit to Corsica in 1948, interwoven with experiences and researches spaced through the next 20 years'. Among her many writings on Corsica (one hopes they may be brought together and published in book form one day) are 'Cardinal Fesch, a grand collector' (*Apollo*, London, November 1967), a fine introduction to the Fesch collection in Ajaccio when the museum is reopened; 'Rediscovery of Roman Corsica' (*Geographical Magazine*, London, March 1960). Her latest book is *Napoleon and his Parents on the Threshold of History* (London, 1987). Dorothy Carrington (Frederica, Lady Rose) read English at Lady Margaret Hall, Oxford, has lectured in many countries, was decorated in 1986 by Jack Lang, French Minister of Culture, as Chevalier de l'Ordre des Arts et des Lettres and in the same year was one of three historians to represent Corsica at the XVI Consortium on Revolutionary Europe (1750–1850—French and American Revolutions and the Corsican Revolution 1729–69 against Genoa) at the State University of Florida, Talahassee, Florida.

Mérimée, Prosper. *Colomba* (Paris, 1840). Mérimée (1803–70), travelling in Corsica in 1839 as inspector of ancient monuments for the French Government (reported in his *Notes d'un voyage archéologique en Corse*, Paris 1840) met at the village of Fozzano, 21km E of Propriano in the SW of the island, the 64-year-old widow Colomba Bartoli, *née* Carabelli, who had been at the heart of a vendetta between her family and the Durazzo in 1833. The two fortified houses of the respective families are still there. Taking the story of this vendetta as his inspiration but transferring the scene to the north of the island, Mérimée wrote his novel about 'Colonel Sir Thomas Nevil, a distinguished Irish officer of the English army...and his daughter Lydia' who become involved with the participants in a vendetta. There have been several translations of this lively and convincing evocation of the Corsican approach to life, honour and vengeance. Mérimée's short story 'Mateo Falcone' is a vignette of the code of honour in face of betrayal which overrides even paternal love. The history of the real vendetta in Fozzano is told by Dorothy Carrington in *Granite Island*.

Moracchini-Mazel, Geneviève. *Corse Romane* (Paris, 1972). Profusely illustrated with photographs and ground plans of romanesque churches, this invaluable book for dedicated church-watchers incorporates a translation of the French text into English by Alan McLeer—and into German by G. Checher. Among the author's other books, only in French, are *Les Monuments paléo-chrétiens de Corse* (Paris, 1967), *Les Eglises Romanes de Corse* (Paris, 1967), and, with the collaboration of Dorothy Carrington, *Trésors oubliés des églises de Corse* (Paris, 1959).

Biographies and works of general interest. Among the books in English, most of which are out of print but can be consulted in many libraries, the best life of Paoli to date is *Pasquale Paoli: an Enlightened Hero* by Peter Adam Thresher (London, 1970). There are biographies of Theodor von Neuhof, who ruled as Theodore I, King of Corsica, from April–November 1736, by Valerie Pirie, *His Majesty of Corsica* (London, 1939), and by Aylmer Vallance, *The Summer King* (London,

1956). Perhaps his most lasting memorial is the tablet erected to his memory by Horace Walpole when the debt-ridden Neuhof died in London in 1756. It is still on the wall of the air-raid-damaged church of St. Anne's, Soho, London, above that to the memory of Hazlitt. More readily noticed in Soho is a pub called 'The King of Corsica'.

The Anglo-Corsican Kingdom lasted a little longer than that of Theodore—it was proclaimed in June 1794 and ended in September 1796 with the departure of Sir Gilbert Elliot, the Viceroy. The second volume of the three-volume *Life and Letters* of this humane, liberal and aristocratic Scot (his education in Paris was supervised by David Hume and he spoke fluent French and Italian) was prepared by his great-niece, Emma Eleanor Elliot, Countess of Minto (London, 1874). He was the best kind of British administrator, his love of Corsica was genuine and he in turn was held in affection by Corsicans. When he was created Baron Minto in 1797 he chose to have the Corsican Moor's head emblem incorporated in his arms. His letters retain a freshness that evokes the island of his time. An indication of his feeling for Corsica is his enthusiastic likening of it to Scotland—'but with a fine climate'!

An ingenious comparison between his native Corsica and Scotland was made by Joseph Chiari who served the Free French cause in the UK during the Second World War. *The Scented Isle: a parallel between Corsica and the Scottish Highlands* was published in Glasgow, 1945. Equally ingenious and readable is Chiari's *Corsica: Columbus's Isle* (London, 1960), a lively presentation of Calvi's claims to be Columbus's birthplace. The energetic Scottish spinster Thomasina Campbell demonstrated her love for Corsica in her *Notes on the Island of Corsica* (London, 1868). The title page states that she is 'of Moniack Castle, Scotland', there is a frontispiece of the forest of Valdoniello by her friend Edward Lear and many a reference in the lively accounts of her Corsican travels to *her* native land.

A selection of books in French. *Corse: les Guides Bleus* (Hachette, Paris, 1983) conforms to the high standard of this series, particularly for those travellers who know more, or wish to know more, about French history. A reasonably good knowledge of French is required to make the most of this and of the *Michelin Guide* (Clermont-Ferrand, 1983). For bibliographical details of books and guides to the Corsican Parc Naturel Régional and the GR 20 long distance path, see the end of Rte 16.

de la Torre, Michel. *Corse: l'art et la nature des 360 communes de la Corse* (Paris, Nathan: Promotion Culturelle, 1985). An inexpensive paperback for the pocket, one of a series covering all the *départements* of France, giving compressed details of history, prehistoric sites, architecture, museums, folklore, sports, etc. Available in nearly all Corsican bookshops and at many newsagents.

Ettori, Fernand and others. *Corse: Ecologie, Economie, Art, Littérature, Langue, Histoire, Traditions populaires* (Le Puy, 1984, Ency-clopédies Regionales/Christine Bonneton). Six contributors, mostly academics, each dealing with a particular aspect of Corsican life, make this profusely illustrated and beautifully produced book of 370 pages—at the price of a luncheon—worthwhile before-and-after travel reading for the serious researcher with a good command of French. It can be bought in most good bookshops in both Corsica and mainland France.

Panassié, Louis and Verdeaux, Laurent. *L'Ame Corse* (Paris, 1979). A large-format, good introduction to and souvenir of Corsica with not-too-difficult text and many fine photographs in colour (17 of them taken by Jonathan Robertson, who taught History of Art at Bristol University before going to live in Corsica with his Corsican wife).

Grosjean, Roger. *La Corse avant l'histoire* (Paris, 1981). 'I had a premonition, at Filitosa, that I had stumbled on a find of great significance...I reported (those) statue-menhirs....Organised prehistoric research in Corsica had to wait for several years until the arrival of Roger Grosjean. Together we went to Filitosa. We saw the statues Jean Cesari had shown me...' (Dorothy Carrington: *Granite Island*, Chapter 3). In the past 35 years Roger Grosjean has had the satisfaction of seeing and generally overseeing the prodigious archaeological discoveries in Corsica. Member of the Centre National de la Réchérche Scientifique and Director of the Centre de Préhistoire Corse and of the Filitosa investigations, this book is a clearly written guide to the Corsican sites, illustrated with photographs, drawings, charts and plans. Among Grosjean's many other books is a 32-page illustrated guide to Filitosa, on sale at the site and, with his other publications, in bookshops throughout Corsica.

PRACTICAL INFORMATION

Approaches to Corsica

By Air: At the present time there are no direct flights from the UK to Corsica but there are frequent Air France and Air Inter connecting flights from Paris, Nice and Marseille to Ajaccio, Bastia, Calvi and Figari. In summer there are Air Alpes flights from Nice, Chambéry and Hyéres to Ajaccio, Bastia, Figari and Propriano. Full and up-to-date information from all French Tourist and Air France offices. Among UK companies specialising in travel/hotel/package holidays to Corsica are French Leave, French Travel Service, Cox and King.

By Rail and Boat: For information contact French Railways Ltd (SNCF), French Railways House, 179 Piccadilly, London, W1V 0BA (tel. 01-409 1224), and Continental Shipping (SEN), 179 Piccadilly, London W1V 9DB (tel. 01-491 4968).
Motorail: There are no through journeys, contact SNCF (tel. 01-409 3518) and Continental Shipping (see above).

Ferries and passenger boats: There are car-ferry and passenger services to Ajaccio, Bastia, Calvi, l'Ile Rousse and Propriano from Marseille, Toulon and Nice, varying in frequency according to season. Run by the State SNCM (*Société Nationale Maritime Corse-Méditerranée*) all details may be obtained from French Tourist Offices.
Corsica Ferries provide services between Genoa, Savona, San Remo, La Spezia, Leghorn to Bastia and Calvi, varying according to season. Information from both French and Italian Tourist Offices.

General information on travel to Corsica can be obtained from the French Government Tourist Office, 178 Piccadilly, London W1. Their offices in the USA are at: 610 Fifth Av., New York; 645 N Midrigan Av., Chicago; 9401 Wilshire Blvd, Beverly Hills; 360 Post St, San Francisco, 2050 Stemmons Freeway, Dallas. In Canada, at 1840 Ouest, Rue Sherbrooke, Montreal and 372 Bay St, Toronto.

Travel in Corsica

Motoring: Main roads in Corsica are good and well-maintained. Those in the mountains are often narrow, with passing places, and many tight bends. Very large cars or those towing caravans may experience occasional difficulties. Check with local people before setting off on a minor mountain road. Car hire can be arranged in most towns, at airports and larger places on the coast. In summer arrange hire as far ahead as possible.

Railway: The building of the Corsican railway system is a triumph of 19C engineering since the greater distance, and the most difficult part through mountains, was constructed from 1883 and only the final sections, through less difficult terrain, from Ghisonaccia to Solenzara, opened in 1930, and from Solenzara to Porto Vecchio, opened in 1935, were built in the present century. The total length of the network was 365km and there were plans to extend the line S from Porto Vecchio to Bonifacio. During the Second World War the railroad suffered heavily, 18 bridges being destroyed on the E coast section alone and four iron bridges and one stone bridge destroyed on the Bastia-Ponte Nuovo section. The retreating Germans also destroyed tunnels, galleries in the mountainside, and systematically demolished control systems, locomotives, rolling stock and station buildings. This trail of ruin was followed by the rise of the motor vehicle, improvement of roads and the decline of rail traffic and profits. The E coast section has never been brought back into use and the southernmost station before the track turns W and inland is Casamozza, half an hour from Bastia, on the way to Ponte Leccia, an hour and 47km from Bastia. The first part of this line, from Bastia to Biguglia, is now used as a 15-minute journey for commuters to Bastia. There are about six trains daily to and from Ponte Leccia where the railway divides into two lines. One goes N to the W coast and becomes the 'tramway de la Balagne' serving l'Ile Rousse, Algajola, and the beaches as far as Calvi. There are two trains daily from Ponte Leccia to and from Calvi. The distance from Bastia to Calvi is 120km and the time taken for a single journey is 3 hours. The other line turns S from Ponte Leccia to Francardo, Corte, Venaco, Vizzavona and stations in between to Ajaccio Gare and Ajaccio Port. There are four trains to and from the two places daily. The distance from Bastia to Ajaccio is 158km and the time taken for a single journey is 3.45 hours.

The Corsican railway is a wonderful way of seeing the landscape and particularly where it winds above ravines, over viaducts and bridges built despite all natural obstacles. The most picturesque section is that from Bastia to Ajaccio and the other branch is virtually a superb taxi service by diesel coach and trailers to the Balagne beaches. The rolling stock has been modernised and the system was made part of the French Railway organisation, the SNCF, at the beginning of 1983. Information is therefore available from offices of French Railways and French Tourist Information offices in all countries.

Sport

The Sea: Nearly everywhere around the 1000km coastline of Corsica there are ports, coves, creeks, estuaries and bays, making the island an ideal place for sailing. Boats of all sizes are on hire; windsurfers and submarine anglers and divers can rent equipment quite easily. (La Ligue Corse de Voile, fossés de la Citadelle, 20000 Ajaccio–21–07–79. Club nautique bastiais, quai Sud du Vieux Port, 20200 Bastia–31–27–78.)

There is good fishing around the coasts and in the mountain rivers and lakes. The fish available and equipment necessary vary considerably but the local Bureau d'Initiative can give advice and information.

The Rivers: The fast-running mountain rivers of Corsica now attract those interested in trying out their skills in canoes and kayaks. Equipment can be hired from March–May when the rivers are in

spate. (M. Santonacci, route des Sanguinaires, 20000 Ajaccio–21–39–
46.)

Pony Trekking: An excellent way of getting to know Corsica and very
well organised. (Association Régionale du Tourisme Equestre Corse,
Pinetu, Lucciana, 20290 Borgo–36–03–27.)

The Mountains: For a description of Corsica's long-distance mountain path, the GR 20, *see* Central Corsica 3 Le Parc Naturel Régional
de la Corse—the GR 20. (Informations Sentiers Randonnée GR, 8
avenue Marceau, 75008 Paris. Association Muntagne corse in liberta,
immeuble Girolata, avenue Napoléon III, 20000 Ajaccio–23–17–42
evenings. Informations Parc Naturel Régional de la Corse, Palais
Lantivy, 20000 Ajaccio–21–56–54.)

Ski: Haut-Asco (1480–1820m) Asco 20276. 76km from Bastia, 120km
from Ajaccio. Downhill, departure point for high-level ski route and
for climbing Monte Cinto (2710m). Two teleskis. Hotel-restaurant tel.
47–81–08.

Ghisoni (1580–1850m) Ghisoni 20227. 37km from Ghisonaccia, the
Station de Ski du Renoso is a downhill ski and mountain walking
centre in the Renoso (2357m) region. Two teleskis. A Parc Naturel
refuge with 15 beds and a hotel-restaurant (35 beds).

Vergio (1400–1600m). Vergio 20224. tel. 48–00–01. 100km from
Bastia, 80km from Ajaccio. Both downhill and cross-country and
mountain walking on the GR 20. Two teleskis. Hotel, bar, restaurant.
Chalet, village de vacance at Aïtone and hotel at Evisa.

Bastelica (1600m) Bastelica 20119 tel. 28–71–73 41km from Ajaccio.
Cross country ski centre. Hotels, bergeries and chalet.

Evisa (835m) Evisa 20126 tel. 26–20–08 70km from Ajaccio 20km
from Porto. Cross-country ski and mountain walks. Six hotels.

Quenza (805m) Quenza 20122 tel. 78–60–97 90km from Ajaccio,
50km from Porto-Vecchio, 45km from Sartène. The Centre Ecole de
ski de fond Coscione-Alta Rocca. Cross country ski and mountain
walking. Two bergeries and Parc Naturel refuge.

Zicavo (1600m) Zicavo 20132 tel. 24–40–05 60km from Ajaccio,
150km from Bastia, 80km from Corte Centre de ski de fond de
l'Incudine. Cross country ski and mountain walking. Three *refuges*
and one hotel-restaurant.

I THE WEST COAST

1 Ajaccio

Ajaccio (Aiacciu; 54,603 inhab.) is situated in the *Golfe d'Ajaccio*, the biggest gulf on the Corsican coast, measuring some 20km N to S and about 20km at its widest extent W to E. The town of Ajaccio is set along the shore in a wide S-facing bay on the N shore of the Golfe and is protected by a crescent of mountains on the landward side. It is to this position that it owes its exceptionally pleasant climate, mild in winter and warm in summer. Although sometimes very hot, the heat is alleviated by the sea breezes. Ajaccio's old town is at sea level, the streets of the business and office districts extend N while the mainly residential areas climb the slopes of the hills and have expanded W along the coast road to the Iles Sanguinaires. With its white buildings, palms and plane trees, it is the most French Mediterranean of Corsican towns, just as Bastia reflects the atmosphere and style of the W coast Italian ports. As the greatest distance in sightseeing is under 2km it is an ideal place to visit on foot.

Since 1975, when Corsica was divided into two départements of France, Ajaccio has been the Préfecture of the Corse du Sud, or capital of the southern region. In the same way Bastia is the capital and préfecture of the northern region—Haute Corse. In the past each town was for a while capital of Corsica. Bastia held the position in Genoese times and under France up to 1811 when Napoleon, who was said to have done so at his mother's request, made his home town the capital and reduced Bastia to a sous-préfecture, one of the many reasons for the Glasgow-Edinburgh or New York-Boston style of long-standing rivalry between Bastia and Ajaccio.

According to legend the name of the town is derived from Ajax but more probably it comes from *adjacium*, meaning a place where shepherds stopped on the way to the mountains with their flocks during the transhumance. The Romans came here and so, in the 10C, did the Saracens who destroyed it. Ajaccio subsequently passed under control of several of the warring clans including, in the late 14C, the Lords of Cinarca (the Cinarchesi), their enemies the Lecas, the Kings of Aragon, and Genoa. Unable to keep the Corsicans under control, Genoa ceded the island to the Banque or Office of Saint Georges, a powerful financial corporation with its own tough army. The Banque was responsible for fortifying the ports and setting up watchtowers.

Its rule ended in 1463 and, after Genoa again took control, Ajaccio passed to France in 1553 and then back to Genoa in 1559. The French began building the citadel which was completed by the Genoese who established firm authority over both the harbour which the citadel dominated and over Ajaccio itself from which Corsicans were banned. Genoa ruled despotically from 1562 until 1729 and the outbreak of the National Corsican Rebellion. There followed 40 years of confusion and fighting in the island, with repeated French intervention. In 1735 Paoli was elected General of the Nation and, after the defeat of his troops at Ponte Nuovo on 8 May 1769 by the French, he retired to England. Since that time Corsica has been French except for a brief period (1790–96) when Paoli returned in triumph and presided over the formation of the Anglo-Corsican Kingdom, with Sir Gilbert Elliot as Viceroy. In 1795 Paoli went into a second and final exile in England and in October 1796 the British left Corsica and the French returned.

In June 1793 Napoleon Bonaparte, a 24-year-old army officer, fled Ajaccio, sending his mother, Letizia (née Ramolino), and her younger children to Toulon. Their house was looted by the Paolists and, by an ironical coincidence, on the arrival of the British troops, Hudson Lowe, who was later to be in charge of the Emperor in exile at Saint Helena, was billeted in the Bonaparte house. In 1793, on the advice of Napoleon, the Convention divided Corsica into two regions. No longer known as the En Deçà des Monts and l'Au delà des Monts (meaning the areas to the E and W of the central mountains) they were re-named the

Départements of the Golo and the Liamone. Ajaccio was capital of the latter. In 1811 the two were reunited into one département, Corsica, with Ajaccio as sole capital of the island, and remained so until the reversion to two départements in 1975, Haute Corse and Corse du Sud.

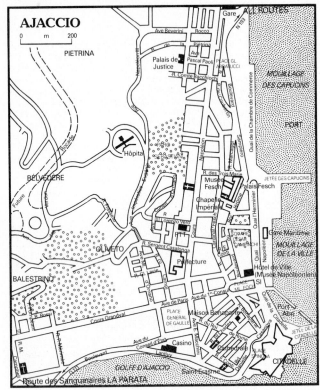

Ajaccio's history is very much that of Corsica as a whole: a succession of colonisations, occupations and foreign military intervention. The town is uniquely distinguished in two ways. Firstly as the birthplace of Napoleon Bonaparte (15 August 1769) and secondly as the first French town to be liberated from Axis occupation in World War II (9 September 1943) by the local Resistance forces. These were joined on 13 September by the 1st Battaillon de Choc, the first France Libre unit to set foot on French soil. The unit of 109 men had been brought from Algiers by the submarine 'Casabianca', commanded by Captain l'Herminier, which had frequently made earlier voyages to bring arms and supplies to the Corsican Resistance forces.

The PLACE GENERAL DE GAULLE is a good starting point with the Old Town to the SE and the modern parts of the town to the N. This large square, called until 1945 the Place du Diamant (the Diamanti family property was here) is rather characterless and around which (1986) much building of shopping centres, hotels, etc. is going on. It is a favourite spot for those Ajacciens who linger over a drink on a café terrace or sit on the stone public benches and look out to the Golfe or inland towards the rising strata of the suburbs. The square contains a *statue of Napoleon*, one of the town's many monuments to its most famous son.

Here he is depicted in Roman dress, on horseback, surrounded by his four be-togaed brothers: Lucien (1775–1840), Prince of Canino; Joseph (1768–1844), King of Spain; Louis (1778–1846), King of Holland; and Jérôme (1784–1860), King of Westphalia. The monument was cast in bronze by Barye in 1865 from plans by Violet-le-Duc. According to the eye of the beholder it is magnificent, pompous, grandiose, majestic, or comic, in the vein of 'A funny thing happened on the way to the Forum'. Sometimes referred to as 'The Inkstand', it is better to wait for this information be offered by an Ajaccien.

The Old Town extends to the E and S of the Place de Gaulle. From the Place follow the Avenue E. Macchini down to the sea and the Boulevard Lantivy where to the right is the Casino (and a large car park under the Place de Gaulle). Turn left and follow the quay to the turning into the Boulevard Danielle Casanova, a Resistance heroine (1909–43) who died in Auschwitz. The Place Spinola, half way along the Boulevard D. Casanova, faces the gateway to the **Citadelle** (begun by the French in 1554 and finished by the Genoese when the French left in 1559). It is massive, and until the invention of heavy naval artillery and aircraft must have been impregnable, as Genoa intended, built as one with the base of the rocky peninsula. Now a military installation and barracks, it is not open to the public. Follow the Boulevard Casanova to the Quai de la Citadelle and turn right to follow the *Jetée de la Citadelle* (200m long) from which there are fine views of the port, the town and the hills and mountains to the N and NE.

Alternatively, on leaving the Place de Gaulle take the Av. E. Macchini until the second turn left into the Rue Forcioli Conti, then again second left into the Rue St. Charles, at the corner of which is the **Cathedral of Ajaccio**, dedicated to Notre-Dame de Misericorde, *la Madonuccia*. It was built in Venetian Renaissance style (1554–93) to the plans of Pope Gregory XIII's architect, Giacomo della Porta. The proportions were reduced by Joseph Moscardi, the bishop of the time, who thought the building work would take too long. Reference to this is made (in Latin) in a frieze inscription above the entrance to the cathedral which records that the bishop in 1593, Joseph Giustiniani (whose arms were set above the plaque), laid the last stone. 'What wouldn't he have given to have laid the first'.

INTERIOR. Above the altar of the 1st chapel to the left, a Delacroix *Vierge du Sacré Coeur*. The chapel is decorated with stuccoes attributed to Tintoretto. To the right of the main door the white marble font which served at the baptism of Napoleon Bonaparte on 21 July 1771 (he was 21 months old). The first pillar on the left of the nave has a plaque in red marble bearing Napoleon's wish expressed shortly before his death: 'Si on proscrit mon cadavre comme on a proscrit ma personne, je souhaite qu'on m'inhume auprès de mes ancêtres dans la Cathédrale d'Ajaccio en Corse' (If my corpse is exiled [from Paris] as my living body has been I would wish to be buried beside my forebears in the Cathedral of Ajaccio in Corsica). The Bonapartes had traditionally been buried in their family vault in the cathedral and this continued until the Imperial Chapel (see Palais Fesch) was completed in 1858 on the orders of Napoleon III. 2nd chapel to the left, sculptures (1739) by the Genoese architect Garibaldi Solari, three 17C frescoes. The 3rd chapel on the left contains 15 small 17C paintings on the theme of the mystery of the Rosary. In 1811 Napoleon's sister, Elisa Bacciochi, Princess of Lucca and Piombino, Grand Duchess of Tuscany, presented to the cathedral the white marble high altar surmounted by four columns of Italian black marble veined with yellow. An 18C marble statue, the Immaculate Conception, in the 2nd chapel to the right.

On the right in the Rue Forcioli Conti, just before it joins the Rue Casanova, is the church of *St. Erasme*. Built in 1602, it was the chapel of the Jesuit college until the expulsion of the Jesuits. Later, during the Revolution, it was used as offices, was subsequently returned to being a chapel and was restored in 1932 and 1978. Erasmus is the patron saint of sailors and the chapel contains models of sailing ships as well as three Christs on the Cross which are carried in a religious maritime procession on 2 June of each year.

The Rue Saint Charles (formerly Rue Malerba) running NE from the Cathedral leads (200m) to the *Maison Bonaparte* or, as it was called when Napoleon was born there on 8 April 1769, the Casa Buonaparte. Built late 17–early 18C, it became the family home in 1743 and carries the Bonaparte arms on the façade. Facing the house is a small tree-shaded square, the *Place Letizia*, named for Napoleon's mother, in the middle of which is a bust of Napoleon's son, the roi de Rome, as a child, by Vézin (1936).

Napoleon's birthplace, Maison Bonaparte, Ajaccio

The **Maison Bonaparte** has since 1923 been a museum. (Open in summer: 1 May–30 September every day except Sunday afternoon and Monday morning 09.00–12.00 and 14.00–18.00. In winter: 1 October–30 April, every day except Sunday afternoons and Monday mornings, 10.00–12.00 and 14.00–17.00. There is a charge for the partly-guided visit which lasts about 40 minutes.)

On the ground floor a sedan chair in which, it is believed, Napoleon's mother, feeling the pains of oncoming childbirth, was brought back from the service in the cathedral to the house for the future emperor to be born. On the first floor the salon which Madame Letizia had enlarged and refurbished in Louis XVI style, upholstered in red damask (now reproduction). The work was carried out with her compensation money awarded by the Directoire in 1798 for the damage done by Paolist and British troops in 1794. Next to it is Madame Mère's bedroom with a big Louis XV bed. In the 'chambre natale' is the couch on which Napoleon was born. The 12m-long gallery with Italian inlaid wardrobes and looking-glasses give the room an air which it is unlikely to have had at the end of the 18C. Two small rooms with white walls contrast with the general décor. One of them is said to be Napoleon's room from which he escaped from the over-enthusiastic acclaim of his supporters in 1799. General Bonaparte, as he then was, together with Berthier and Murat let themselves out by way of a trap door to the ground floor.

On the second floor are four rooms. In the first of these are genealogical trees, portraits of the Bonaparte parents, personal possessions of Napoleon and of his father and, in facsimile, the *acte de reconnaissance de noblesse* of the Bonaparte family, which was approved by the Conseil Supérieur de la Corse, 13 September 1771. In another room are portraits of Napoleon's siblings and the third opens to an alcove where Napoleon may have slept on his return from the Egyptian campaign. A fourth room is given over to Napoleon III, the Empress Eugénie and their visit to Corsica (1860).

Bust of Napoleon's son, l'Aiglon, Roi de Rome, by Vezin, in the Place Letitzia opposite the Maison Bonaparte

Continue along the Rue St. Charles to where it meets the Rue Bonaparte, the *carrugio dritto* which divided the old Genoese city into the E district of Macello, a poor area mainly occupied by butchers, and the Petite Vendée to the W where the rich trades-people lived. The Rue Bonaparte leads to the PLACE MARÉCHAL FOCH, formerly called the Piazza Porta because it was the site of the only gate leading into the Genoese city (demolished in 1813). The square, well-shaded by palms and planes, is open on the E side to the port (many restaurants specialising in lobster and fish). In the centre of the square is a fountain (1827; by Maglioli, Ajaccian painter and sculptor) surrounded by four lions with woollen-toy expressions, and a statue of Bonaparte as First Consul, toga-wrapped, by Laboureur. A small statue, set in the niche of a house on the S side of the square, of *La Madunnuccia*, Notre Dame de Misericorde, patron of Ajaccio, bears an inscription in Latin: 'They have placed me here as guardian'. It recalls the appeal for protection from the plague of 1656 then raging in Genoa. The feast of the Miséricorde, 18 March, is celebrated each year by the citizens of Ajaccio.

On the N side of the square the *Hôtel de Ville* (1826) has the Syndicat d'Initiative office for Ajaccio and Corsica and the **Musée Napoléonien** (open summer 09.00–12.00 and 14.30–17.30, including Sunday, winter 09.00–12.00 and 14.00–17.00, Sundays and public holidays excepted. Same ticket covers the Musée Fesch). The museum is on the first floor of the Hôtel de Ville and contains portraits of the Bonaparte family, including a Winterhalter of Napoleon III with the Empress Eugénie and the Prince Imperial (son of Napoleon III, killed by Zulus in South Africa in 1879 while serving with the British Army). The baptism certificate dated 21 July 1771 shows that Napoleon was baptised at the same time as his sister Marianne, born on 1 July that year. The death mask taken at Saint Helena is here, in bronze. Collection of medals and coins, the latter commemorating outstanding events from 1797–1876.

Leaving the Place Foch by the W end, turn right into the narrow and busy Rue Cardinal Fesch to reach the **Palais Fesch and Musée**. (Open summer 09.00–12.00 and 14.30–17.30 including Sunday, except holidays; winter 09.00–12.00 and 14.00–17.00 excluding Sundays and holidays.) The palais was built between 1827 and 1837 under the direction of Cardinal Fesch (1763–1839), Archbishop of Lyons and half brother of Napoleon's mother, née Letizia Ramolino. There is a statue (1850) of the cardinal in the central court of the three buildings.

The N wing houses on the ground floor the LIBRARY, founded in 1800 by Lucien Bonaparte, then Minister of the Interior. It contains more than 50,000 volumes, including many valuable collections donated to the library. Many works on Corsica and Corsican history, rare first editions and medieval manuscripts. Reading room open to the public.

The MUSEUM is on the first floor above the library. From 1974 extensive reorganisation was carried out over a period of more than ten years to bring the museum into line with the cardinal's original intentions when he endowed it with his collection of 1200 paintings. Work continues to restore the Palais to its original state; in the past it has been variously used as a barracks and a high school. The collection in the *Great Gallery* is composed chiefly of paintings of the Italian school from the 14–18C including paintings by Botticelli (1444–1510), Cosimo Tura (1431–95), Titian (1485?–1576), Veronese (1528–88), Poussin (1594–1665), and Dughet (1615–75). The *Small*

Gallery or Bacchiochi Gallery contains paintings of the Flemish, Dutch and French schools, which were given to the town of Ajaccio by Felix Bacchiochi, husband of Napoleon's sister Elisa. In the *Salle des Reliques* are religious objects which belonged to Cardinal Fesch. Portrait of the cardinal by Pasqualini and furniture from the cardinal's residence in Rome.

The S wing of the Palais, the CHAPELLE IMPERIALE (1855–58) was built in Renaissance style on the orders of Napoleon III. It fulfilled a stated wish by Cardinal Fesch (1763–1839) that the remains of the Bonapartes be brought together in one place. The Imperial Chapel was left to the French nation in 1923 by Prince Victor Napoleon.

Nine members of the family are buried there: Napoleon's mother, born Letizia Ramolino (1750–1836); Charles (formerly Carlo), Napoleon's father (1746–85); Charles-Lucien (1803–57), son of Lucien and nephew of Napoleon; Napoleon-Charles (1839–99), grandson of Lucien and son of Charles-Lucien; two of Napoleon-Charles's daughters, Zenaide (1861–63) and Eugénie (1872–1949); Cardinal Fesch (1763–1839), Napoleon's half-uncle.

At the top of the vault stairway are the tombs of Prince Victor (uncle of the present prince, descended from Jérôme Bonaparte) and Princess Clementine. The remains of Napoleon's father were brought from Montpellier in 1951.

Above the main altar hangs the Coptic Crucifix which the then General Bonaparte brought back from Egypt, he had 'borrowed' it, as he put it. After the campaign he gave the crucifix to his mother. The interior of the dome, the walls of the choir and the pendentives are decorated in trompe l'oeil by the Ajaccio artist Jérôme Maglioli who also designed the fountain of the four lions in the Place Foch.

The Rue Fesch joins to the N the Cours Napoleon, the 800m-long principal street of the town running from the Place General de Gaulle in the S to the Palais de Justice (1873) and the railway station in the N. This avenue, shaded by orange trees and bordered with elegant shops and smart cafés is the fashionable centre of Ajaccio. It has little of architectural or historical interest. About half way along the Cours the church of *Saint Roch* (1895) has good modern stained glass of 1956 by Gabriel Loire. The enormous *Préfecture*, just to the S of the Post Office and at the lower end of the Cours, has in the entrance hall a 3C sarcophagus.

The main avenue running from the Place de Gaulle in the E to the Place d'Austerlitz (formerly Place du Casone) in the W is of similar length to the Cours Napoleon. It begins as the Cours Grandval and half way up becomes the Boulevard General Leclerc. This has nothing of the commercial bustle of the Cours Napoleon and is mainly residential, with apartment blocks, offices, clinics and villas set in large gardens. About 250m along (right) is the *Anglican church*, compact, brown and pebbly, set in its own small yard off the street. Now deconsecrated and waiting to be put to a new use, it was built in the 1860s, largely at the instigation of an intrepid Scottish spinster, Thomasina Campbell (there is still a Rue Campbell on the other side of the main road).

The church was raised for the growing British colony's spiritual needs so that they might stroll, top-hatted and be-bonneted, to divine service from their wooded Balestrino hillside and well-appointed villas which they, in a British upper middle class tradition that never dies, referred to as cottages.

Miss Campbell's 'Notes on the Island of Corsica', and the 'Journal of a Landscape Painter in Corsica' by her friend Edward Lear, attracted other

English. They set a minor fashion for Victorians who wanted to get away from it all and who ended up recreating much of what they had left behind when they got there. Few, if any of them, emulated Thomasina's travels throughout the island. More interested in botanising than bandits, she dedicated her book to 'those in search of health and enjoyment', writing 'So pleasant and fertile does this valley [of the Ortolu that rises on the Vacca Morta in the SW] appear, it is hardly possible to believe malaria *can* exist there; probably the imagination predisposes the system for the disease, for every ailment, from indigestion to a cold in the head, is here called "the fever". Porridge, cod liver oil and no nonsense probably carried Thomasina through.

On the Boulevard Leclerc is the monument to Fred Scamaroni, leading Corsican Resistance fighter. He was sent from London as an agent of the Free French by General de Gaulle, head of the Free French opposition to Nazi-occupied and Pétainist France, in 1941. Scamaroni was subsequently arrested, and poisoned himself in prison rather than run the risk of talking under torture. The PLACE D'AUSTERLITZ is dominated by the gigantic **monument of Napoleon** by Seurre (1938). The original, which now stands in the grand courtyard of the Invalides in Paris, from 1833 to 1863 surmounted the column in the Place Vendôme, Paris.

It is Napoleon in his most familiar stance, dressed in frock coat and bicorne hat. He is looking down the Cours Grandval and over the town of Ajaccio. Alone of the many statues in the town, it has majesty and grandeur. At the base of the monument is a cave where it is said that the young Napoleon, who was sent away to school when he was nine, may have played.

A. Expeditions inland from Ajaccio

MONTE SALARIO AND THE SALARIO FOUNTAIN, 5km from the Place Austerlitz. Leaving Ajaccio, a road just before the Place leads off to the right (marked) and at just under 5km reaches the *Salario fountain*. Actually a spring with a faucet, it was said in the past to have been an area populated by salamanders, thence *funta Salamandra*. One might see a lizard now and then but there is a good view over the surrounding countryside which is even better from the summit of *Monte Salario* (311m) reached easily by a stony track. From here one can see the valley of Saint Antonine, the former prison of Castelluccio and the pinnacles of Punta di Liza (790m) to the NW. A track called the Chemin de la Serra leads down directly into the town.

LES MILELLI: leaving Ajaccio to the N, either by way of the Boulevard Sampiero or by the Cours Napoléon (the latter is busier), take the D 61 and follow the clear 'Monuments Historiques Les Milelli' signs NW for under 5km to the former Bonaparte property (today it belongs to the town of Ajaccio and is open to the public). This plain, solid, small-windowed and architecturally unremarkable house conveys a stronger sense of Napoleon's deep Corsican roots than does the Maison Bonaparte in Ajaccio.

It was to les Milelli that Napoleon's mother on 25 May 1793, accompanied by her half-brother Abbé Fesch, brought her two daughters from her house in the Rue Malerba which was then threatened, and later commandeered by, the Paolists and their British supporters. The party left les Milelli during the night of 1 June, skirting Ajaccio to reach the Tour de Capitello (S of the present airport) where Bonaparte and 50 men, who had been put ashore by the French navy, were planning an attack on the town. This plan became impossible and Napoleon, his family and his men boarded their vessel, reached Calvi on 3 June and subsequently Toulon.

B. Les Iles Sanguinaires

Les Iles Sanguinaires can be reached either by road or by boat (3-hour round trip, leaving twice a day at 09.00 and 15.00 from the Quai Napoleon), a voyage of 18.5km to *La Grande Sanguinaire* (or *Mezzo Mare*) from Ajaccio through the N of the Golfe d'Ajaccio. The boat stays there one hour before making the return trip, giving time to walk on this, the largest islet of the tour (1200m long by 300m wide, highest point 80m). A lighthouse with a flashing beam visible for 56km stands here and Alphonse Daudet lived on the islet during part of 1863. From both the shore and from the lighthouse there are very good views of the gulf and of Ajaccio.

Although the granite of these islets glows fiery red at sundown (one of the essential sights of Corsica) the name is less likely to be connected with this than with the Golfe de Sagone which the isles separate from the Golfe d'Ajaccio; on old maps they are named as *Sagonares insulae*.

To reach the islands by road take the Boulevard Lantivy E along the coast from the Place de Gaulle, passing (2km) the *Chapelle des Grecs*, where the Greek refugees came in 1731 before settling at Cargèse. Founded in 1632, some lines from Joseph Bonaparte's memoirs are chiselled above the entrance. A 'Couronnement de la Vierge entre des saints et les donateurs' recalls the foundation of the chapel by Artilia Pozzo di Borgo, widow of the commandant of the Corsican Papal troops, in 1619. View over the gulf from behind the chapel. Just beyond the chapel is the striking cemetery with family vaults and tombstones spread thickly over the steep hillside.

The road is *en corniche*, cut into the granite and hugging the shore. The road leads past sandy beaches, Scudo (on the road) and Vignola (off road to N), before reaching the *Pointe de la Parata* (Punta di a Parata) crowned by a tower built by the Genoese (1608) in defence against the Moorish raiders. (There is a car park at the foot of the promontory.) A footpath leads to the end of the point (about 35 minutes there and back) from which there is a superb view of the islets. (Restaurant and bar by the car park.) If possible, and if the sky is clear, the Sanguinaires should be seen in the light of the setting sun. A touristic cliché perhaps but one of the most worthwhile.

C. Castello di a Punta and Alata

Leave Ajaccio by the Boulevard Sampiero and take the D 61 to Alata passing through (7km) the Col de Pruno (Faccia di Campo 216m) on the high ridge of the peninsula running between the Golfe of Ajaccio to the S and the Golfe de Lava to the NW. Take the road to the left at the col (good views of the gulf). 13km from Ajaccio are the burned ruins of the **Castello di a Punta** or Château de Pozzo-di-Borgo. Standing on a terrace at 600m, it was built by the Pozzo-di-Borgo family (1886–94) of materials brought from the Tuileries which had been burned in 1871. There was a faithful reproduction of one of the

Tuileries pavilions. The iron railings come from Saint Cloud. The N façade, overlooking the Golfe de Sagone, used to be at the Place du Carrousel, the S façade, overlooking the Golfe d'Ajaccio once fronted the Jardin des Tuileries. An inscription explains: 'Jérôme, du Pozzo di Borgo, and Charles, his son, had this building constructed with stones from the Tuileries Palace (burned in 1871), to preserve for the Corsican people a precious souvenir of the French mother country'. The castle used to be open to the public and one could see the faithful reconstructions of once-familiar Parisian buildings, fine furniture and paintings. Like the Tuileries and the old Hôtel de Paris, from which a marble group of the Four Seasons had been brought, the Castle in its turn was burned down (1980) but the contents were saved. Still worth going to see (no entry fee) for the outstanding views.

Motors are not allowed on the track that continues to the Punta (even more outstanding views). Allow an hour there and back by the clearly marked footpath. The tower (restored) that one passes is all that remains of the Pozzo di Borgo village, razed by Barbary pirates in 1594. From the *Punta* (780m) on which stands a telecommunications (Corsica-mainland) relay station, one can see: NE the peaks (usually snow-covered) of Monte Renoso and Monte d'Oro; N the Golfe de Lava and the Golfe de Sagone; S the Golfe d'Ajaccio; SW the Punta di a Parata and the Sanguinaires.

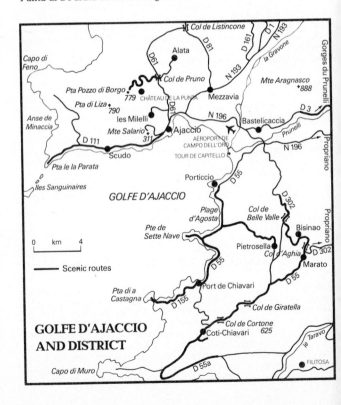

If, instead of turning left from the D 61 at the Col de Pruno, one carries along the D 61, 10km from Ajaccio is the village of *Alata* (450m, 552 inhab.). Built like a balcony on the side of the Serra mountain, it commands extensive views over the Golfe d'Ajaccio. This is the centre of the countryside dominated for centuries by the Pozzo di Borgo family, one of whose castles, the *Château de Mattone*, now in ruins, stands to the left of the D 61 just before the Col de Pruno. At Alata was born in 1764 the most famous of the Pozzo di Borgo family, Comte Charles-André (originally Carlo Andrea).

He was elected Député for Corsica in 1791. In 1793 he campaigned with Paoli for Corsican independence from France. In 1794 he supported Paoli and the Anglo-Corsican kingdom and was outlawed together with Charles Bonaparte and left for England when the French reoccupied Corsica in 1796. In 1803 Charles-André became private adviser to Czar Alexander I and worked to strengthen the coalition between Russia, Austria and Great Britain against his own arch-enemy Bonaparte, who put pressure on Russia to get rid of him, whereupon he returned to England. The Czar invited him back to Russia in 1812 during the Russian campaign. He advised the Czar to burn Moscow, and he was near Wellington at Waterloo where he was wounded. He later advocated exiling Napoleon to Saint Helena, was Russian ambassador to the court of Louis XVIII in Paris until 1834 and then Russian ambassador in London 1834–39. He died in Paris in 1842. There is something very Corsican about the lifelong enmity between Napoleon and Pozzo di Borgo, as he came to be called. At the time of Napoleon's birth the Bonaparte house in Ajaccio was shared with distant Pozzo di Borgo cousins. Perhaps a vendetta concerning political ideas developed. As Jacques Grigori summed it up: 'Napoleon fut partisan d'une Europe française, Pozzo di Borgo d'une France européene'. Their differing stances were rooted in diametrically opposed ambitions for Corsica, to which their Corsican nationality lent a bitter inflexibility.

2   From Ajaccio to Propriano and Sartène

A. The Inland Route: Ajaccio to Propriano.

ROAD (N 196) 74.5km.—21.5km *Cauro*. (—*Bastelica* 20km to E).—51.5km *Petreto-Bicchisano*.—61.5km *Sollacaro* and *Filitosa* (to W of road).—65.5km *Olmeto*.

Taking the inland route first, leave Ajaccio by the Boulevard Sampiero to reach the N 196 which skirts the E side of the Ajaccio Campo del Oro Airport, crossing two rivers, the Gravona and the Prunelli. At 12.5km from Ajaccio, at the Prunelli crossing, the coast road goes off to the right. Follow the N 196 to Cauro, 21.5km from Ajaccio, passing less than 2km from a tiny hamlet called *Barracone*, scene of the assassination of Sampiero Corso on 17 January 1567 (for history of Sampiero see Bastelica). The village is overlooked by the ruins of two medieval castles on the two hills which dominate it. To Bastelica (20km) take the D 27.

DETOUR TO BASTELICA. To visit Bastelica is to get to know the heart of the island. It is, in fact, only 40km from Ajaccio by the D 23. The road climbs steadily for about 10km to the Bocca di Marcuccio (661m) and then descends (1km) through the Bastelica pine forest to the Pont di Zipitoli over the Eze, the main tributary of the Prunelli. A road to the

right mounts the Eze valley on the left bank of the river, taking a
5km-longer but dramatic route to Bastelica.

On the D 27 5km beyond the bridge at the Bocca di Menta (756m) a
road (left) skirts the N shore of the Tolla reservoir, built 1956–64, and
winds by way of *Ocana* (350m, 308 inhab.) through the Gorges de
Prunelli to rejoin the N 196 to Ajaccio just N of Cauro. NW of this lies
the central Corsican forest and mountain barrier, which includes the
Monte Renoso and Monte Giovanni peaks and ranges.

Should you come from the N and off the Corsican main transversal
road, the N 193, from Bocognano, then it is 25km to Bastelica by the D
27, a picturesque but narrower and more winding road.

Bastelica (800m, 2000 inhab.) is set in a saucer surrounded by
chestnut trees and virtually encircled by mountains (climbing trips to
Monte Renoso; 2352m). Its hamlets are scattered within its sheltered
position, containing many old and elegant houses with fine doorways
and windows. There is a good late 19C statue in bronze opposite the
church of Bastelica's hamlet of Santo. The church is in decent 19C
style but of no particular interest.

Statue of Sampiero Corso, Bastelica

Bastelica is of special significance for Corsicans. It was in one of the six Bastelica hamlets, Dominicacci, that on 23 May 1498 was born Sampiero Corso, a great Corsican hero who is remembered with Pasquale Paoli and Napoleon Bonaparte. Called 'the most Corsican of Corsicans' because of his implacable hatred for the Genoese who ruled the island, in 1555 he tried to enlist the help of France, which he had served with distinction as a soldier. He succeeded, only to be betrayed in 1559 when France did a deal with the Genoese and handed Corsica back to them. Sampiero travelled throughout the courts of Europe to enlist help, but got none so, in 1564 he landed in Corsica, in the Gulf of Valinco, with an invasion 'army' of 20 Corsicans and 25 Frenchmen. He rallied many supporters and fought on for three years, until he was assassinated in an ambush by the Genoese and their Corsican allies on 17 January 1567. Among those who plotted to have Sampiero killed were members of the Ornano family to which his wife Vanina belonged. Sampiero had strangled her, believing her to have been in league with the Genoese. Tall, broad, bearded and handsome, Sampiero came from mountain shepherd stock and had the physical attributes of a hero, which part he played in the Shakespearean drama of his life and death.

Having taken the detour to Bastelica, return to the N 196 at *Cauro* (370m, 780 inhab.), dominated by two hills on each of which are the ruins of the respective châteaux of the della Rocca and Bianca families.

Boswell, visiting Corsica to meet 'a people actually fighting for liberty', having parted from Corsica's leader Paoli (whose advice to James was to go home and get married) on 27 October 1765 at Sollacaro, just N of Olmeto, fell sick of the tertian ague (or malaria). He was much heartened however by the company of 'a great swarthy priest who had never been out of Corsica' who had, with two other Corsicans, taken a castle garrisoned by 15 Genoese. 'I have often heard them say [reported Boswell] "Our women would be enough against the Genoese." I was returning to Corte but...at Cauro I had a fine view of Ajaccio and its environs....I was lodged at Cauro in the house of Signor Peraldi...before supper Signor Peraldi and a young abbé of Ajaccio entertained me with some airs on the violin.' His host also put on a show for Boswell of Corsican dances which appeared to have 'the idea of an admirable war dance'. On his way to Cauro Boswell had stayed at Ornano 'where I saw the ruins of the seat where the great Sampiero had his residence: They were a pretty droll society of monks...when I told them I was an Englishman "Ay, Ay," said one of them, "as was well observed by a reverend bishop, when talking of your pretended reformation, *Angli olim angeli nunc diaboli*" [Once the English were angels, now they are devils]. I looked upon this as an honest effusion of spiritual zeal. The fathers took good care of me in temporals.'

In Cauro turn left and S down the 'N 196 through mountain foothill country but with nothing of arresting interest on the road itself. 30km from Cauro is *Petreto Bicchisano* (Pitretu Bicchisgia, 550m, 1200 inhab.). Really two villages face to face, the former, Petreto, being the higher of the two and on the D 420 and Bicchisano being the lower village on the N 196, from which there is a view over the Taravo valley. These two villages stand at a point where ancient pathways came to a crossroads and, as always, there is much to be explored in the district. For example, there is the megalithic complex of *Settiva* in the mountains close by, with the Furchiccioli peak (1335m) at the centre. The possible routes are so complicated that those wishing to get there should ask in the village. Persistence will elicit more-or-less precise directions, so try your luck in local cafés and shops and with the curé, if you can find him.

10km S of Petreto-Bicchisano on the N 196 is the Col de Celaccia (594m) from which the D 307 to the right leads to (2km) *Sollacaro* (Suddacaro, 450m, 550 inhab.), a fine old Corsican village filled with the history of the island. It was a former seat of the d'Istria family of whom Vincentello d'Istria was a 15C Viceroy of the King of Aragon. A fortified house, built in the 16C to replace the old castle, is still inhabited by descendants of the family, or was until recently.

Dumas stayed there in 1841 for a few days which inspired his novel 'The Corsican Brothers' which, however, has next to nothing to do with Corsica which evidently meant little to him. Boswell arrived here in October 1765 after a fortnight of fairly rough travelling from Centuri. 'My journey over the mountains was very entertaining. I past some immense ridges and vast woods.' On arrival 'I was shewn into Paoli's room. I found him alone, and was struck with his appearance. He is tall, strong, and well made; of a fair complexion, a sensible, free and open countenance, and a manly, and noble carriage. He was then in his fortieth year. He was drest in green and gold...I had stood in the presence of many a prince, but I never had such a trial as in the presence of Paoli....For ten minutes we walked backwards and forwards through the room, hardly saying a word, while he looked at me, with a stedfast, keen and penetrating eye, as if he searched my very soul....I then ventured to address him with this compliment to the Corsicans: "Sir, I am upon my travels, and have lately visited Rome. I am come from seeing the ruins of one brave and free people: I now see the rise of another." This naturally went down well and Boswell spent a week in Paoli's company.

Just beyond the northern edge of .Sollacaro the D 57 goes left and in under 8km reaches the **Station Préhistorique de Filitosa**, Corsica's major prehistoric site, which remained practically undiscovered and ignored for nearly 5000 years.

Towards the end of summer the grass has been worn away and the statues take on a dusty and weary appearance but visit Filitosa in early spring when the banks of the streams and the meadow are bright with flowers, the olive trees are green and the inquisitive cows pose beside the statues, and you can comprehend why successive peoples chose this rocky height set in a verdant saucer. At such a time, particularly very early in the morning, there is something enchanted about it which gives life and colour to the archaeological remains.

As late as 1948 Dorothy Carrington, who was staying with the Cesari family on whose land Filitosa stands, was taken by her hosts 'to look at the statues'. 'I had been prepared for disappointment,' she wrote in 'Granite Island', 'right up to the instant when I reached the spot...but the block of granite lying before us on the ground, six feet long or more, was without doubt carved by the human hand in the human form....The head was clearly shaped: a large round head with protruding ears, sinister close-set eyes and a faint indication of mouth and nose. Neck and shoulders were carved from the block; but the body was simply a flattened shaft of stone, with a ridge, just discernible, crossing it diagonally: not an arm, it seemed, but a sword. It was still monstrously impressive, this hero-image lying on its back in the maquis worn by uncounted centuries of wind and rain. The head recalled nothing I had seen so much as one of Picasso's more brutal drawings.' Dorothy Carrington helped to draw academic attention to Filitosa where archaeological excavation began in earnest in 1954.

The name of the archaeologist Roger Grosjean is inseparable from the systematic discovery and interpretation of Filitosa. His invaluable guidebook, 'Filitosa, haut lieu de la Corse préhistorique', is on sale in the bar and restaurant belonging to the Cesari family where tickets for the museum and the site are also bought. There is a clearly marked parking place at the entrance to the hamlet.

In the MUSEUM are three restored statues. Left, as one enters, is the upper part of a figure known as Scalsa-Murta, 1400–1350 BC. He carries a sword held vertically, his back is protected by armour and he is helmeted. Two holes in the helmet may have held horns, Viking

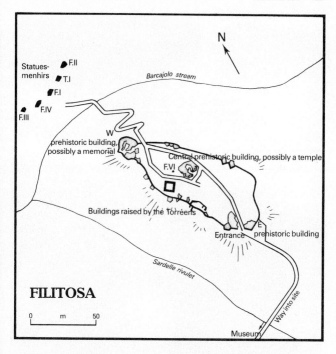

FILITOSA

style. Facing the door is 'Filitosa XII' whose hands and arms are indicated in the sculpture, and a head called Tappa II. The impact of first meeting with these megalithic statues is unfortunately lessened by the inadequate lighting and a number of potted evergreen plants, creating an effect half-cemetery and half Palm Court.

A tree-bordered track leads downhill from the museum, crossing the Sardelle stream. About 80m on the right stands Filitosa V, the largest of Corsican statue-menhirs. He bears a sword, held vertically, and is also armed with a dagger. After crossing the Sardelle, the track makes a 90° turn to the left to enter the OPPIDUM OF FILITOSA, 130m long by an average of 40m wide, set on a boat-shaped spur of rock between the Sardelle and the Barcajolo Rivers which join 100m to the W. There is a surrounding wall of massive blocks of stone, supposedly raised by the 'Torréens' (so named by Grosjean because they built tower-like fortresses, usually on the tops of hills). The Torréens re-used statues sculpted by the megalithic people they defeated after invading and ranging through the southern part of Corsica. The *East monument* is a tumulus and the *Central Monument* was a Torréen building used for religious purposes. Here again statues from an earlier age were incorporated into the walls but have since been retrieved (for example Filitosa IX, with its clearly defined features, to the right of the entrance). The *West monument*, at the point of the rocky spur was, according to Grosjean, both for religious use and for

Statue-menhirs at Filitosa

defence. The central part is divided into two, and it has been calculated that the last time it was used was about 1200 BC.

A steep path to the right of the W monument leads down to a pasture where the Baracolo is crossed. On the other side five statue-menhirs have been set up in front of an ancient olive tree. Three of them, armed, date from the megalithic era.

To reach *Propriano* there is a choice of two routes. One is to return to Sollacaro and the Col de Cellacia, turn right and proceed S on the N 196. From here on there is a view out to the Golfe de Valinco and at (4km) **Olmeto** (Ulmetu 360m, 1300 inhab.), a large village terraced on the S slopes of the Punta di Buturettu (870m) and surrounded by olive groves from which it has traditionally made its living. It is a typical old Corsican village, with ancient stone houses and mellow-tiled roofs. Situated some 6km from the long sandy shore of the Gulf of Valinco, the Plage de Baraci, Olmeto is now launched into the business of tourism. On a peak to the E, facing the village, stand the ruins of *Castello della Rocca*, 14C stronghold of Arrigo de la Rocca, great grandson of Giudice.

A ferocious patriot, Arrigo de la Rocca enlisted the King of Aragon on his side and returned to Corsica in 1372 and hounded out the Genoese from everywhere but their citadels of Calvi and Bonifacio. As Count of Corsica he ruled the island wisely and well for four years before dying in 1401 at Vizzavona of a 'stomach ailment'. There was a lot of it about at the time and he, like so many, was probably poisoned.

Fiction brings greater renown to places than fact. Olmeto is famous because Colomba Carabelli, the original of Prosper Merimée's heroine Colomba in the novel of that name, died in Olmeto aged 96 in 1861.

On the way to (9km) *Propriano*, a turning to the left after the bridge over the Baraci stream brings one to (1km) the *Baraci baths* (open 1 March–mid October). These are baths of sulphur and salt water at 47°C for the treatment of rheumatism, arthritis and skin afflictions.

The alternative route to Propriano from Filitosa (18km) is by the D 57, S along the lower valley of the Tavaro to where it meets the D 157. Continue straight along this road which hugs the coast and the sandy beaches of the Golfe di Valinco most of the way, joining the N 196 4km outside Propriano.

B. The Coastal Route: Ajaccio to Propriano and Sartène

ROAD (D 55 and 55A, D 757, D 157, N 196) 124km.—40km *Coti-Chiavari*.— 79km *Propriano*.

Leave Ajaccio by the N 196 and immediately after crossing the Piscatello bridge over the Prunelli, just past the *Campo del Oro airport*, turn right onto the D 55. 3km beyond the bridge and 1km by a track to the shore and the mouth of the Prunelli is the *Tour di Capitello*.

The tower is in good condition although seriously cracked by Bonaparte's attempt to blow it up. The Tour di Capitello played two parts in the history of the Bonapartes. First was in April 1793 when Bonaparte with 50 men and a cannon installed himself there with the intention of attacking Ajaccio while the French fleet bombarded the Paolists and their British allies. A storm held the French ships offshore and Bonaparte and his men were besieged in the

*Tomb at Olmeto, typical of Edward Lear's interpretation of
Corsican scenic grandeur*

tower for several days until they managed to get out and rejoin the
fleet. In June 1793 Bonaparte met his mother, two sisters, and his
uncle, Abbé Fesch, at the tower and took them off to Toulon.

This stretch of the coastline has been much developed recently for
tourism. A *village des vacances* is followed by the new development
at Porticcio and the road continues along the Plage d'Agosta. The

D 55 hugs the shore closely as far as the Plage de Verghia and the tiny port of *Chiavari*. From here the D 155 goes out in the direction of the *Punta di a Castagna* from which there is a fine view of the Golfe d'Ajaccio. To reach the point there is a 30-minute round-trip on foot from the hamlet of *Portigliolo*. At the Plage de Verghia the D 55 goes due S and away from the sea to the village of *Coti-Chiavari* (Coti Chjavari 500m, 352 inhab.) which is 40km from Ajaccio and 40km from Propriano. It is a terraced village with a nearby television relay station and a military camp set on a height. Both are out of bounds but the service road may be used to reach a twin peak (581m) from which there are views over the Gulfs of Ajaccio and Valinco. To avoid crossing the rocky spine of the peninsula that ends in the Capu di Muru the D 55 goes to the hamlet of Acqua Doria before turning W and crossing the foothills on its way to the Taravo valley and Propriano. A few hundred metres to the S of Acqua Doria a turning to the right is marked *Capu di Muru* 5km. It leads not only to the cape but also to a number of isolated and fine beaches, but the track is unmetalled, very rough, and muddy after rain. On the way to the Taravo valley and the D 757 (later becoming the D 157 where it crosses the Taravo) there is a turning to the right to *Serra di Ferro* (A Sarra di Farru, 528 inhab.) which has nearby a beach of fine sand.

Immediately before the D 157 makes a right angle to cross the Taravo, a minor road, D 757, goes straight (2.6km) to *Porto Pollo*, a small port on the E of a tiny peninsula. Protected from the W wind, it was formerly a haven for sailing ships loading charcoal and for fishing boats. Now it is a delightful and modest seaside village with a few hotels, a restaurant and a camping site.

From the bridge over the Taravo it is 14km to Propriano which looks N from the S shore of the Golfe de Valinco.

Propriano (Pruprià, 3000 inhab.) is the port serving Sartène (13km) and the Sartenais district which produces wine, honey and fruit, and pastures cows, goats and sheep for their milk and cheese. Propriano is also roughly mid-way between Ajaccio (74km) and Bonifacio (67km) and 76km from Porto Vecchio. SNCM car ferries ply to and from Marseille and the marina is (1986) being greatly enlarged.

There has been a port here since at least the 2C BC. Greeks, Romans and Carthaginians left traces of their visits here and so did Turkish and Barbary raiders. It was occupied by the Pisans in the 10C and by the Genoese in the 13C. It was here that Sampiero Corso landed to begin his conquest of Corsica. By the end of the 18C, mostly due to the barbarian raids, there was little left of the town. Only four houses were reported there in 1794. Its long history of settlement is due to the rock called Scoglio Longo which shelters the harbour from the W and NW winds. The harbour jetties were built on this rock at the beginning of this century. Although fishing and maritime trade have not increased, tourism has brought a new prosperity to Propriano.

The town has had such a rough history that there is little of architectural interest. It consists mainly of one long street running from where the N 196 comes into town from the N down to the port. In general the luxury hotels are in the northern and higher part and the restaurants border the main street and the port.

The route to Sartène lies along the valley of the Rizzanese (50km long, rising at the foot of the Incudine). Take the N 196 out of Propriano as for Campomoro but cross the Rizzanese 6km from Propriano by the Pont de Rena Bianca. There are two menhirs, marked on the map and signposted to the right of the road, called *u Frate et a Suora* (monk and nun), illicit lovers turned to stone as they fled from Sartène and divine wrath. The road follows the river valley until it meets the D 69 coming in from the left when it turns due S for Sartène.

Spin'a Cavallu, 13C bridge over the Rizzanese (its single arch gives it the 'horse's back' name)

The D 69 is one of those splendid, winding exploratory roads through Corsica which, given time, are so rewarding to follow. After branching E from the N 196, the main road to Sartène from Propriano, on the left (4.5km) is the 13C Genoese bridge *Spin'a Cavallu* (the horse's back). Beautifully proportioned, it consists of a single arch. Turning N to run along the valley of the Chiavone, a tributary of the Rizzanese, the road reaches (25km) *Aullène* (Auddè, 834km, 821 inhab.) on the left bank of the Cascione. The village is set among the sweet chestnut groves and on the W edge of the Parc Naturel, in and out of which the D 69 wends its way up to Vivario and the N 193.

The S extremity of the Golfe de Valinco is the *Punta di Campomoro* (the camp of the Moors) which looks N to Porto Pollo across the gulf. It is 16km on a narrow road but worth a visit. Leave Propriano by the N 196 in the direction of Sartène and after 3km, having crossed the Rena Bianca bridge over the Rizzanese river, turn right onto the D 121 which follows the river closely and skirts around the S edge of Propriano-Tavaria airport (not international) and the racetrack. At 8.5km from Propriano there is a fine beach at *Portigliolo* (not to be confused with the beach of the same name near the Punta di Castagna mentioned above). 3km further on is *Belvédère-Campomoro* (Belvédère-Campu-Moru, 120 inhab.), a village set on a terrace with a view across the whole gulf. The road goes down towards the sea, and a track to the left leads to the menhir, 2.50m high, of Capu-di-Logu.

Campomoro, at 16km from Propriano, is in an isolated position out on the point which makes it both very attractive and discourages tourists. Beach of fine sand. A half- hour's walk or gentle climb up through the maquis brings you to the Genoese tower on the Punta di Campomoro (built to prevent the Moors setting up camp again?). For those who enjoy walking this is an ideal area. There are no roads for 10km as the crow or seagull flies between the Punta di Campomoro and *Tizzano*, set in a deep and narrow cove, on the W coast to the S (19km from Sartène). Tizzano has a small port overlooked by the ruins of an old fort.

3km to the NE on the D 48, the road to Sartène, is the megalithic complex of **Palaggiu** (Pagliaju) which Roger Grosjean calls, in his 'La Corse avant l'histoire', 'the most important in the Mediterranean countries, comprising 258 monoliths of which three are stele statues, set out in seven alignments'. Serious excavation began in the mid 1960s and continues. It was also in the 1960s that important discoveries were made on the plateau of Cauria. A road to the right off the D 48 just past the Alignments of Palaggiu, going towards Sartène, leads in 5km to the site. The direction is clearly marked and so is the site itself. The DOLMEN OF FONTANACCIA (in Corsican, Stazzona del Diavolo—the devil's forge) is the finest and best-preserved dolmen in Corsica, complete with funeral chamber and roof, measuring 2.60m by 1.60m with a height of 1.80m. There is a signpost to the *Alignment of Rinaiu* and a walk of 400m to the collection of 45 menhirs. At the *Alignment of Stantari* (signposted) 25 menhirs have been found and in this area Roger Grosjean, since 1964, has discovered eight statue-menhirs representing Bronze Age warriors. It is worthwhile to spend some time in the excellent *Musée de Préhistoire Corse* at Sartène (see Rte 3) before visiting these and other sites in the area.

To visit Tizzano and Palaggiu without returning to the outskirts of Propriano go back to Belvédère by the D 12 and take the only right out of the village, signposted to *Grossa* (400m, 80 inhab.). Just off the road in a cul de sac, it is a small village of old men in black suits and homburgs and old women dressed entirely in black, their head shawls giving them an almost Oriental look. Perhaps the younger people are all away at work but there is a strong impression of a lost village of old people. Records of Grossa's population at the present time vary between 58 and 80 and even its altitude fluctuates in reference books between 325 and 400m, suggesting it is not of close concern to outsiders. The Hachette *Guide Bleu—Corse* has an interesting note that it is 'one of the few villages in this region to have been depopulated by malaria' which is strange in this terrain of mountains of around 500m high. It was here in Grossa in 1388 that Giovanni della Grossa was born. During an eventful working life as a lawyer he was pro-Genoa in sentiment but when he retired he went back to his native village and wrote the most valuable surviving chronicle of life in medieval Corsica.

All the roads in these bare mountains wind around but both the D 21 and the D 321, which takes a detour to the village of Bilia, meet up with the N 196 at Bocca Albitrina, 2.5km S of Sartène.

3   From Sartène to Bonifacio through le Sartenais

ROAD (N 196) 54km—24km *col di Roccapina.*—29km *Monacia d'Aullene* (N of the road).—34km *Pianottoli-Caldarello.*—49km *Col d'Arbia.*

Sartène (Sarté, 330km, 6000 inhab.) is sous-préfecture of Corse du Sud.

The most famous description is by Prosper Mérimée: 'la plus corse des villes corses'. The quotation is as famous as Edinburgh being called 'the Athens of the North' and Sartène could very well be called 'la plus écossaise des villes corses'. The tall, solid, granite houses, austere to the point of grimness, the narrow streets and steps of the Old Town are reminiscent of Edinburgh or Stirling.

Coming into Sartène from the S by the N 196 you cross the Pont de la Scalella and from the bridge there is the impression of a town built into and forming part of the great cliff that faces you. The fortified appearance is for good reason: the Barbary pirates landed on the coast and made their way inland to lay siege to Sartène. In 1583 they took the town and carried off 400 citizens into slavery in Algiers. These raids continued until the 18C. Another reason for the semi-fortified status of the houses was that Sartène kept alive the old Corsican traditions of honour and the vendetta for longer than any other Corsican town. Not only was there violent rivalry between families but also between different parts of the town down through the 19C. Now, under the Communist majority town council, Sartène is one of the cleanest and best run towns in Corsica.

The strong attachment of the Sartenais to tradition is most strongly expressed in the Eve of Good Friday Procession du Catenacciu (literally the 'Chained one' from *catena*, a chain). The identity of the man who leads the procession, dressed in a red robe and hood through which only his eyes are glimpsed, is a closely guarded secret known only to the priest. This principal role of the Penitent Rouge is much sought after and has to be 'booked' many years ahead. Often it was a bandit or murderer or someone guilty of a crime which he wished to expiate by walking barefoot for three hours through the tortuous and candle-lit streets of the old town, bearing a wooden cross (31.5kg) and dragging a metal chain (14kg) shackled to his right ankle. The Grand Penitent is followed and aided, when he stumbles or falls (often due to the pressure of the crowds curious to discover his identity) by the Penitent Blanc, also anonymous, representing Simon de Cyrène who aided our Lord. He in turn is followed by hooded Penitents Noirs.

The procession starts from the Eglise Sainte Marie, close to the Hôtel de Ville and the Place de la Libération, at 21.30 and returns after midnight to the Place de la Libération with the effigy of the dead Christ from the church lying on a shroud and borne by the Penitents Noirs. An old Corsican chant, 'Perdono mio Dio', is repeated endlessly and sung by the crowd until the last moment when the silent throng is addressed and blessed by the priest. The effect of the whole ceremony is strongly medieval, chilling rather than moving, and deeply impressive with the constant chanting, the sound of the chain dragged over the stones and the almost palpable excitement bordering on hysteria of the packed crowd lining the route where the windows of houses are lit with candles. Not to be missed if one is there or nearby at Eastertide. Get to the route early and remember that as well as the ecstatic religious side there is a considerable degree of commercial exploitation. During the rest of the year the cross and chain used in the procession may be seen hanging from the N wall inside the church of Sainte Marie. (There is also a Catenacciu procession the same evening in Propriano. It is less crowded, less exploited, less impressive, but being simpler it is more moving.)

GOLFE DE VALINCO PROPRIANO AND SARTÈNE

Sartène

The centre of Sartène is the Place de la Libération which has a market and cafés. An archway under the Hôtel de Ville, formerly the Palace of the Genoese Governors, leads into the Old Town and the Middle Ages. At 100m (SW and downhill) from the Hôtel de Ville to the right of an alley is an *echaugette*—a 12C watch tower and one of the few relics of the wall that originally surrounded the town. The old town is very well signposted, as is the more modern part of Sartène. One of the great advantages of its situation on the side of a hill is that it is possible to walk everywhere. Follow the signposts to the hospital, and from there to the Musée de Préhistoire Corse which is a few minutes walk from the Place de la Libération, or by steps leading down from the Boulevard Jacques Nicolai.

The **Musée de Préhistoire Corse** (open 10.00–12.00 and 14.00–18.00 every day, Sundays and public holidays included, 15 June–14 September; rest of the year 10.00–12.00 and 14.00–17.00, public holidays excepted; free) is housed in a former prison built in 1843, actually a delightful yet solid granite manorial building. Created by Roger Grosjean, there is a comprehensive exhibition of objects dating from 6000–500 BC discovered in Corsica during the archaeological excavations carried out since 1955.

Room I. Neolithic (6000–4000 BC) pottery decorated with patterns made by shells or pointed instruments; primitive tools made from local stone and flints. Room II. (3500–3000 BC) tools and arrowheads, grindstones, fired pottery. Vases, cups, and copper, gold and silver ornaments from 3000–1800 BC. Room III. Human bones burned and placed in spaces under rocks, the Taffoni-Hypogées culture; serpentine stone rings and pendants. Room IV. Bronze Age (1600–1200 BC) pottery, pieces of bronze weapons retrieved from the 'torre' settlements. Room V. Late Bronze Age (1200–700 BC) Torréen pottery, imported pottery from Italy, bronze objects. Early Iron Age Pottery, decorated with 'combed' effects or incised, arms and weapons in iron, ornaments in bronze. In the main room there is the reconstruction of an Iron Age cremation burial, menhir statues, and a dolmen. Large photographs of the principal archaeological sites in Corsica and explanatory wall charts.

To reach (54km) Bonifacio leave Sartène by the S-bound N 196. On the edge of the town on the right is the *San Damiano monastery* (318m) from which there is a view of Sartène, the estuary of the Rizzanese and the Gulf of Valinco. The Penitent Rouge spends the day and night here in constant prayer before the Good Friday procession. Built in the 19C, the monastery, which is inhabited by a community of Belgian monks who are responsible for the repair and maintenance of the building, is not of outstanding architectural interest.

The journey S is through the pleasant cultivated country of the Sartenais, mostly vineyards where often the local wine, honest, unadulterated and not rough, is on sale by the bottle or case.

LE SARTENAIS could almost be northern France or even southern England: there are farmhouses and scattered cottages but practically no villages along this road which crosses (20km) the River Ortolo (Ortolo rises on the Puntadella Vacca Morta, 18km long). 4km *Col de Roccapina* (150m), view of the pink granite rocks of Roccapina and a Genoese tower. The most famous of the rocks is supposed to resemble a lion couchant (personally I have never been struck by this) and to the right of it, the head of an elephant. (There is a restaurant and bar called l'Oasis du Lion and a good parking place across the road from which Lion and Elephant can be recognised, admired and photographed.) The next tower along this coast is the *Tour d'Olmeto* perched out on a point.

5km A road to the left leads to the village of *Monacia d'Aullène* (2km) (A Munacia d'Auddè, 120m, 1008 inhab.), well-known for its excellent wines. Monacia is also a good starting point from which to commence the climb to l'Uomo di Cagna (1217m). This 'Man of Cagna' consists of a great spherical block of about 10m in diameter balanced on top of a slender base, giving the impression of a human form from many points in the southern plains (it marks the S end of the central mountain ranges of Corsica). The ascent of the 'man' itself is for experienced rock climbers only and the first climb to the top of the head dates only from 14 June 1970. The walk to the foot of l'Uomu takes about 2½hrs and the reward is a breathtaking view of Bonifacio and Sardinia.

5km *Pianottoli-Caldarello* (Pianottuli Caldareddu 80m, 881 inhab.). The first part of this village, Pianottoli, is on the N 196 and Caldarello, 1km to the S, has its houses scattered about in a great tumble and jumble of rocks. Until the 17C caves and grottoes among the rocks were inhabited and they still give shelter to farm animals. In the past the local people spent the summer in the mountains because of the heat and malaria on the seaboard, returning in the fall for the grape harvest. Now there is extensive cultivation of vines to produce the Figari wines.

After 2km the D 22 leads left to *Figari-Sud Corse Airport* (5.5km), served by Air France and France Inter (not international). Opened in 1975, its traffic has increased greatly year by year.

1km beyond the turning to the airport the road crosses the Figari by the *Pont de Figari*. Here the narrow Baie de Figari is watched over by the 13C Genoese tower. 2km beyond the Figari bridge the D 859 turns left to Sotta and Porto Vecchio. From here to Bonifacio the road passes through an unpopulated and somewhat desolate country of maquis, interspersed with cork-oaks and boulders, followed by marshes and meres. 10km *Col d'Arbia* (138m) guarded by the granite peak of la Trinité (219m) and bristling with wireless aerials.

Just beyond the col a road leads right to the *Trinité monastery*, a former hermitage, built on a terrace in the shade of ilex and olive trees from which there is a view over to Bonifacio. Centre of pilgrimage on Trinity Sunday and on the feast of the Nativity of the Virgin Mary on 8 September. Small church containing ex votoes.

Bonifacio (Bonifaziu, 3015 inhab.) is totally unlike any other town in Corsica, of which it is the most southerly—and indeed the most southern town of all France.

To the N is an extensive region of scrub (or *garigue*) growing on the inhospitable granite which in the past effectively shut off Bonifacio, set apart on a mighty plinth of limestone and chalk, from the rest of the 'granite island'. The nearest town is the Sardinian port of Santa-Teresa di Gallura, 12km across the Straits of Bonifacio, while the nearest Corsican town, Porto Vecchio, is 27km away. There is a special Bonifacien dialect derived from ancient Ligurian and often not understood by Corsicans from other districts.

The town is built on a long high promontory whose cliffs fall sheer to the sea. Between the promontory and the mainland to the N is a fjord 1600m long and 100–150m wide. This is and was Bonifacio's port. There is a *port de plaisance* now at the E end.

It is believed that the first description of Bonifacio was made by Homer in The Odyssey (Book X). Odysseus tells of arriving at the fortress of Lamos held by the Laestrygons and coming into a good harbour protected all around by an unbroken wall of rock with two jutting headlands guarding the narrow entrance. The Greeks went ashore and near the settlement met a girl drawing water from the spring of Artacia that supplied the town. Her father the king, being of the cannibal persuasion, began murdering the Greeks and started to eat one. The Greeks fled to their boats but the Laestrygons dropped boulders from the cliffs, holing the boats, while others speared the swimmers 'like fish' in preparation for a feast. The topography described certainly sounds uncommonly like Bonifacio.

Originally called Giola, Bonifacio owes its later name to Bonifacio II of Lucca who took the town for Louis the Debonair. He ousted the marauding Saracens for a while but they subsequently returned and may have remained there until the mid 12C. In 1187 the Genoese took the town, built the citadel, banished the inhabitants and replaced them with Ligurian families. It became virtually an autonomous republic while still acknowledging Genoa. Besieged by the

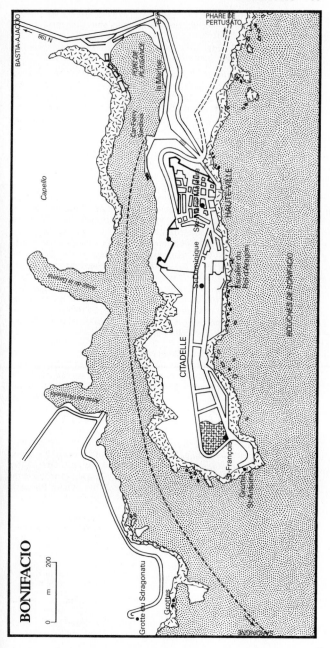

BONIFACIO

BASTIA-AJACCIO
N 198

PHARE DE
PERTUSATO

PORT DE PLAISANCE
la Marine

Cavallo Sottano

Capello

Madonetta Di Co litre

Sémaphore di the litre

m   0   200

Grotte du Sdragonatu

Grottes

SARDAIGNE

CITADELLE

HAUTE-VILLE

Ste-Marie-Majeure

St-Dominique

Escalier du
Roi-d'Aragon

François

Cimetière
St-François

BOUCHES DE BONIFACIO

Aragonese in 1420, the French and their Turkish allies set siege to the town in 1554. Bonaparte entered peacefully as a young artillery officer and spent several months there in early 1793.

From the main port car ferries leave for Sardinia and boats make excursions to the grottoes and along the shore below the cliffs.

The only main road into Bonifacio is the N 196 and where it finishes at the E end of the Marina there are two car parks. The QUAI JEROME COMPARETTI along the S of the harbour is the centre of commercial life with shops, cafés, restaurants, taxi rank, embarkation point for boat trips to the grottoes and the Lavezzi Islands, bus agency, and the excellent *aquarium* in a cave in the rock: comprehensive and interesting presentation of fish and crustaceans from the surrounding waters. Off the Quai Banda del Ferro is the fishing port, further W beyond that and off the Quai Sotta Portigliola is the Customs shed and the embarkation point for the car ferries to Sardinia, a busy and thriving part of the town's tourist industry.

To drive up to the old town on leaving the Marina car park do not turn right along the Quai Comparetti but go straight into the Avenue Charles de Gaulle which winds its way up to the top of the rock where a left turn leads into the Rue Fred Scamaroni. In Ajaccio there is a monument to this Corsican Resistance envoy of de Gaulle (see Rte 1, Ajaccio). Follow the Rue Scamaroni into the Place Fondaco-Montepagano. (There is a car park next to the Foreign Legion monument.) On the way up from the port and immediately before coming into the Avenue de Gaulle on the right is the *war memorial*, a grey granite Roman column discovered on the islet of Bainzo (San Bainsu). At the far end of the Avenue de Gaulle, by the turn into the Rue Fred Scamaroni one enters the Citadel by the Porte Neuve (1854) or Porte de France as it is usually known.

To reach La Ville Haute (the Citadel and the Old Town) on foot follow the Quai Comparetti to the Place St. Erasme then climb the steps of the Montée Rastello. The small church (*St. Erasme*) on the right was that of the fishermen, barred from the town by the Genoese. Striking in its simplicity, it has a model wooden sailing boat hung from the timbered roof, constructed like an upturned boat. The Montée Rastello passes underneath the Avenue de Gaulle and is succeeded by another flight of steps, the Montée Saint Roch, which leads to the *Col Saint Roch* (32m) where there is a natural belvedere, looking over the harbour on one side and out to sea on the other, beyond the great white blocks of limestone that have fallen from the cliff. One of the largest is called, inevitably, the 'grain de sable'. The sheer white cliffs and the peninsular isolation of Bonifacio recall the Dorset Purbeck coast and Portland.

To the left of the Col Saint Roch a path marked at the beginning by a black wooden cross leads to the *Pertusato semaphore and lighthouse* (for opening times ask at the Office de Tourisme, 12 Rue Longue, together with the Mairie in the centre of the Old Town). This is a walk of about 45 minutes along the ridge. The lighthouse stands 90m above sea level and its light can be seen for 27km. There is a fine view of the Bonifacio peninsula, the granite mass of the Trinité to the W and the northern shore of Sardinia. The lighthouse may also be reached (5km) by car, taking the D 58 out of Bonifacio and then the first to the right.

The *Chapelle St. Roch* (closed to the public) was built on the spot where died the last victim of the plague of 1528 during which Bonifacio lost two thirds of its population. The Montée St. Roch continues to climb and enters the *Bastion de l'Etendard* by the Porte de Genes, until the 19C the only gate to the old town. The 1598 drawbridge mechanism and the massive gates can still be seen. Pass through the gateway and turn to the right into the Place d'Armes which contains the plinths of four late 15C grain silos which, with others on the Place Manichella, provisioned the Bonifaciens during sieges.

Opposite the Porte de Gênes take the Rue du Corps de Garde which runs alongside the N wall of L'EGLISE SAINTE-MARIE, formerly the cathedral church, begun by the Pisans at the end of the 12C and refashioned with Gothic additions by the Genoese during later centuries. The vast *loggia* in front of the church, where the notables of the town used to meet and where proclamations were made, is built over a great water cistern (now dry and transformed into a conference hall). The *podesta*, the ruling magistrate, dispensed justice here twice a week and his palace (fragments of a 13C colonnade) was opposite the church. The square four-storey campanile (14–15C) is possibly Aragonese in inspiration.

Bonifacio

The *interior* is dark. On entering, directly on the left is a 3C Roman sarcophagus, now a receptacle for holy water. Above it is a 1465 Genoese tabernacle, beautifully sculpted and representing the torso of Christ, arms crossed at the wrists, the delicate long-fingered hands showing the nail wounds, supported by eight mourning cherubs. The largest is at the base, his chubby form and curly head seemingly supporting with difficulty the weight of the complete tabernacle. A carved octagonal casket in ivory and ebony is said to have contained relics of Saint Boniface. It is northern Italian, end of 14C. It may be necessary to ask for permission to see this casket and a so-called relic of the True Cross which are kept in a locked cupboard in the sacristy. Formerly in times of storm the relic, said to have been given to Bonifacio by 'a princess' who escaped shipwreck in the Straits of Bonifacio, used to be carried onto the terrace of the Place Manichella, 65m above the roaring waves. The clergy blessed the waves in the hope of bringing calm, in the presence of as many Bonifaciens as could get there.

A *jardin des vestiges* has been made around the ruins of the medieval town walls. This public garden may be visited, and apart from the ruins now brought to light there are views of Cap Pertusato, the Straits of Bonifacio, the old houses of the town seemingly perched on the edge of the stupendous cliffs, and the coast of Sardinia. When visiting the jardin des vestiges and the ramparts it is helpful to take a pamphlet, containing a plan published by the Bonifacio Office du Tourisme entitled 'Visite des Remparts: du siege de 1553 aux jardins des vestiges'. To quote the opening sentence on the history of Bonifacio 'Everything hinges on the siege of 1553...'. Bonifacio (like Calvi, always faithful to Genoa) was besieged from the sea by the French and Turks, commanded by the corsair Dragut and aided from the landward side by Sampiero Corso's troops in revolt against Genoa.

Apart from the path along the ridge of the plateau towards the lighthouse of Pertusato there is a cliff walk, *Promenade pédestre des Falaises*, which starts from the S end of the sweet-sounding Rue du chante de Mai, on the other side of the Rue Doria. Go through the Rue Doria in the other direction and turn left into the Rue des Pagnas from the Place Montepagano. At the end is *l'Escalier du roi d'Aragon*, constructed in the summer of 1420 when the Spanish fleet besieged Bonifacio.

There is a legend that this stairway of 187 steps cut into the cliff face from the shore to the level of the Haute Ville was made in a single night. A self-deprecatory Corsican joke playing on their unjustified reputation for indolence declares 'It certainly was not Corsican workmen who did it'. In fact, these steps had served during earlier centuries as a route for Bonifaciens to draw water from the St. Barthélémy well which is fed by a subterranean lake under the plateau (possibly the Articia fountain of The Odyssey?).

The Citadel occupies the whole of the W end of the peninsula and for 20 years from 1963 it was out of bounds to the public as the main garrison of the Foreign Legion. Although the Legion has now left there is still a military presence but the short walk (less than 500m) to the end of the promontory allows a visit to the two old windmills, one of which has just been restored, and the ruins of the *Franciscan monastery* and the church of *Saint François*, built in 1390 and now being restored. The church contains a single nave, very plain and austere, a fine marble font and a white marble flagstone over the tomb of Rinuccio Spinola, bishop of Ajaccio (died 1437). Nearby is a large cemetery, worth visiting for the variety of Baroque tombs. Opposite the gateway into the Citadel is the *monument to the Foreign Legion*, or more precisely to those of the Legion who died during the Sud-Oranais campaigns of 1897–1902. It originally stood in the main square of Saïda and was brought from Algeria in 1962 and set up in Bonifacio a year later when the Legion's garrison was formed and stationed at the Caserne Montlaur.

On the S side of the Citadel stands the church of *Saint Dominique*. Begun by the Knights Templars in 1270 to take the place of a romanesque church of which no trace remains, it was given to the Dominicans in 1307 and the church itself was finished in 1343. It has recently undergone a careful and thorough restoration. A very simple gothic church on whose pillars separating the aisles from the nave are delicate and moving small paintings (18C) of the Fifteen Mysteries of the Rosary. In the *Resurrection*, Christ seems to dance on the tomb as do the other two figures; it is admirably joyous. The white marble 18C altar is encrusted with coloured stones and comes from the church of Saint François. A Vierge du Rosaire with portraits of aldermen was given in thanks for the raising of the siege in 1553. There is an 18C Descent from the Cross. Two statues, kept in the sacristy, a Mater Dolorosa and a Sainte Marthe (Pisan workmanship of the 14 or 15C) are carried in the Good Friday procession as is the 800kg carved wood *Martyre de St. Barthélémy*. Turbanned infidels are flaying the saint alive and a small dog is being held back from picking up the saintly scraps.

Excursions from Bonifacio

Boat trips from Bonifacio to the Iles de Lavezzi, Baïnzo and Cavallo. (In good weather there are usually two trips a day, of an hour's duration. Information at the port.) These granite isles are vestiges of the isthmus that once connected Corsica and Sardinia. No trees but a variety of flowers, and seabirds nest there. The Iles de Lavezzi have been a nature reserve since 1982.

On 15 February 1855 the frigate 'Sémillante', bound for the Crimea with reinforcements, struck one of the Lavezzi rocks with the loss of all 773 soldiers and sailors aboard. The bodies recovered were buried on one of the islets. Alphonse Daudet, sailing between Sardinia and Corsica with some seagoing Customs companions, spent a night beside the cemetery ten years after the wreck. He relates in one of the 'Lettres de Mon Moulin' an eye-witness account by a leprous old shepherd of the 'Sémillante' striking the rocks. In 1893 a French steamer foundered on the same reef but without loss of life.

The sea caves and the Bonifacio coast. (Trip of 45 minutes from the Marine where there is a ticket office labelled 'Grottes et Falaises'.) The caves, Le Camere, Le Bain de Venus and the Sdragonatu, are in the S-facing cliffs to the N just beyond the inlet to the harbour fjord. The Sdragonatu is lit by the sunlight coming through a great natural cleft which is, by coincidence, roughly the shape of Corsica. The light, reflected by the red rocks and the violet-greenish water, creates the effect of a stage set. As the boat rounds the point one gets the best possible view of the town of Bonifacio with houses perched on the edge of the cliffs, of the King of Aragon's staircase, the Grain of Sand rock and the Saint Barthélémy spring. Everything that has or is said to have happened comes alive in the observer's mind: the Laestrygons hurling boulders down upon the Greek ships, the sieges in the Middle Ages, the hacking of the stairway into the cliff face.

Boats to Sardinia. Daily service to Santa Teresa di Gallura, Palau and La Maddalena (frequency according to season, duration of voyage under an hour, car ferry). Information from the offices of Corsica Ferries and Tirrenia at the port.

Beaches in the Bonifacio region. All that rugged history and landscape sharpens the appetite for the beach. For the *Plage de Cala-Longa* take the D 58, fork left at 3km to the D 258 and reach the beach in 3km. For the *Plage de la Rondinara* take the N 198 towards Porto Vecchio. Turn right at 11km to Suartone and continue for 4km until

the road ends within sight of the sea. For the *Plage du Gurzago* take
the D 58 for 6km to Gurzago on the shores of the Gulfu di Sant'
Amanza.

4   Le Désert des Agriates and the Valley of the Ostriconi

A. Le Désert des Agriates

Corsica, blessed with a widely varied landscape, even has its own
desert, not the Sheik of Araby kind with horizon to horizon sand, but
as defined by the OED, an 'uninhabited and uncultivated tract of
country, a wilderness'.

The D 81 road from l'Ile Rousse to Saint-Florent (46km) enters the
Désert des Agriates 18km from l'Ile Rousse at *Pont d'Ostriconi*,
crossing the river of that name which rises on the slopes of Monte Asto
(1535m) and runs 22km to empty into the Mediterranean at the Anse
de Paraiola. The road follows the S edge of the desert, uncultivated
and devoid of human presence and buildings apart from the occasional shepherd's hut. One point of entry into the desert is from the
Bocca di Vezzu (312m) which is roughly half-way along the D 81 and
the pass between the valleys of the Ostriconi and the Zente. From
here one can see over the Golfe de Saint-Florent to Cap Corse. From
the col a road to the left leads to the coast, about 11km which proves
very rough going to an ordinary car although vehicles like Range
Rovers or Jeeps should have no difficulty. For the walker there is a
toughish 3-hour walk that brings the more energetic and adventurous
traveller to the shoreline, where there are many deserted creeks
between the Punta di Malfulcu and the Punta Negra. It is by taking a
walk now and then that one gets to know and appreciate the wildness
and solitude of the desert. This remote area of maquis, although more
and more abandoned, has sparse grazing lands for the now-depleted
herds of cattle. Time and patience needed for such a trip on foot
through the rocky wilds to the N shore and back.

There is another road or track up to the coast, to the left immediately
before reaching the hamlet of *Casta*. Again this is negotiable by
rugged and high-slung motors but there is always a chance of getting
stuck on the loose surface stones or slithering sideways after rain. But
whether taking it on tyres or on foot ignore the first and second
turnings to the right because both of them go into the desert and then
just stop. The main track skirts the W slopes of Monte Genova,
following the line of the River Zente to its outlet into the Golfe de
Saint-Florent in a mini-lagoon beyond which is the sandy Plage de
Saleccia. There are footpaths to the Étang de Loto to the E and along
the N coast to the *Punta Mortella* and the ruins of a Genoese tower.
Just beyond Casta the D 81 comes out of the desert and passes
between the two sectors of an Army firing range before turning NE
towards the sea and Saint-Florent (18km from Casta).

B. The Valley of the Ostriconi

Although S and out of the desert area, the Ostriconi valley is again something different from anything else in Corsica and, given time, is worth exploring. Coming from l'Ile Rousse take the D 8 to the right 2km beyond Pont d'Ostriconi. The road travels S along the lower slopes of the E side of the valley along which the settlements are strung out thinly. This used to be a district of agriculture, beef herds and olive groves but since World War II it has turned to sheep and goats. The Ostriconi valley is 18km long and 6–8km wide and is neither of the Balagne nor of the Nebbio but a small corridor region between the two, taking its name from Lama, one of the villages. The farmers in the valley were the last in Corsica to retain the use of draft oxen.

10km from the Pont d'Ostriconi is *Urtaca* (360m, 228 inhab.), set in a bowl of the reddish mountains. In fine weather there is a worthwhile but not entirely easy walk along a mule track over the Tenda range by the Bocca di San Pancrazio (969m) to *San Pietro di Tenda* in the Nebbio, a distance of 10km.

3km beyond Urtaca is *Lama* (480m, 301 inhab.), perched on a rocky spur, with tall narrow houses above steep and narrow streets, a very 'Old Corsican' village in atmosphere and appearance. *La Maison Bertola* has rooms with frescoes depicting Italian Renaissance poets. Views from the village the length of the Ostriconi valley right to the sea. A not-too-hard 6km walk along a track to the side of Monte Asto (1535m) on the lower slopes of which Lama is built.

4km S along the D 8 is *Pietralba* (Petralba 450m, 513 inhab.). Traces of the Romans have been found in this village which occupies a high, dry, commanding position. Once a great sheep-raising centre, sheep still form the main livelihood. Another village of narrow streets with, above the present village, the ruins of a much older hamlet. The parish church has a bell-tower incorporating Roman building stones. Splendid panorama from the village to the Balagne coast. An ancient stone-paved track that was for centuries the link between the Balagne and the Eastern Plain provides a fine 5½-hour walk (about 6.5km) by the Bocca di Tenda (1219m) to *Pieve* in the Nebbio.

The D 8 in 4.5km reaches the N 197, 8km NW of *Ponte Leccia* which, situated at the junction with the N 193, opens the way to Bastia and Ajaccio. To return to the Désert des Agriates and the D 81, turn right on the N 197 which winds its way up the valley of the Lagani stream for 11km, then right onto the D 12 to *Novella* (400m, 97 inhab.), a village of fine old houses, many with elegant porches. Some ruins of the 11C *Château de San Colombano*. View to the Désert des Agriates from the *Col de Colombano*. This picturesque region may also be appreciated from the train which tunnels frequently close to Novella. The D 12 passes through deserted country to join (10km) the D 81 within a few hundred metres of the junction with the D 8.

5   La Balagne

A self-contained region of some 861km² and nearly 17,000 inhab., the **Balagne** (A Balagna) is a fertile area of NW Corsica, running from

Calvi on the coast, N along the coastline (50km) to the estuary of the
Ostriconi, beyond which is the Désert des Agriates.

A district of plains and rolling hills, it is flanked by the Mediterranean to the N and W, and the forests of Bonifato and Tartagine to
the S. Further S lies the central Corsican mountain range in which,
outstanding and often visible from most of the Balagne, are the peaks
(from N to S) of Monte Grosso (1938m), Monte Padro (2393m) and
Monte Cinto, the highest mountain in the island at 2710m. The rivers
of the Balagne are, starting with the Ostriconi in the N which is the
divide between the Balagne and the Agriates and is divided from the
Balagne proper by a range of low mountains, the Lozari and Régina
which reach the sea at Lozari, the Fiume Secco, the Bartasca and the
Ficarella, which all reach the sea near Calvi. To the S of the Balagne,
the Filosorma is irrigated by the Marsolino and the Fango which flow
into a common estuary in the Golfe de Galéria.

The fertility of the Balagne which earned it the title of the Garden of
Corsica also brought invaders seeking its riches of oil, fruit, cereals,
flocks and herds. Phoenicians, Greeks, Etruscans, Romans and Moors
all came to plunder or settle. Nowadays there is a flourishing tourist
industry along the coast and, through an active irrigation programme
dating from 1977, a revival of olive oil and wine production, both
along the coastal area and in the inland hillside villages.

After Ajaccio and its environs it is probably the Balagne that is the
best known and most popular holiday region of Corsica for British and
American visitors. The Garden of Corsica is also known as Holy
Balagne on account of its many fine churches, mainly built during
Pisan domination in the 11th and 12C. Their construction owed much
to the feudal overlords, sent at Papal instigation to drive out the
Moors, who fortified and occupied the area. The Genoese built
fortresses at Calvi and Algajola and l'Ile Rousse was Paoli's fortified
port to rival Calvi.

A. Along the coast: from Lozari to l'Ile Rousse and Calvi

ROAD (N 197) 29km.—7km *l'Ile Rousse.*—17km *Algajola.*

To the N of the Ostriconi River is the W part of the Désert des Agriates.
The D 81 from St. Florent reaches the Mediterranean 2km beyond the
Pont d'Ostriconi and hugs the coast for 9km as far as *Lozari* where
there is a *village des vacances.*

Much more than a holiday centre, it is organised to show those who stay there
what the Balagne, past and present, has to offer to visitors and is closely
concerned with promoting local history and local employment. It is very much
part of the Balagne and those who stay there may learn much about Corsican
traditions and history in general and about this part of the island in particular.

7km along the coast road, the N 197, brings one to **l'Ile Rousse** (l'Isula
Rossa, 2645 inhab.). This 'Red Isle' merits its name. Islets of orange-
red granite offshore (now joined to the mainland) glow a deep red in
the evening sunlight reflected from the sea.

L'Ile Rousse owes its existence to Paoli who decided that there should be a
western port that was Corsican and opposed to the Genoese-held ports of Calvi
and Algajola, respectively 24km and 9km along the coast to the SW. L'Ile Rousse

had been a Roman settlement called not suprisingly, Rubico Rocega, but had declined after the Romans left. Paoli, in founding l'Ile Rousse, said that he was building 'a gallows to hang Calvi', intending to put the port out of business. There was discussion at the time (1758) of calling the new port Paolina and in 1769 of calling it Vaux after the Comte de Vaux, commandant in chief of the French forces in Corsica. Its old name remained, however, and l'Ile Rousse it still is, a port exporting olive oil and dairy produce destined for Roquefort, as well as the other products of the Balagne. Of increasing importance to the local economy however is its status as an expanding tourist centre, a favourite with British holidaymakers because of its high sunshine rate and currently attracting more than eight per cent of visitors coming in to Corsican ports.

The centre of l'Ile Rousse is the spacious, plane-shaded PLACE PAOLI. Above a fountain in the centre is a white marble statue of Paoli who surveys with a stony eye the petanque players in the square. On the W side is the large baroque church of the Immaculate Conception, restored 1930–35 after damage by fire in 1914. There is nothing of particular interest in the church except its welcome simplicity. On the N side of the square is a covered market beyond which one goes into the OLD TOWN, and narrow paved streets leading down to the sea. At the end of the Rue Notre-Dame is the Place Tino Rossi, touching and fitting because he brought more fame to Corsica than anyone other than Napoleon Bonaparte. Could there be a Vera Lynn Square in England or a Bing Crosby Garden in the USA? On the landward side of the square, beside the Hôtel de Ville, is a partly ruined and much-restored tower carrying an inscription about the founding of the town by Paoli. To the N of the Place Paoli is a splendid old-style hotel, formerly the Château Piccioni which became for a time, as the Hôtel Napoléon Bonaparte, the most luxurious hotel in the island.

The town has many cafés and restaurants, and the railway station from which the *tramway de la Balagne*, part of the island railway system, goes to Algajola and Calvi and, in the other direction, to Belgodère and Ponte Leccia and the line down to Ajaccio or up to Bastia.

The island of *Petra* or *Isula Rossa* is now joined to the town by a raised causeway. At its extremity is the lighthouse and from the open space around it there is a fine view over l'Ile Rousse to the Balagne hills behind, the village of Monticello and the neighbouring small islands.

Algajola (Algaiola, 174 inhab.) is 9km from l'Ile Rousse. Genoese Algajola was the place where the lieutenant governor of the Calvi area lived. The Genoese built the fortifications in 1664 after the Turks had sacked the town; they are today in ruins except for the Citadel, which may have been rebuilt in the 17C. There is not much to see but there is a well-preserved 17C Descente de Croix in the church. Up the hillside are the granite quarries from which was hewn the granite for the base of the Vendôme column in Paris.

At the *Marine de Sant'Ambrogio*, 2km S, is a Club Méditerranée with all that goes with it: pool, tennis courts, bars and so forth, and a harbour for small pleasure craft.

At *Lumio*, 3km from Sant'Ambrogio, the church of SAN PIETRO E SAN PAOLO is built of red granite in romanesque style. It stands 1km outside the village of Lumio at a hairpin bend in the R 197 to Calvi. Built in the 11C, it was restored in the 18C with, set into the façade, two curly-maned lions brought from some earlier building where, in Tuscan fashion, they may have flanked a small porch. Although the church does not compare with, for example, Murato, it stands with dignified calm at the end of its churchyard approached along a path

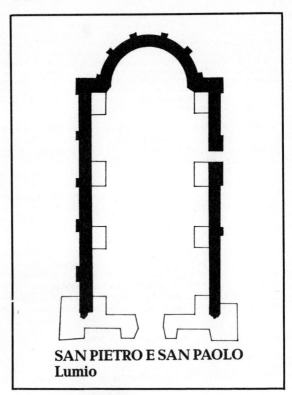

SAN PIETRO E SAN PAOLO
Lumio

between lilac bushes and is well worth a visit. From Lumio it is 8km W along the N 197 to Calvi.

Calvi (3684 inhab., sous-préfecture of the Haute Corse) has been fought over, besieged, destroyed, endlessly rebuilt and is still solidly there.

During the second half of the 13C it was disputed by warring factions of local landowners until the citizens appealed to the Genoese for protection. The town was rebuilt and fortified in 1268 by Giovaniello de Loreto and the Calvesi were accorded special rights and privileges by the Republic of Genoa to which it remained 'semper fidelis' through the centuries. The town's history is that of a fortress port prepared to repel all comers, whether raiders from the North African coast, the Royal Navy, or the assaults of Corsican nationalists like Paoli who founded l'Ile Rousse as a rival port to Calvi.

When in July 1793 Paoli appealed to England for support against the French the Royal Navy besieged Calvi. From 16 June to 5 August the town resisted 6000

British and Paolist supporters. Forced back by French ships, including 'l'Orient' commanded by the gallant Luce de Casabianca, the British shelled the town from the heights of La Serra. It was during these land and sea attacks that Captain Nelson was wounded by rock splinters and lost the sight of his right eye. The Royal Navy eventually took the town after having damaged it severely by bombardment. Two years later the British pulled out and in 1796 Calvi was French again.

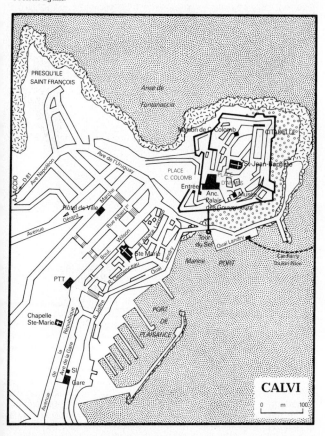

The town is built on a traditional Corsican or accepted medieval plan, the chosen site being difficult to reach from seaward, where it is protected by cliffs, and so placed geographically that the possibility of attack from landward is also reduced. Calvi has all of this. The port, entered from the Golfe de Calvi, is sheltered from the W wind by the promontory on which the Citadelle stands. There is deep water in the anchorage for the ships that export the produce of the Balagne: grapes, olives, cereals, figs and other fruits; and also for fishing boats, steamboats and sailing vessels.

Calvi is roughly divided into two parts: the Citadelle, built on the rocky promontory and virtually impregnable until the arrival of the aeroplane, containing the Haute-Ville with its maze of ancient narrow streets and the Port or Marine district, the Basse-Ville, with a broad quay, ships lying at anchor, cafés and restaurants along the quayside and, towering protectively above it all, the Citadelle's honey-coloured ramparts.

Auld Acquaintance—M. Ignace Bianconi, hôtelier at Calvi, formed enduring friendships with wartime British troops

The Citadelle and the Old Walled Town. Although it is possible to reach the Citadelle and the Old Town by car the effect is greater if one explores on foot. Cross the Place Christophe Colomb, pausing to read the commemoration of the last struggle for liberty: '1943 First landing on French soil [by French troops] at Ajaccio 13–14 September where the volunteers of the 1st Shock Battalion met and joined up with the forces of resistance. In this citadel of Calvi the 1st Battalion forged its spirit and its arms...300 of its members died for their country'. Calvi is proud of its history and reputation as a training centre for the crack regiments of the French Army including the French Foreign Legion.

The only entrance to the Citadelle was formerly guarded by a drawbridge, portcullis and armoured gates. Over the gateway are the arms of Calvi and the words that celebrate the town's long loyalty to Genoa, 'Civitas Calvi semper fidelis', accorded by the Republic of Genoa in 1562 after the town had heroically withstood the sieges of 1553 and 1555 by French and Turkish forces and Sampiero's Corsicans, rebels or partisans according to point of view.

A tour of the RAMPARTS encircling this fortified granite promontory rising nearly 80m sheer from the sea gives spectacular views over the Golfe de Calvi to the SE and over to the inland villages and orchards of the Balagne with the mountains rising beyond. To the W there is a view over the Marine and the Lower Town and beyond to the Saint François Peninsula and the Golfe and Point of Revellata on which stands a lighthouse.

After completing the tour of the ramparts one comes back to the Place des Armes which is dominated by the former *Palace of the Genoese Governors*, begun in the 13C and enlarged in 1554 (between the two sieges by the Franco-Turkish-Sampiero forces), by the Bank of Saint George. The old palace, of massive construction, is now the Sampiero Barracks (not open to the public), occupied since 1967 by the Foreign Legion 2nd Parachute Regiment.

On the far side of the Place des Armes the cathedral church of **Saint John the Baptist** stands on the highest point of the rock on which the old city is built. Built in the 13C, it suffered in the 1553 siege and was severely damaged by fire in the explosion of the Palace powder magazine in 1567. Rebuilt in 1570 and raised to cathedral status in 1576, it is in the form of a Greek cross and surmounted by a cupola.

Inside, under the dome are what appear to be theatre boxes protected by grilles. Here sat the wives of local dignitaries when they attended mass; the grilles were to protect them from the curious or lustful eyes of the common people. To the left of the entrance are marble baptismal fonts dated 1568. The carved and painted *pulpit* was given by the people of Calvi in 1757. The central panel portrays John the Baptist and is flanked by the symbols of the four evangelists.

The *high altar* is marble and surmounted by a triptych (1498), the work of the Ligurian artist Barbagelata and a copy of his master Mazone's painting for the church of Santa Maria di Castello in Genoa. The work was commissioned and paid for by two Calvesi. The central panel has gone but there remain an Annunciation and six figures of patron saints of Calvi. Below the triptych is a portrayal of Saint Nicolas and three children, the work of 'primitive' local artists.

To the right of the choir, above the altar, is the ebony *Christ of the Miracles* which was displayed above the ramparts to the besieging Turks who at the sight of it fell back and lifted the siege. Above the altar to the left of the choir is the wooden *Virgin of the Rosary* (16C) from Seville. The Andalucian custom is followed by dressing the figure in a sequence of robes for different holy days: for example she wears mourning black on Good Friday.

One of Calvi's most notable families, the Baglioni, are buried below the cupola. In 1400 a member of this family overheard two men plotting to deliver the town to the Aragonese forces. Shouting 'Liberta! Liberta!' he cut them down with his sword and in gratitude the Calvesi added 'Liberta' to his surname. He and his descendants are so-called to this day.

The 15C *Oratoire Saint-Antoine* has over the main door a carved late portrayal of the saint with his piglet, flanked by St. Francis of Assisi, St. John the Baptist and members of the Franciscan order. The Oratory is now the religious art museum of the Balagne, 15–18C. Damaged 16C frescoes and panels of a 15C altar-piece repainted in 1677. Fine collection of ecclesiastical vestments (17–18C). Ivory Christ attributed to the Florentine sculptor Sansovino (died 1570). Permanent exhibition in other rooms of the history and archaeology of Calvi, with Roman, Pisan, Genoese and French exhibits, many recovered from the seabed.

Look at the *wall plaque* commemorating Columbus's birth in the Rue Colombo (formerly the street of the weavers, Rue des Tisserands, Carrugio del Filo). This states categorically that: 'Ici est né en 1441 Christophe Colomb, immortalisé par la decouverte du Nouvelle Monde, alors que Calvi était sous la domination génoise; mort à Valladolid le 20 mai 1500'.

Calvi claims to be the birthplace of Christopher Columbus. Joseph Chiari, a Corsican diplomat long resident in the UK, put forward a well-argued and spirited case for Columbus's having been born here. The claim rests on the fact that he was Genoese (as was Calvi at that time). Another famous figure connected with Calvi is the real-life Don Juan, Miguel de Leca y Colonna y Manara y Vincentello. He was born in Seville in 1627 of a father from Calvi and a mother from the Balagne village of Montemaggiore.

From the Place Christophe Colomb follow the Rue Albert 1er to where, on the right, approached by stepped terraces through well-tended gardens, is the *Hôtel de Ville* (open 08.30–12.00 and 14.00–16.00, except Saturday, Sunday and public holidays). The Council Chamber has some paintings given by Cardinal Fesch (whose main collection belongs to Ajaccio), three of which are said to be by Rubens. Others are of 17C Italian provenance.

The Basse Ville containing the Marine, the Port de Plaisance and the quays, is overlooked by the church of *Sainte Marie Majeure*. It was begun in 1765 on the site of earlier churches destroyed during the Barbarian incursions in the 5C and later in the 16C, the cupola belonging to the second quarter of the 19C. Follow the Boulevard Wilson 230m S to just beyond where it becomes the Avenue de la République. On the right stands the *Chapelle Sainte-Marie*, rebuilt in the 14C incorporating vestiges of the 4C basilica. At the NE corner of the Marine on the Quai Landry is the *Tour de Sel*, storehouse for salt, originally a strongly fortified lookout tower.

To visit the *Chapelle de la Madona di a Serra*, 6km SW of Calvi, take the D 81 from the Avenue Napoléon, clearly marked as the road to Ajaccio. A turn to the left at 4km leads in 2km to the chapel, standing 216m high on the summit of a hill. A 19C building on the site of a 15C sanctuary destroyed during the 1794 siege of Calvi, the chapel is of no architectural interest but contains a painting on parchment over the altar of the Immaculate Conception with a Franciscan monk 'en donateur'. On 8 September (Feast of the Nativity of the Virgin) or the following Sunday there is a procession to the chapel from Calvi. A footpath to the left leads back to Calvi in 40–50 minutes. The visit is recommended above all for the view from the chapel NE across the Gulf and town of Calvi, E across the Calenzana valley to the Monte Grosso, and NW to the Revellata peninsula and out to sea.

Punta di a Revellata. Taking the same road, the D 83 to Ajaccio from Calvi, take at 4km the turning to the right (almost opposite the turn to the Chapelle de la Madona di a Serra) to the point (2.5km) where there is a lighthouse and an oceanographic centre founded by Liège University. View over the Golfo di a Revellata and to the Citadel of Calvi. It may be impossible to drive all the way to the point but there is a footpath. Another footpath also leads back to Calvi (two hours).

Boat Excursions from Calvi to La Grotte des Veaux Marins, (3 hours there and back), to sea-caves once inhabited by Mediterranean seals. Fine views of the cliffs of the Revellata Point. Day trips to the landlocked fishing port of Girolata and to Porto. Details obtainable at the Port of Calvi or the Tourist Office, Place de la Gare.

RELIGIOUS FESTIVALS IN CALVI AND DISTRICT. *Maundy Thursday.* Canistrelli procession in the town. The name *Canistrelli* comes from the biscuit made with eggs baked in Corsica at Easter and called in other parts of the island caccavelli. *Good Friday.* Granitola (the snail) procession 21.00–23.00—barefoot, hooded penitents carry a life-size statue of the dead Christ followed by a statue of the Virgin Mary in mourning. *Assumption of the Virgin.* 15–18 August, three days of games, fireworks, processions, etc. *Pilgrimage of our Lady of the Serra.* 8 September (or the following Sunday).

B. Belgodère to Corbara: some Inland Villages of the Balagne

ROAD (D 71) 29km.—10km *Speloncato* (to left of road).—16.5km *Muro*—24km *Aregno.*—26.5km *Pigna.*

Instead of taking the N 199 from Lozari to l'Ile Rousse, take the N 197 going directly S from Lozari for 8km to *Belgodère* (Belgudè, 310m, 535 inhab.). This is a 'balcony' village with its natural protection enhanced by an old fort, on a jutting rock, now in ruins, overlooking the olive groves and orchards of the fertile Prato valley. The village owes its name, meaning 'beau plaisir' or pleasant place, to its situation. The best view over the valley is from the ruins of the old fort, reached by a narrow lane and steps. The church of *Saint Thomas de Belgodère,* founded in 1269 by André Malaspina, marquis de Massa, contains a painting (late 16C) on wood of the Virgin and Child between two apostles and members of the fraternity who donated the painting.

Leave Belgodère by the D 71 in the direction of Calvi. At 4.5km on the other side of the hamlet of Costa the road rounds the *Convent of Tuani,* now a private house.—10km beyond Belgodère, S of the D 71 on the minor D 63 a left turn is marked to *Speloncato* (Spiluncatu, 550m, 265 inhab.), built on an outcrop of Monte Tolo (1332m). The rocks on either side of the village have numerous grottoes, the most famous being the *Pietra Tafonata* (Pierced Stone), 8m long and 6–7m wide. On 8 April and 8 September at around 18.00 the setting sun goes temporarily out of view and reappears for a few instants, shining through the hole in the rock. Narrow streets of tall granite houses. From the village there are superb views over the Balagne to the sea.

Return to the D 71 by the D 663 and on reaching it turn left, passing two villages, *Nessa* and *Feliceto,* which lie on detour roads. These are worth visiting, set among great chestnut trees and olive groves. During harvesting, green or orange nets are spread beneath the olive trees to catch the fruit. The trees may be up to eight centuries old but many groves have been destroyed by fire.

6.5km beyond Speloncato is **Muro** (Müru, 320m, 433 inhab.), a village consisting principally of a main street of houses on one side only, the other being the open side of a 'balcony' poised above a precipitous drop down to gardens, orchards and olive groves. On the street the church of *the Annunciation,* too large for the village, is one of Corsica's baroque masterpieces. Interior a riot of polychromatic marble covering the altar, altar rail, pulpit and organ loft. Note inscription inside: 'On 4 March 1798, Ash Wednesday, part of the roof of the church fell in during the service and killed 59 parishioners'. Local oral tradition has it that at the moment this took place the priest in Calenzana interrupted his sermon to ask his congregation to pray for the parishioners of Muro and their church.

Near the end of the village street is a tall square house, once a centre for the cultivation of silkworms imported from Syria and fed on mulberry leaves from trees in the Regina valley below. The building was originally two storeys higher but these were removed as being unsafe (heeding the warning of the church?).

In many places along the D 71 there are fine views across the Balagne countryside and also from the villages lying along the road, Avapessa, Cateri (a folkcraft centre) and, 2km W along the D 71 leading to the N 197 coast road, *Lavatoggio* (Lavatoghju, 200m, 204 inhab.) with a vista over the Algajola Bay and to the surrounding villages.

Take the D 151 N from Cateri and then at 500m the D 143 to *Sant'Antonino* (Sant Antuninu, 500m, 113 inhab.) set on a ridge between two valleys. The village of old houses, many carefully restored, rises up the hillside in narrow sloping streets. Cars must be parked close to the church which is set on a greensward plateau kept cropped by the sheep and goats which wander over it. There is a remarkable eagle's eye view over the Balagne to the sea and inland to the mountains.

Return to the D 151 and turn right for under 1km to reach *Aregno* (Aregnu, 219m, 534 inhab.), a village set among orange and lemon groves. Just before reaching the village there is a cemetery on the right, in the middle of which stands one of the triumphs of Pisan Romanesque architecture, the church of LA TRINITÀ (mid 12C) which is also dedicated to San Giovanni Battista. The first sight of it is stunning.

Exterior. The façade, of contrasting light and dark stones in a complicated chequerboard pattern, and of three unequally divided storeys, is ornamented with bold sculptures in high relief. To the left of the W door is the standing figure of a woman in a long dress, hands on hips, her head covered by a round cap. To the right of the door sits the figure of a naked and bald man (Moses?) holding on his knees what might be the tablets of the Law. Under the apex of the pediment is a seated male figure with the ankle of the left leg resting on the knee of the right leg. It is obvious that the W door was originally surmounted by a low rounded arch without a tympanum. Moracchini-Mazel writes in 'Corse Romane' that 'It was the restoration carried out at the end of the 19C which replaced the lower arch by a monolithic lintel. This is to be discovered if one studies old drawings of the church'. The nave roof is now covered in round tiles but that of the semi-circular apse has preserved its *teghie* (flat stones).

Interior. The single nave is admirably bare and on the N wall there are two frescoes. The first represents *Quatre Docteurs de l'Eglise latine* (Augustine, Gregory, Jerome and Ambrose). The fresco, dated 17 May 1458, was probably the work of a local artist. Jerome, for example, is given in the Corsican form of Gilormi. The second fresco, dated 1449, depicts Saint Michael slaying the dragon, his expression that of a matador confident of tail and ears.

2.5km N of Aregno is *Pigna* (230m, 101 inhab.), lying just off the D 151 to the left, its houses huddled on the summit of a hill with olive groves on the slopes and overlooking the curve of Algajola Bay. Along

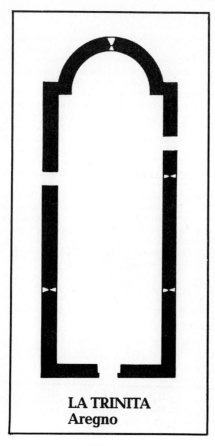

LA TRINITA
Aregno

the winding narrow lanes, paved or sometimes with steps, many houses are occupied by people engaged in handicrafts including weaving, pottery, basketry, woodcarving and candlemaking. This *artisinat* (or cottage industry) flourishes as a co-operative association called La Corsicada, founded in 1964 and increased in size more than tenfold since. It has as its aim the revival of old village crafts, producing locally everything needed by the community of shepherds, farmers and housewives. The materials employed include metal, wood, wool, clay and osier. This village is not a souvenir trap. It is informative and interesting to see how traditional crafts are still practised and taught to young apprentices. One can buy objects but, with customary Corsican courtesy, it is left to the customer to ask.

1km N of Pigna is the *Couvent de Corbara*, founded in 1456 by the Franciscans who occupied it until 1792. It was abandoned at the time of the Revolution until in 1857 the monastery was re-founded by the Dominicans. In 1884 they established their Studium Provinciale there, a college teaching theology and religious philosophy to local students. Paoli stayed frequently at Corbara. There is a footpath, or more correctly, a mule-path from the convent (80 minutes there and back) to *Monte Sant'Angelo* (562m) with a view over the Balagne, the Agriates Desert and the W coast of Cap Corse.

Corbara (Curbara, 17m, 467 inhab.), long known as the 'key to the Balagne', is a large village spread out over the slopes of the grandiloquently-named Monte Guido (a hill rather than a mountain). Ruins of the Castel de Guido and the Castel de Corbara. The Savelli de Guido family were the rulers hereabouts from the beginning of the 14C. They built a château (c 1375) at Corbara, in effect a fortified castle which the Genoese pulled down in the early 16C as being a threat to their rule, whereupon the stubborn Savelli restored Castel de Guido which the Roman prince Guido de Savelli had built in 816. He had been made Count of Balagne after despatching the Saracens. The village of Corbara has almost a North African or southern Spanish air with its narrow streets, Barbary fig cactus and covered passageways. The 18C church of *the Annunciation* is another baroque triumph in polychromatic marble (1750) imported from Liguria or Tuscany.

3km N of Corbara the D 151 joins the N 197 running NE to l'Ile Rousse and SW to Algajola and Calvi.

C. Balagne villages inland from l'Ile Rousse

From l'Ile Rousse itself there are easily-accessible villages, such as *Monticello* (200m, 345 inhab.). From l'Ile Rousse take the D 63 which winds up the hillside to this village with a large square, shops, and a calm relatively untroubled by tourism. The views down to the coast at l'Ile Rousse, over the cultivated fields, vineyards and orchards, are alone worth the climb to the village. Take the D 263 from Monticello, a winding road, to *Santa Reparata di Balagna* (260m, 727 inhab.), of no intrinsic interest but very typical of the Balagne villages of this area, with wide views across the lower-lying Balagne lands.

D. Balagne villages inland from Calvi

Calenzana is easily accessible from the main N 197 Calvi–l'Ile Rousse coastal road. At 4.5km from Calvi, going E towards l'Ile Rousse, take the D 151 to the right which follows the valley of the Bartasca and in 13km reaches **Calenzana** (Calinzana, 250m, 1700 inhab.). This is a very large village, almost a small town (it would be accounted a town in Devon or New Hampshire) complete with a surreptitious urban air about it. I first went there with an entertaining and ebullient Calvais who pointed out to me that 'the large villas with the very high walls belong to the gangsters who run Marseille, the small villas with lower walls belong to their lawyers. And if you are looking for the priest, he is the man in jeans sitting over there at the café.'

Set among olive and almond trees, against the slopes of Monte Grosso, Calenzana is the starting point of the GR 20, the long-distance mountain walk that ends up at Conca, near Porto Vecchio, in the SE of Corsica. Anybody in the village will show you how to climb up the stony alleys to get to the route. The church of *Saint Blaise* (end 17C, finished in 1715) is of breathtaking proportions. Much polychromatic marble inside and the black-and-white tiled floor sloping (one can check it against the edges of memorials along the walls) towards the W door ('Lets the water out when there's a flood from the mountain', the Monte Grosso, a local informed me). The polychrome marble altar is of 1767. There is some cunning trompe l'oeil of 1880 and medallions around the ceiling of the 18C nave depicting St. Blaise administering to a child patient.

The clock tower bears an inscription to one of the most famous Corsican legends allied to hard history. It has to be retold straight-faced, legend, history, myth and all. In 1729 the Corsicans rose against the Genoese rulers. The Genoese hired German soldiers to help them put down the Corsican nationalists (there was a profitable deal in the Germans' favour, incidentally). On 2 February 1732 Genoese troops, supported by 500–800 German mercenaries, did battle in Calenzana. One version says that the citizens of Calenzana attacked the invaders with agricultural weapons, scythes, sickles, hayforks and spades, but another, more romantic, version says that the villagers hid until the German mercenaries were well into the village and then hurled down beehives, complete with buzzing tenants. The unhappy German soldiers, stung to distraction, rushed to the fountains for relief where they were butchered by the under-armed but adequately knived Calenzenais. The number of Germans killed varies in the telling from 100–800, but those who fell were buried on the spot in a mass grave called the Cimetière des Allemands (the Campu santu di i Tedeschi).

1km from Calenzana is the church of *Sainte Restitute* who since the 5C has been one of the most popular Corsican martyrs. She was beheaded in 303 on the orders of the Emperor Diocletian. Two processions, the first on Easter Monday, the second the first Sunday after 21 May. Sarcophagus of the saint, in Carrara marble, from the late 4C, was until 1951 concealed under a cover in a 15C tomb decorated with frescoes, described by Geneviève Moracchini-Mazel as 'naive and touching paintings belonging to the art of miniatures as though the painter had tried to reproduce a manuscript which he held in his hands'.

24km from Calvi along the D 451 lies *Montemaggiore* (400m, 215 inhab.), a 'terrace' village set at the end of a rocky spur above the basins of the Secco and the Ficarella, overlooking the Gulf of Calvi. Large baroque church but more interesting is the romanesque church of *Saint Rainier* (San Raniero) about 1km above the village, set in the middle of olive groves. Built second half of the 12C, black and white granite. Some good marble sculptures both inside and outside the church.

6   From Calvi to Porto and Ajaccio

ROAD (D 81) 164km.—23km *Argentella.*—58km *Bocca a Croce.*—67.5km *Partinello.*—81km *Porto.*—93km *Piana.*—112.5km *Cargèse.*

Leaving Calvi by the D 81, which cuts across the foot of the Revellata peninsula and passes close to the chapel of Notre Dame de la Serra (see Rte 5), this winding road keeps for the most part within sight of the sea (although there are few easy tracks down to the shore).

16.5km from Calvi the road turns S and inland from the *Capo a u Cavallo* to which there is a track (2km) to the semaphore (295m). Magnificent view from this point: to the E the Cinto range and further ranges of high mountains in the Corsican interior above the pine forests and maquis, to the N Cap Corse and to the S the serrated W coastline of the island. When the weather is very clear the Alpes Maritimes on the French mainland to the NW can be seen.

22.6km from Calvi *Argentella*, which owes its name to the silver-bearing lead sulphide or galena formerly mined there, the ore being shipped from the nearby tiny port of Crovani. Mine buildings now abandoned ruins. A further 5km S is the Bocca Bassa (120m), a col taking the road over the *Punta di Ciutonne*, view over the gulf of Galéria and the village of the same name tucked into the NNE-facing slopes of the Capu Tondu (840m).

To reach *Galéria* (524 inhab.) turn right off the D 81 after the bridge over the Fango, on to the D 351. Sandy beach between the village and the mouth of the Fango to the N. In summer the boat from Calvi stops mid-morning at Galéria on its way to Girolata and Porto and late afternoon on the return journey. Details from the Mariani agency in Calvi.

From the Galéria turning the D 81 winds it way through the Fango Forest to the Bocca a Palmarella (374m). The D 35 turns left at le Fango, to follow the Fango valley into the Parc Naturel Régional (see Rte 16).

To the W of the D 81 lies *Girolata*, magnificently isolated except for footpaths and the summertime cruise boats mentioned above. It is a small fishing port at the farthest inland point of the Golfe de Girolata, set on a promontory with wooded and maquis-covered hills inland and its own Genoese watchtower, one of many along the coast. Girolata makes its living from lobster fishing and from the summer tourist boats that stop briefly there.
   The footpaths by which Girolata may be reached go down from the D 81, that from the Col di Palmarella being the shortest and most direct as well as the hardest on the way back. A second one leads down from a col about 1km to the S of the Palmarella pass. It is not easy to find and goes down by way of a collection of small houses marked on the map as Tuara and passing a sandy bay just below the Source de Tuara. A third way starting from the col called Bocca a Croce (272m), a few kilometres further S along the D 81, also leads to Girolata by way of a maquis-bordered mule track down to the Source de Tuara and joins pathway No. 2. (I prefer the last, as giving the greatest variety of landscape and views to Capo d'Osani, the rocky promontory of red stone separating the Golfe de Girolata from the Golfe de Porto.)

1km S of the Bocca a Croce a turning to the right, the D 424, leads to the hamlet of *Osani*, above which is a prehistoric circle on which there is little information available. From Osani a track descends (4.5km) to a lonely pebble beach at *Gratelle*. The going is not easy, either there or on the return journey. The beach at *Caspio*, 3km from Partinello on the D 324, is easier to get to.

10km S of the Bocca a Croce along the D 81 is *Partinello* (Partinellu, 207m, 254 inhab.). A further 13.5km brings one to **Porto** (335m, 605 inhab.), forming part of the commune of Ota and built in the form of an amphitheatre at the foot of Capo d'Ota (1220m). (At 5.5km from the village of Porto the D 124 winds up into the hills to *Ota* which is built, so to speak, in layers on the hillside, with a number of small but very good restaurants.) Porto itself is set at the point where the Gulf of that name penetrates furthest inland. Possessing one of the most beautiful situations not only in Corsica but in the whole of the Mediterranean, Porto has suffered the consequences. There are too many tourists and too many hotels put up too quickly, the little bay has been transformed into a marina and at the entrance to this village of half-finished hotels and boutiques is one of the most hilarious one-way systems I have ever seen. Porto is expanding into its new buildings, shops, hotels and new persona. The basic attractions of the place, the Genoese tower, the eucalyptus groves and the almost Chinese-style wooden bridge over the estuary of the Vaita, remain, but Porto itself has changed almost beyond recognition in the past 20 years.

Take the D 81 S out of Porto. After it crosses the River Vaita, the road turns right to follow the Vaita valley almost to the sea and then turns SW along the coast within sight or reach of Corsica's most astonishing coastal strip, LES CALANQUES, (Les Calanche, E Calanche; same pronunciation however they are spelt). Red spires, steeples, seemingly sculptured heads and shapes, all of granite ranging in colour through reds and pinks, often rise up sheer from the sea for 300–400m. The best centre from which to observe these (and do not try rock climbing on them) is from *Piana* (A Piana, 661 inhab.) at 93km from Calvi, 71km from Ajaccio (many good hotels). It hangs above the Gulf of Porto, with a large white church of *Sainte-Marie* (18C) and a fine campanile. Les Calanques and Piana form perhaps the best-known sights of Corsica and, although by no means typical of the island, are well worth seeing, particularly at sunrise and sunset.

Little less than 20km S of Piana is **Cargèse** (Carghjese, 907 inhab.) (the pronunciation varies between a soft or a hard 'g').

Cargèse was founded in 1676 by Greek refugees from Turkish rule who asked the Genoese rulers of Corsica for the right to settle on the W coast of the island. The Genoese (often, and for the most part rightly, criticised for their harsh rule in Corsica) allowed 730 Greeks who had arrived in Genoa in March 1676 to leave in May of that year to set up their new homes. The Genoese unfortunately took little account of the native Corsicans' attitude to this apparently generous gesture and in 1731 the Corsicans, finding themselves excluded from the traditional pastures to which the shepherds of the Niolo and Vico brought their flocks, burned the Greek villages and the inhabitants took refuge in Ajaccio. Once Corsica became French (1769) the Greek village and church were rebuilt at Cargèse and 110 Greek families returned there with a grant of 22 hectares per family. Over the years the Greek and Corsican families of Cargèse worked out a way of living together and tolerated each others' Roman Catholic and Greek Orthodox churches. Between 300 and 400 Greeks, observing the Orthodox faith, still live in Cargèse. To confuse this ecumenical example a little further, families of Greek settlers went to Algeria in the 19C and established the village of Sidi Merouan. After the Algerian war some of their descendants returned and took their place again in Cargèse's Greek community.

The *Greek Orthodox church* was built in the second half of the 19C, decorated with the ikons donated by the Greeks in the late 17C. The ikon of a winged Saint John the Baptist (16C), splendidly coloured in blue, green and grey, is remarkable and is signed by 'a monk of Saint Athos'. The early 19C *Roman Catholic church*, facing the Orthodox building, has an extravagantly decorated trompe l'oeil interior, and must be one of the last churches to have been decorated in a flamboyantly baroque style. The two churches, facing each other in location as well as in faith, and reached through peaceful gardens full of poppies, fig-trees and nasturtiums, form the heart of Cargèse. Down the hill there is a rather run-down fishing port which revives in the summer. Cargèse is built on the S side of a rocky promontory from which the D 81 goes due E inland and then sharply S, following the coast closely (with fine views over the Mediterranean shore) and rounding the capes of the Gulf of Sagone until reaching the site of historic *Sagone*.

The Romans founded a town here which became the seat of a bishopric in the 6C. In the Middle Ages the diocese of Sagone was enormous, but in the 12C it was put under that of Pisa. By the 16C Sagone had become unfit to live in (possibly malaria was the cause): the town was in ruins, the cathedral had to be demolished and in 1572 Pope Gregory XIII directed that the bishopric be transferred to Vico. In 1625 Urban VIII, having decided that Sagone was more-or-less abandoned, transferred the bishopric from its temporary seat at Vico to Calvi. Just beyond the bridge over the Sagone a narrow road to the right leads to the ruins of the cathedral of *Sant'Appiano* (early 12C). Archaeological excavations have discovered a wall of an apse which might have been part of the original basilica (4th or 5C). Near the sanctuary there is a menhir but nothing of its archaeological history is known.

13.5km from Cargèse is the port and village of *Sagone*, set on the estuary of the river of the same name. The Sagone River rises on the slopes of San Angelo (San Anghiulu, 1272m) and is some 20km long from source to estuary, creating a wide delta which is responsible for the extensive sandy beaches. The Golfe de Sagone runs from the Punta di Cargèse in the N to Capo di Feno in the S. 4km S of Sagone the D 81 crosses the marshy delta of the Liamone, which runs 46km from where it rises on the Cimatella. The sand which it brings down, as in the case of the Sagone, has built up into a sandbar to enclose a lagoon.

At the *Punta Capigliolo* (Genoese tower) the D 81 makes a right-angle turn to the E and along the coast to the tiny seaside resort of *Tiuccia* on the shore of the Gulfu di u Liscia, a gulf within a gulf, whose S point (not on the D 81 but on a minor track which hugs the shore) is *Punta di Palmentoju* where another Genoese tower faces that of Capigliolo 3km across the Gulf.

On the hillside beyond the shoreline buildings stand the ruins of the *Castello Capraia*, formerly the stronghold of a famous or perhaps notorious Corsican family, the counts of Cinarca (Cinarchesi) who achieved great power during the struggles between Genoa and Pisa in the 13C. One of them, Sinucello de la Rocca, who earned the name of Giudici, 'Judge', because of his impartial administration of justice, succeeded for a while in ruling the whole of Corsica. Nevertheless the struggles returned and one of his many bastard sons betrayed him to the Genoese, in one of whose mainland dungeons he died in 1312, blind and nearly 100 years old.

The area of the CINARCA, which lies to the E of the D 81, is that of the basin of the Liscia river (today it is the canton of Sari d'Orcino). Surrounded by mountains, it is well-watered and very fertile, 'a garden amidst the maquis' as it is often described. It has citrus groves, olives, peaches, maize, vineyards, sweet chestnuts and pastures. The D 601, turning left off the D 81 less than 3km S of Tiuccia, leads by a narrow and winding road to (7.5km) *Casaglione* (Casaglio, 272 inhab.). The church of San Frediano contains a painting dated 1505 of the Crucifixion.

Leaving Casaglione, 3.5km to the W on the D 25 is the Bocca di San Antonio (358m). Alternatively, turn right along the D 1 to (3.5km) *Sari d'Orcino* (Sari d'Urcinu, 300m, 390 inhab.), two hamlets spread in a semi-circle above the Liscia valley, cultivating olives and citrus fruits. Extensive views over the valley and the Golfe de Sagone. This short tour gives a good idea of this small and verdant area but although the signposting is usually good a large-scale map of the area is advisable so as not to waste time if driving. It is also a most pleasant walking area.

Return to the D 81 at Calcatoggio and continue S 11km to meet the main N 194 road, from where it is 5km to Ajaccio.

A. Vico and local excursions

Before leaving the region of the Sagone Gulf, instead of following the D 81 S down the coast, take the D 70 to the left out of Sagone and in 20km cross the Col de San Antoine (496m). The road forks almost immediately and to reach Vico take the right fork. The other road also leads to Vico but in a circular and more complicated route.

21km from Sagone, **Vico** (Vicu 400m, 2000 inhab.) is a small town set on well-wooded hillsides overlooking the fertile valley of the Upper Liamone with its olive groves and sweet chestnut woods. To the E is the mountain of *la Sposata* (Punta di a Spusata). It owes its name (the Bride) to the legend that a beautiful local girl, having married a rich husband, left her old widowed mother penniless. The mother cursed her daughter for her flinty heart and the daughter turned to stone. The outline of the mountain could be thought to resemble a woman on horseback. In 1572, after Sagone had fallen into decay, the bishopric was moved for a while to Vico.

Less than 2km S of Vico is the *monastery of St. François*, founded by Gianpolo di Leca in 1481. The Franciscans left in 1793 and in 1836 the Oblats of Marie Immaculée settled there. The convent church is 17C and has a polychrome marble altar (1698) and massive carved chestnut wood sacristy furnishings. This church contains a crucified Christ in wood, said to be the oldest in Corsica. It predates the foundation of the monastery in 1481 and is believed to have been brought from Italy by the founding monks.

Some 4km to the S of Vico, on a massive rock, stood the castle of the Leca family. In the Middle Ages this was one of the most important and powerful families in W Corsica. The castle was a fortress during the long struggle against Genoa, and after 1453 against the forces of the Banque (or Office) of Saint Georges, a Genoese business organisation with its own private army. Murder, treachery and clan warfare continued and in 1459 22 members of the Leca family were captured and had their throats cut by order of the Genoese Governor, Antonio Spinola. Three hundred years later the curé of Guagno, Dominique Leca, known as Circinello, spent his life fighting for Corsican independence. In 1769, when Paoli retired to England, Father Dominique continued the fight for freedom, this time against the new rulers, the French. Leading a small band of partisans, he continued his guerrilla warfare for a further three years and died, having excaped prison or assassination, of exposure and exhaustion in the Fiumorbo. He has never been forgotten by the mountain people of this region and a memorial was erected in Guagno in 1937.

Vico is a good centre for exploring the district. Take the D 23 E from Vico for 12km to reach *Guagno les Bains* (480m, 120 inhab.) which has two hot springs, recommended in the 16C and exploited by the French in the 18C. After a long period of dilapidation the spa centre has been rebuilt and great efforts made to attract visitors. The top spring (37°C) of 'l'Occhio' on the D 323 (turning to the left off the D 23) was long used in treatment of the eyes as its name suggests, and the lower spring called Venturini (52°C) is used in the treatment of rheumatism, skin afflictions, arthritis and sciatica. Even without taking the waters there is a pleasant journey along the lush Fiume Grosso valley.

Guagno (Guagnu, 800m, 1100 inhab.), 8.5km beyond Les Bains, overlooks the valleys of the Fiume Grosso and the Albelli. Set in thick woods of sweet chestnuts, oaks and Corsican pines and larches, it makes a good starting point for mountain expeditions. Guagno is 3km inside the W border of the Parc Naturel Régional (see Rte 16) and walkers may join up with the GR 20 mountain path at Bocca a la Soglia and near the Bocca Manganello.

B. Vico to Evisa

By following the D 70 N from Vico one reaches the D 84 in 23km. One can then take the D 84 NE, crossing the Parc Naturel Régional diagonally to meet the N 193 N of Corte, or, alternatively, go left to Evisa and take the D 84 back to the coast at Porto. The D 70 leaves Vico to the N to become a climbing, winding mountain road. 2km beyond the Chapelle St. Roch (755m) on the left there is a right turn for *Renno* (6km) (Rennu, 900m, 172 inhab.), a collection of hamlets among chestnuts, walnut orchards, and holm oak trees. It is claimed that, together with those of Bastelica, the *pommes reinettes*, or pippin dessert apples, are the best in Corsica. Sheep, pigs and chickens are raised here and there is a St. Roch Fair held on 16, 17 and 18 August, with a pilgrimage to the Chapelle St. Roch.

Return to the D 70 and continue N to the Col de Sevi (1100m). There is a good and fairly easy walk from the Col, leading up to *l'Incinosa* or Chieragella (1510m) where there is a panoramic view over to the Gulf of Porto, about 2 hours there and back. The D 70 continues high and winding, at just under 1000m, until it begins the descent to the valley of the Tavulella and the village of *Cristinacce* (E Cristinacce, 835m, 128 inhab.), its houses built on the steep chestnut-covered slopes of Capo di Melo (1564m). The D 70 climbs for 3.5km through thick chestnut woods, (this is the southern border of the Fôret d'Aïtone) to the Bocca a Zora (897m). Fork left here on the D 24 or continue on the D 70 for less than 2km to the first turning to the left, a hairpin turn signposted (2km) to Evisa.

C. Evisa and local excursions

Evisa (835m, 723 inhab.), one of the most beautiful of Corsican villages, stands on a rocky spur that separates the upper valley of the Porto River from the ravine of the Aïtone stream. It is the gateway to the Aïtone Forest and a good centre for expeditions by car or on foot. Possible excursions from Evisa include the 12km by car to the *Col de Vergio* (1477m) through the forest of towering straight Corsican pines, fir trees, beech and holm oaks. The col is the highest point (1464m) for a motor road in Corsica and is the gateway E to the Niolo which, in turn, is the road connecting the valleys of the Porto and the Golo. The Station de Ski at Verghio is open, according to state of the snow, from December to April (two ski lifts, restaurant, hotel, bar, equipment hire; open in summer for mountain expeditions). The GR

20 long-distance path passes within a few 100m of the hotel and actually crosses the D 84 close by.

The other expeditions from Evisa can only be undertaken on foot. On the D 84, 4.5km N of Evisa and 1km beyond the Maison Forestière de Catagnone, is the *village de vacance* called *Le Paesolu d'Aïtone*. Immediately beyond the Paesolu is a turning to the left, the *Route Forestière 9a*, which leads off to a 6–7 hour walk by way of the Bocca a u Saltu (1350m, refuge hut), the Col de Cuccavera (1475m) above the pines of the Lindinosa Forest and the Bocca di Guagnerola (1837m) to the River Golo and the GR 20 leading down to the D 84 near the Col and Station at Verghio. It is essential to carry the map of 'Corse Nord de Calvi à Vizzavona, No. 20 Itineraires Pedestres; Scale 1:50,000', Editions Didier & Richard, Institut Geographique National.

Other walks from Evisa include the 2-hour round journey to Le Belvédère. From Evisa, 3km along the D 84 in the direction of Verghio, a track leads off left and winds among the pines to a rocky spur, the *Belvédère* (975m), poised above the Aïtone torrent. There is an impressive view of great jumbled red rocks beyond which the sea is glimpsed. Taking the same road towards the Col de Vergio, turn left into the first *route forestière* for the Aïtone waterfall and the sparse ruins of the watermill, about 2½ hours there and back.

Leaving Evisa by the D 84 in the direction of Porto, after 1km there is a sharp bend at the church of *Saint Cipriano*. From this point there is a view of the Porto valley, the village of Ota and out to the Golfe of Porto. In fact along the 20km to Porto there are many self-evident stopping places from which to admire the view down the valley and, to the right, the *Cirque de la Spelunca*, where the Aïtone joins the Porto River, a massive red pyramid decorated with finials and crockets of the same red stone. The village of *Ota* (c 1km to the N on the D 124) can be seen set in a basin on the further bank of the Porto with behind it, as a rosy-red backdrop, the Capu d'Ota. At 21km from Evisa the D 84 reaches Porto.

Also starting from Evisa, *Les Gorges de la Spelunca* is one of the easiest and most impressive walks in Corsica. Involving no serious climbing or scrambling, it has to be made on foot, there being no nearer roads than the D 84 on the S bank of the Porto, or the D 124 which turns right off the D 84 (14.5km from Evisa) to cross to the N bank of the Porto at the renovated Genoese Pianella bridge, from which it is 3.5km to the village of Ota. The D 124 continues along the N bank to Porto and the sea (5.5km).

Allow about 3 hours to walk from Evisa to Ota by the Spelunca and about 3¾ hours for the return walk. Leave Evisa by the D 84 in the direction of Porto for 1km to St. Cyprien's Chapel. At the end of the cemetery wall, take the path to the right (waymarked in red). It zigzags down maquis-covered rocky slopes to the Tavulella River which it crosses in a well-shaded spot by the Genoese Pont de Zaglia, just above the Tavulella's confluence with the Aïtone (at roughly 1½ hours from Evisa). The path follows the precipitous S bank of the red granite ravine, high above the torrent. After 1 hour's further walk the path reaches the D 124 road at the Deux Ponts d'Ota where the Aïtone and the Onca meet to become the River Porto. There is a bridge over each river. Carry on downstream for 3km to *Ota* (335m, 605 inhab.), built in an amphitheatre below the Capu d'Ota (1220m). The commune of Ota, to which Porto belongs, is in a very fertile area producing chestnuts, olives, vines and vegetables. Many of the houses retain outside stairways, a local feature. There are good restaurants in this village and it is worth coming 5.5km up from Porto when it becomes too crowded and hot in summer to have a meal in the fresh evening air.

II THE EAST COAST

7 Bastia

Bastia (55,000 inhab.) is the Préfecture of Haute Corse.

2000 years ago the site of the present town was a Roman colony; after the
Romans left there was a fishing village called Porto Cardo on what is now the
Vieux Port. In 1380 the occupying Genoese built a fortress or 'bastiglia' (hence
Bastia) overlooking Cardo harbour, which they enlarged, to guard against attack
both from the unruly Corsicans inland and enemies planning invasion across the
Tuscan Straits. The citadel was built 1480–1521 and the town became a garrison
and the seat of the Genoese governors of Corsica who moved from the less easily
defended Biguglia to the S. Bastia remained chief town of the island until the
French Revolution when, in 1791, the Convention divided Corsica into two
départements, with Ajaccio the capital of one and Bastia of the other. This
division lasted for 20 years until 1811 when the island came under one
administration again with the capital moved to Napoleon's birthplace, Ajaccio.
There has always been rivalry between the two towns, each vaunting its past
glories, and the cliché description has been forged that Ajaccio is the cultural
centre of Corsica and Bastia the industrial capital where 'feet are on the ground
and hands at work'. Now that they each administer one of the two départements
of the island, jealousy and resentment have lessened although there are still
obvious differences between the two towns: Ajaccio in atmosphere and architecture is very 'French' while Bastia is much more 'Italian'.

Although the town now looks prosperous and solid it has suffered siege and
depredation over the centuries, the most recent being the damage inflicted
during September–October 1943. De Gaulle awarded the town the Croix de
Guerre avec palme for 'the courage and spirit of its citizens' resistance', in the
same spirit as Malta was awarded the George Cross.

Bastia consists of two parts, the Terra Vecchia and the Terra Nova.
Pay no attention to these terms, there is nothing new about the Terra
Nova which was the original quartier built, fortified and walled by the
Genoese in 1480–1521.

The 20km drive to Bastia from the Bastia–Poretta airport is not the
most attractive introduction to the town. The airport is (sensibly) in the
flat eastern plain near the sea but also close to the N 193 which runs N
between the Biguglia Lagoon on the right and the mountains on the
left. Smallholdings give way to suburban industrial estates: small
factories, showrooms of agricultural machinery and packing plants
where everything is collected and wrapped, from grapes and
tomatoes to wine and refrigerators. Until the end of 1983, when the
tunnel under the Vieux Port was opened to take road traffic into the
heart of Bastia, the town was entered by a comparatively narrow
street thick with traffic, winding down a hill with side streets leading
steeply down to the port on the right beyond the massive walls of the
citadel, and on the left tall Italianate tenements, gay with drying
laundry splashing colours against the speckled old walls.

Now the new expressway from the coast road goes under the
Citadel and the Vieux Port and continues along the edge of the Bassin
St. Nicolas, with the Place St. Nicolas on the left, to the Nouveau Port
and the embarkation points for ferries to Marseille, Toulon, Nice,
Genoa, Leghorn and Sardinia. Bastia, Corsica's largest port and town,
is best seen, in its layout of a series of rising terraces, from the sea. At
almost any time of the day or night there seems to be a large ship,
usually a car ferry, either just coming into or leaving the port.

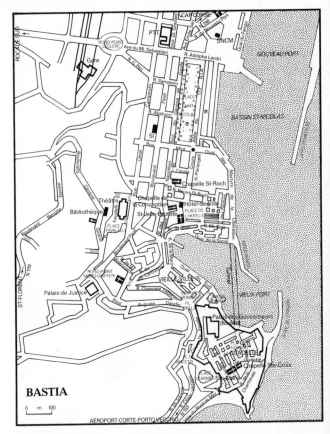

BASTIA FROM NORTH TO SOUTH. In the N of the town, close to the Nouveau Port and the ferry boat arrival and departure point, much of practical use to the visitor is grouped. The D 80 goes N from here through the suburb of Toga and up the E coast of Cap Corse; the *Post Office* is a block away on the Boulevard du General Graziani; the buses for Cap Corse leave from the Rue du Nouveau Port, those for Bonifacio, Porto Vecchio, Piedicroce and Solenzara leave from the Avenue Maréchal Sebastiani, close to the Post Office. The avenue itself leads to the Rond-Point Leclerc and the *railway station* from which there are trains to Ponte Leccia, Ile Rousse, Calvi, Ajaccio, Corte, Venaco, Vizzavona, Bocognano and intermediate stations. There is a *Tourist Information office* on the N side of the Place Saint Nicolas, Opposite the Centre Administratif and just over the road from the embarkation point on the Nouveau Port. The main *Syndicat d'Initiative* is on the Boulevard Paoli, between the Rue Abatucci and the Rue Miot.

The PLACE SAINT NICOLAS, an imposing and very large square (300m long), is open on the seaward side, being built on a terrace overlooking the port. The other side is lined with cafés and shops and the Place itself is shaded by palm and plane trees beneath which at most times, but particularly in the evening, several games of *boules* are usually in progress. There is a constant parade of strollers past the bandstand and the statue of Napoleon wrapped up in a toga. The statue is not by a Corsican but by the Florentine sculptor Bartolini. There is a car park under the square and another between the E side and the expressway that runs along the sea front.

Parallel to the Place Saint Nicolas and running several blocks to the S of it towards the Old Town are three streets forming the main and smartest shopping district. From E to W, or from the Place Saint Nicolas inland, they are the Boulevard du General de Gaulle (becomes the Rue Napoléon S of the Place); the Boulevard Paoli which continues under the same name to the Palais de Justice; the Rue César Campinchi which joins the Boulevard Paoli, at its S end just below the theatre in the Place Favalli. Across the next street to the W, the Boulevard du General Giraud, is the impressive *Municipal Library* of over 80,000 books, many rare, including a 'Decameron' of 1529, as well as an extensive collection of Corsican interest. This part of Bastia and further W becomes progressively steeper. Shorter routes for pedestrians involve many flights of steps.

Chapelle Saint Roch, Bastia

On the Rue Napoléon, between the S side of the Place Saint Nicolas and the Place de l'Hôtel de Ville is the *Chapelle Saint Roch*, built in 1604 by the Confrérie de Saint Roch. The interior is richly decorated and carefully preserved, with finely carved pews, and a gilt 1740 organ.

150m to the S where the Rue Napoleon becomes the Rue des Terrasses is the **Chapelle de la Conception**, built in 1611 by the Confrérie de la Conception. The interior is even richer, the walls hung with crimson damask, cut-glass chandeliers hang from the painted ceiling. There is carved panelling and over the altar a copy of Murillo's *Immaculate Conception*. The sacristy is a small museum of religious art and the statue of the Holy Virgin is carried in procession on 8 December to the Church of St. Jean-Baptiste. The interior of the chapel is so regal in fact that it was used by the Corsican Estates when in session during the French monarchy and by Sir Gilbert Elliot for the first meeting of the Anglo-Corsican Parliament in February 1795. In front of the chapel is a small square with a pebble mosaic of a face wearing a very enigmatic expression and with beams radiating from the head, more a sun figure than a Christian saint.

On the seaward-side of the chapel is the Place de l'Hôtel de Ville, in the centre of a collection of narrow streets leading to the port. Lively market in the square every morning. At the S side of the square is the back of the church of *Saint Jean-Baptiste*, built mid 17C, enlarged and much decorated inside in the 18C. Some Italian pictures from Cardinal Fesch's collection and pulpit, altar and baptismal fonts in Corsican polychromatic marble. The twin towers and the imposing façade dating from 1666 dominate the Vieux Port and more than anything else, including the Citadel, are a visual representation of Bastia. The best view of the Vieux Port, the tall well-weathered houses of the Terra Vecchia and, of course, of the church of Saint Jean-Baptiste, is from the Jetée du Dragon which projects from below the Citadel towards the Môle Genois, the two arms protecting the Vieux Port.

Around the Vieux Port and in the labyrinthian narrow streets, many with steps, are the restaurants and bistros to suit all tastes and pockets. There are cafés and bars and places where traditional Corsican songs and guitar music are performed. It is much less touristy than most seaports and if you ask for or hunt out restaurants where the Bastiais eat it is there you will do best.

To reach the TERRA NOVA follow the street round the inland side of the Vieux Port by way of the Rue de la Marine and the Quai du Sud to the *Jardin Romieu*, reached from the quai by an elegant double staircase. The garden is a shady terrace under the ramparts and within the Terra Nova, the new town set up in 1480, fortified, and with the buildings around the Keep turned into the Governor's Palace, with a campanile added to the main façade in 1530. Through the centuries it has retained the distinctive style which the Genoese set upon their towns, nor was this style marred by the restoration in the reign of Louis XVI.

To reach the **Citadel** turn left at the top of the steps from the Jardin Romieu into the Cours du Docteur-Favale and the entrance is a few steps along on the left. Bastia takes its name from the 'bastiglia' or 'bastille' and the bastia itself is the great round tower, in very good condition, at the right-hand corner of the Palais des Gouverneurs. It is the oldest surviving part of the original fortifications raised in 1378 by the Genoese governor Leonello Lomellino after he had been burned out of his fortress at Biguglia by the supporters of what would now be called the Corsican 'resistance'.

The galleries in the inside court were vandalised when the Governor's Palace was made redundant by Napoleon's choice of Ajaccio as capital and the palace was turned into barracks. A third of the buildings were time-bombed by the Germans before they retreated in September 1943. The War Ministry passed the building over to the Secretary of State for Arts and Letters who restored it to become a museum. The ETHNOGRAPHIC MUSEUM OF CORSICA was created in 1952 (open every day, including Sundays, 09.00–12.00 and 15.00–

Steps to the Jardin Romieu, Bastia

18.00, a small charge is made; out of season the opening times are more restricted, and on certain public holidays the museum is closed. Information from the Tourist office). The order of the displays has been carefully worked out and presented to show how geology and geography gave this relatively isolated island its unique character, and how its zoology, botany, archaeology and entire history have been conditioned as a consequence. The personality of Corsica can be grasped here in an hour or so through prehistory to the Greek and Roman presence, Pisan, Genoese, Aragonese and French occupations and the fortunes of Corsican patriots such as Sampiero Corso and Paoli. There are displays on every aspect of Corsican ways including the life of the peasants and mountain people with the implements they used, the interior of a Niolo shepherd's hut complete with human figures, and artifacts connected with the cultivation and processing of the sweet chestnut.

Next to the museum is a memorial to the 173 and 373 Infantry Regiments and a roll of their battle honours through almost two centuries. At the far end of the courtyard is the CENTRE DU DOCU-MENTATION D'ARCHÉOLOGIE SOUS-MARINE, housed in what was the powder magazine. Collection of anchors, amphorae for oil, olives and wine, and other relics of the cargoes of boats trading in Roman times between Italy and Spain which had to pass through the Straits of Bonifacio and often foundered off the Lavezzi Isles.

On a terrace in the grounds of the Citadel is a more recent marine object, the conning tower of the submarine 'Casabianca'. Having escaped from Toulon on 27 November 1942, the 'Casabianca' reached Algiers and for the rest of the war, under the command of Captain l'Herminier, plied secretly between Algeria and Occupied Corsica, playing an important part in the liberation of Corsica. The submarine was named for the 12-year-old Jacques, son of Luce de Casabianca who commanded the 'Orient' and was killed at Aboukir on

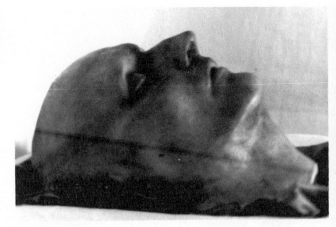

Death mask of Napoleon, in the Citadel Museum, Bastia

10 August 1798. His son, refusing to leave the ship, was killed when it exploded. The poor boy is on permanent duty in Mrs Hemans's poem 'The boy stood on the burning deck'.

Head of Louis XVI, bas-relief from the Bastille in Paris, now in the courtyard of the Citadel Museum, Bastia

Follow the Rue Notre Dame from the Citadel to, on the left, the church of **Sainte-Marie** (1495–1604, restored in 1938). It was elevated to cathedral status in 1570 and retained this distinction until the bishopric of Corsica was transferred to Ajaccio in 1801. The interior is richly baroque with much gold and marble. On the right is an Assumption of the Virgin in chased silver which is carried in procession on 15 August across the Terra Nova and the Terra Vecchia. Above the altar is a painting on wood of the Assumption, dated 1512 and formerly in the Canonica at Mariana (see Rte 8). The two polychromatic statues carved in wood are 17C and represent the Immaculate Conception and Notre Dame du Rosaire. The organ was built in 1845 by the master instrument makers Serassi of Bergamo.

THE CHAPELLE SAINTE CROIX, in the Rue de l'Evêché, is next door to Sainte Marie. Although built in 1543 the additional Louis XV decoration in gold stucco and the bonny cherubs gambolling in the blue ceiling give it something of the air of a ballroom or similar place of entertainment rather than of devotion. But in this chapel is a work of art that is impressive and touching at the same time and acquires a further inspirational quality when one learns its history. A figure of Christ, carved in oak that had been blackened by long immersion in water, is said to have been found floating in the sea by fishermen in 1428. This black *Christ des Miracles* is carried in procession on 3 May and the first catch of the season is offered up to Our Lord by the fishermen of Bastia. The striking appearance and dramatic lighting of the Black Christ should not, however, claim all the visitor's attention as there is another very beautiful Christ, 13C, in this chapel to the right of the entrance.

The Terra Nova covers a relatively small area and is a very self-contained neighbourhood, differing enormously from the rest of Bastia. It is easy to walk along its narrow short streets. Halfway along the Rue du Dragon is the Place Guasco: small, peaceful and tree-shaded, with the atmosphere of a medieval village square. Unless it is very windy or raining it is worth walking some of the way out on to the Jétée du Dragon for the view of Bastia and beyond: to the N Cap Corse, and to the S the Biguglia Lagoon and the great Eastern Plain which is overlooked by Bastia and emphasises why and how the fortress city came to be placed where it is.

8   Bastia to Solenzara: The Eastern Plain

ROAD (N 193 and N 198) 102km.—30km Mariana (to left of road).—70km Aléria.—85km Ghisonaccia.

Buses from Bastia to Solenzara, Porto Vecchio and Bonifacio (and information) from Les Autocars Rapides Bleus, 1 Avenue Maréchal Sebastiani, Bastia (Tel: 31.03.79). Bus services are good and frequent and the great advantage is that the N 198, the straightest and fastest road in Corsica, is never far from the sea.

The history of the Eastern Plain of Corsica, lying between the Tyrrhenian Sea and the central mountain spine of the island, on average 12–16km wide, has been dictated by its geography. Low-lying, it was easy to invade, and in 565–540 BC Phocaean Greeks from Asia Minor settled and built the town of Alalia. In 259 BC Alalia was conquered by the Romans together with the rest of the island. Alalia became Aléria, a military colony with a naval base on the Étang de

Diane with an estimated population of around 20,000 while it was the capital of Rome's Corsican province (259–162 BC). As the power of Rome declined so did Aléria and the Plain of Aléria. The land was no longer drained and cultivated and the water from the mountains turned the fields into marshes where mosquitoes and malaria flourished. This, and invasion by the Vandals in the 5C, drove the inhabitants away from the plain and into the hills, only descending to pasture their beasts in the winter.

The plain remained practically abandoned for some 1500 years and until the present century the average expectation of life among Plain dwellers was 22 years. Baedeker obviously thought things went from bad to worse, referring in 1895 to 'the somewhat bleak and desolate E coast...the malarious plain of Aléria' and deleting 'somewhat' from the 1907 edition of his *Guide*. Periodic incursions and settlement by Pisans, Genoese, Aragonese, French, Italians and Germans brought scant improvement to the area.

It was occupation by the liberating US Army that dispelled the murderous blight that had lain there for a milennium and a half. American forces were stationed in Corsica from 1943–46. Their main enemy was the anopheles mosquito and their weapon was DDT. Once the mosquito had been eliminated the area began to be cultivated again and in 1957 impetus was given towards reclamation by the creation of SOMIVAC (Société pour la mise en valeur de la Corse). 30 years later the cultivated area of the Plain amounts to 80 per cent of agricultural Corsica, producing citrus and other fruits, vines, cereals and vegetables and raising sheep, goats and cattle. Reservoirs in the central Corsican mountains ensure irrigation. In the late 1950s and '60s many of the French colonists (or *pieds noirs*, the name given by the North Africans to those who wear shoes) acquired land in the Plain. They had experience of similar conditions, climate, and crops in North Africa and many of their Arab workers came with them. They set a high standard of farming but this massive incursion of non-Corsican settlers did not, in the early years, take place without strong and sometimes violent opposition from Corsican farmers.

Apart from the overwhelming agricultural importance of the present-day Plain there has been a rapid development of tourism along the magnificent and for the most part sandy coastline broken by a half-dozen lagoons. Baedeker reported in 1895 that the railway from Bastia to Ghisonaccia was 'to be prolonged'. The line was extended to Solenzara in 1930 and thence to Porto Vecchio in 1935. It would eventually have reached Bonifacio had it not been for World War II which began four years later. The Germans, in retreat in 1943, destroyed bridges, tunnels, locomotives, signals, freight vans, passenger cars and stations. Rebuilding was never undertaken so that now the farthest S one can go is to Casamozza on the Golo where the line turns inland to cross to the W coast of Corsica.

Leave Bastia by the N 193, heading S and at 3km look out for the town *cemetery*. On the corner is a stone commemorating the landing on 23 August 1553 of Sampiero Corso (at that time a colonel in the French army), when the French aided by a Turkish fleet invaded and conquered the whole isle with the exception of Calvi and Bastia which held out for Genoa. 2km further on, to the right of the road, is the ruined castle of *Furiani*, set on a hill above the new factories. The Genoese laid siege to the castle in 1729. It was defended and held by Luigi Giafferi, another Corsican hero. 8km *Casatora*, from which the D 82 leads to the Défilé de Lancone and Oletta in the Nebbio (see Rte 13).

On the E slopes of the inland mountains, reached from Casatora by a minor road (2.5km), lies **Biguglia** (270m, 2832 inhab.), capital of Corsica after the destruction of Mariana in the 8C, first under the Pisans and then under the first of the many Genoese occupations. At that time it was the diocesan seat. When Biguglia was taken by the Corsican rebels, led by yet another Corsican hero, Arrigo della Rocca, in 1372, the Genoese moved N and built a fortress, a 'bastiglia' which was the beginning of Bastia. From Biguglia the Étang de Biguglia, a lagoon open to the sea by a narrow mouth to the N, takes its name. Renowned for its eels. The seaward bar has a *village de vacances* called *Pineto*.

The railway follows close to the N 193, crossing it a couple of times. 16km *Borgo* (U Borgu, 320m, 3413 inhab.), 3km to the right from the main road.

Set on a rocky spur overlooking the plain, Borgo contains tall old houses with elegant carved doors and porches. Those who fled the unhealthy plain moved to higher villages such as these. In 1768 Pasquale Paoli defeated the French here after the ignoble treaty between France and Genoa brought the Corsicans out in arms once more.

1.5km S of Borgo to the left is the road to the *Bastia-Poretta Airport* (20km from Bastia, buses from Place de la Gare, Bastia). At the Airport there is a stone to the memory of the writer Antoine de Saint Exupéry who, as a Free French pilot, flew from here on a reconnaissance mission over the Mediterranean from which he never returned.

At the same turning there is another road, the D 107, forking to the left, further S, and reaching in 5.5km the archaeological site of the former Roman city of **Mariana** and the churches of La Canonica and San Parteo.

The Roman general Gaius Marius (157–86 BC) founded two military colonies in Corsica in 93 BC, one at Alalia (Aléria) and the other at Mariana. It would seem that the soldiers sent to the latter were penal battalions raised in Italy who aroused the violent opposition of the Corsicans. Mariana was several times destroyed and rebuilt until in the 5–6C, under the onslaught of the combined forces of mosquitoes and Vandals, the city fell into ruins. The Christian Church was strongly established here from the 4C onwards. The church of **Santa Maria Assunta**, the former Cathedral of Mariana which is known popularly as *La Canonica*, stands 50m to the N of the site of a 4C paleochristian cathedral, remains of which have been brought to light by recent excavations under the foundations of the 12C episcopal palace. The square *baptistry* is flanked by two small apses. In the centre is a piscine, later used as a baptismal pool and now roofed over for protection. The floor is decorated in mosaic (4C) depicting fish, ducks, dolphins and stags, with the Four Rivers of Paradise represented by male heads whose bearded faces are portrayed in the classical style of water gods such as Neptune.

La Canonica, the church of Santa Maria Assunta, the former cathedral of the diocese of the Bishop of Mariana, was consecrated in 1119 by the Archbishop of Pisa. The architectural form was inspired by the Roman basilica: the nave is flanked by two aisles and is 35m long, both wider and higher than the aisles and ending in an oven-shaped apse (*cul de four*). Impressively simple in design, great effect was achieved by the use of *calschiste*, marble quarried at Sisco and Brando in Cap Corse whose colours range through a honey-tinted grey to light greenish-orange and blue. The stone slabs were cut to a remarkable perfection and a feature of this church is that the square 'putlog' holes in the stone, to support the scaffolding, were left unfilled and thus form a pattern in this admirably undecorated interior. The W front reflects the relative heights of the nave and side

aisles: two flattened pilasters on either side mark the width of the
nave, balanced by two broader pilasters at the two corners.

La Canonica, Roman paving

The frescoes inside the W door are an unexpectedly ample decoration
of this austere church. The archivolt is decorated with animals: a lion,
griffons, a wolf, a stag pursued by hounds and a triumphant Lamb of
God. The S façade has no decoration whatsoever, but its rhythmical
proportions are perfect as is the E façade. The Canonica is perhaps the
prototype of Corsican Pisan churches and with the former cathedral of
the Nebbio it is one of the architectural jewels of the island.

The church of **San Parteo de Mariana** stands about 300m to the SW
of the Canonica. Pisan, and of excellent proportions, it was built in the
11–12C (construction possibly interrupted by a Moslem invasion).
Excavation of the fields surrounding the church has revealed a

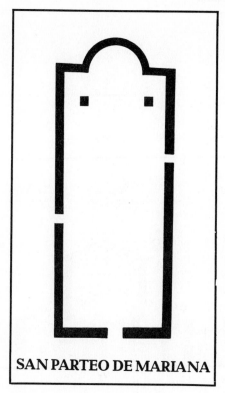

SAN PARTEO DE MARIANA

cemetery, first pagan, then paleochristian and medieval. The present church was built in continuation of an earlier building dedicated to the memory, and possibly housing the relics of, San Parteo, one of Corsica's martyrs (excavation has discovered some foundations). The outstandingly elegant apse is decorated with granite columns and arcadings; some of this material may have come from the ruins of Mariana.

Madame Moracchini-Mazel, whose life's work has been to discover, uncover, classify, protect and describe Corsica's architectural treasures, writes in her excellent book 'Corse Romane' '...it is astounding that a few years ago [in the 1960s], on the direct orders of a company of Paris architects, such a "curious" restoration should have been undertaken. The pediment was reset much too high; the side walls were heightened in grey cement, without trouble being taken to respect the proportions, which the Pisan builders sought as ardently in their apses as did the Greek architects in the façades of their temples...red tiles were used while the original framework was covered by slabs of mauve *teghie* (stone). The best thing for the visitor to do is to try to imagine the outline of the ramparts of the pediments, the level of the side walls and the colour of the roof...'.

The S door lintel has a sculpted decoration of two lions facing each other with comic snarls, a stylised tree between them, their tails

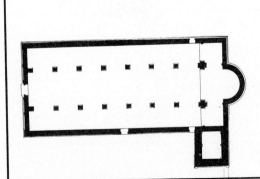

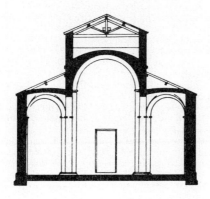

SANTA MARIA
Mariana

looped gracefully: an Oriental design picked up and copied by
European craftsmen from imported woven cloth. The W door lintel
has a string course decorated with sculpted geometrical patterns.

Return to the N 193 by the D 107 but at a T-junction 1.5km beyond
San Parteo turn left into the D 10 and left again when it reaches the
railway which runs parallel to the road for 2km to *Casamozza*, one of
the most important junctions in Corsica. Here, on the River Golo, the
N 193 makes a 90° turn to the right to follow the course of the river
through dramatic ravines to Ponte Leccia and thence to Corte and
Ajaccio. To the S of the road lie the regions of the Casinca and the
Castagniccia (see Rtes 11 and 12).

   In the direction of Solenzara–Ponte Vecchio–Bonifacio the road
continues S as the N 198. Turnings to the right lead to the Casinca
villages and those to the left, such as the D 106, lead, 6.5km beyond
Casamozza, to the beach and *village de vacances* of *Anghione*. 4km
further at *Folelli* the D 506 leads to a fine beach and good hotel at
San Pellegrino. At Folelli the Fium'Alto, a river rising in the
Castagniccia, is crossed and the road runs ever closer to the sea until
reaching (8.5km) *Moriani Plage*, a few hundred metres to the right.
Some of the famous of the past arrived or left from here. Pasquale
Paoli, aged 15, entered his first exile (from the then naval base called
Padulella) with his father Hyacinthe and Luigi Giafferi in 1739 and in
1815 Napoleon landed, having escaped from Elba and before setting
sail for the French mainland. 4km to the S is a new *port de plaisance*,
serving Campoloro, well sheltered by the mountains further inland.
Campoloro itself is rapidly developing, like so many places on the E
coast, into a holiday town. In 2.5km one reaches *Prunete–Cervione*.
6km by the D 71 to the right leads to Cervione and a small road to the
left (about 500m) goes down to one of this coast's finest beaches.

   For 25km from Prunete the road passes through rich farmlands
with orchards, vineyards and cornfields, undramatic but beautiful,
wide and calm; but not so wide that the mountains some 12–15km
inland are not always in view as a backdrop to this intense
cultivation. There are practically no villages until Caterraggio and
Aléria. To the left, clearly marked and 1–2km from the road, are
occasional *villages de vacances*. After crossing the River Bravone at
the hamlet of (another) Casamozza (Marine de Bravone to the right,
2.5km), there is a military firing range lying between the N 198 and
the sea.

   Immediately to the S of the Champ de Tir is the extensive ÉTANG
DE DIANE (600 hectares), a lagoon which served two purposes for the
Romans: as a naval base for Aléria and as a bed to cultivate oysters
which they both consumed and exported to Rome. While Napoleon
was on Elba a boat was sent twice weekly to collect Diane oysters for
him and secretly bring back news from France, no doubt kept as
close as an oyster. An island in the étang is made solely of oyster
shells and there is a road from the N 198 to a store where oysters and
other fish may be bought (although often there is nobody there).

   Caterraggio, 70km from Bastia, on the N bank of the Tavignano
(rises at the Lac de Nino, 1743m) is the spreading modern
counterpart to Aléria. From here it is 3km to the left by the N 200 to a
wide sandy beach at *Padulone*. Cross the Tavignano and continue
1km down the N 198 then right into the D 343, a road clearly marked
with the ancient monument sign (white on dark blue) and arrowed to
Aléria.

Aléria (2500 inhab. in the commune, including Caterraggio.), founded by the Phoceaen Greeks in 540 BC on the plateau about 50m
above sea level on the right bank of the Tavignano.

The settlement dominated the estuary where there had been a trading post since
565 BC. The Phoceaens made it their capital when they were chased out of their
own Asia Minor city of Phoceaea by the Persians. They won the sea battle of
Alalia against an invading force of Etruscans and Carthaginians in 535 BC but
subsequently transferred their capital to Massalia (Marseille), retaining Alalia as
a mercantile link with their new colonies in southern Italy as well as with Greece,
Carthage, Gaul, Sicily and Spain. In 259 BC Alalia was taken by the Romans
from the Carthaginians, who had been in control since 280 BC. The Romans
conquered the whole of Corsica and made the city, with a population of 20,000,
capital of their Corsican province. In AD 81 Sulla established a military base;
subsequently Augustus constructed a naval base in the Étang de Diane and a
mercantile port was built in the loop of the Tavignano. The city flourished until it
was sacked by the Vandals in the 5C and sank into obscurity but was partially
revived on a much smaller scale in the 13C by the Genoese and was a diocesan
seat for 2C. It was still an important place in 1736 when Theodor von Neuhof
landed here before travelling to Alesani where he was crowned King of Corsica.
Prosper Mérimée noted that there were traces of the Roman city remaining in
1840. Some test excavations were made in 1920 but it is only since 1955 that a
systematic archaeological search has been made, and is still (1986) continuing.

The car park for visitors is on the left, just before the village with its
one wide street leading to the square where stands the church of *Saint
Marcel* facing the *Fort de Matra*, built by the Genoese in 1572 and
since 1969 the Musée Jérôme Carcopino (1881–1970, archaeologist
and historian of ancient Rome).

The Musée Jérôme Carcopino (price of entry includes the visit to
the site. Open 15 May–1 October, 8.00–12.30 and 14.00–19.00;
October–May 8.00–12.00 and 14.00–16.00) consists of 12 display
rooms grouped around the central courtyard of the former fort. It
should preferably be visited before going to the site but I have always
found that a second tour of the museum rounds off the whole
experience.

Room 1. Life in Aléria as a city of the Roman Empire: oil lamps,
coins, rings, amphorae, pots and earthenware water pipes. Iron and
bronze objects dominate the metal discoveries, very little silver and
gold. *Room 2.* The evolution of ceramics during the period of the
Roman Empire, the advances in methods of glazing etc. A fine marble
head with ram's horns of Jupiter Ammon (2C), reconstruction of a
Roman tomb. *Room 3.* Pre-Roman Aléria (4–3C BC). Red-figure ware
in which the baked orange clay showing through the painted black
glaze creates the pattern or figures, a method that preceded the
red-glazed pottery which dominated in the Roman period. Examples
of Etruscan and other imported ceramic objects attest to Aléria's
importance as a large trading port. *Room 4.* The showpiece here, and
the most renowned exhibit in the museum, is *attic vase with erotic
figures* ascribed to a master artist of Panaitios, 480 BC. Other objects
recovered from tombs are displayed, such as a curved Greek sword
(5C BC). *Room 5.* This room contains an assembly of objects attesting
to Aléria's rôle in the economic and military development of Corsica
in the ancient Mediterranean world and demonstrating its importance
as a link between the Greek possessions in Spain and Provence and
Greece and the Near East. A display of Greek influence in Corsica in
the 6th, 5th and 4C BC. Note the *crater*, a wide-mouthed vessel for
wine and water (c 425 BC) decorated with a design of a seated
Dionysos in the company of a pair of satyrs and a nymph, by a painter

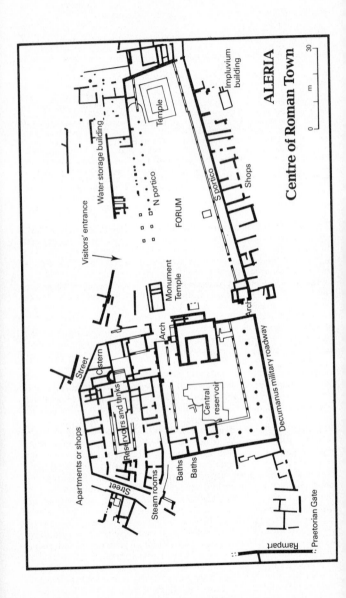

ALÉRIA
Centre of Roman Town

Impluvium building

Temple

Water storage building

N portico

FORUM

S portico

Shops

Visitors' entrance

Monument
Temple

Arch

Arch

Street

Cistern

Reservoirs and tanks

Apartments or shops

Street

Steam rooms

Baths

Baths

Central
reservoir

Decumanus military roadway

Praetorian Gate

Rampart

30
m
0

of Dinos. *Room 6*. Reconstruction of a burial chamber (c 450 BC) containing over 100 objects found in tombs including Etruscan bronze's and Attic pottery. *Room 7*. Objects from the oldest tomb found at Aléria. Two Attic rhytons, drinking vessels, in the forms of the heads of a dog and a mule, of exceptional grace and exquisite workmanship. *Rooms 8–9*. Assorted objects discovered in the tombs. *Room 10*. Attic ceramics and iron weapons from a tomb. *Room 11*. Finely decorated craters and cups including Hercules and the lion, Theseus (450 BC) and Dionysos keeping an eye on the grape harvesting. *Room 12*. A reconstructed tomb set in a cistern, excavated by the Genoese.

The Roman city of Aléria. A pathway leads from the square up a gentle rise to the plateau and the excavations, SW of the village. This archaeological site is unique not only in Corsica but in the whole of France by virtue of discoveries there dating back to the 6C BC. The present excavations began in 1958 and there is undoubtedly much more to be found.

Explanatory boards display clear plans and descriptions of the site.

Aléria

Entry is directly into the FORUM, 90m long running E–W, which was colonnaded and lined with shops. Columns of the N and S porches have been uncovered; of brick originally stuccoed. A small *temple* at the E end of the Forum has a foundation platform of pebbles brought from the bed of the Tavignano. Against its N side is the apse of a later Christian building. Also on the N side of the temple are traces of a large dwelling place known as the *Domus 'au dolium'* because of the discovery in one of the rooms of a huge earthenware jar. At the W end of the Forum is the *Praetorium* from which the Romans ruled the city and the whole of their Corsican colony. Entrance is by an archway

from the period of Sulla Felix of which a column is still standing.
There is a courtyard with water tanks and porches on three sides.
To the N of the Praetorium were the *baths*, the *balneum* with
cisterns and pools and the *caldarium* heated by a system of
underground pipes, the hypocaust, above which lies a decorative
mosaic floor. Additions and alterations to the complex date from 1C
BC–early 5C AD. To the W of the *halneum* lies what is thought to
have been an area for the storage and preservation of fish
including, no doubt, the ubiquitous oyster.

Facing the museum in the Fort de Matra is the former cathedral
church of *St. Marcel*, often locked, but whose most interesting
feature is the inclusion in its 12C walls of blocks of stone from the
ancient Roman city.

Return to the N 198, following the road S and passing on the left
the *Domaine de Casabianda* (no visitors), an open prison where the
inmates are employed in agriculture, a highly successful regime
where valuable agricultural discoveries have resulted from experi-
mentation in crop raising and domestic animal breeding. The
nearby *Réserve National de Casabianda* (1760 hectares) was established in 1951 to ensure the conservation of Corsica's rarer animals
and birds. Eucalyptus nurseries send saplings throughout Corsica
for replacement afforestation in areas ravaged by fire. To the left of
the road is another lagoon, the Étang d'Urbino, where oysters and
mussels are cultivated.

   Ghisonaccia, 15km S of Aléria and 85km S of Bastia (Ghisunac-
cia, 16m, 3366 inhab.), is the 'capital' of the Eastern Plain. Lively
and bustling, it is full of new shops and houses with light industry
making agricultural machines. The population today is four times
what it was 30 years ago. Formerly Ghisonaccia was a large village
whose living depended on the flocks and herds which were the
plain's major source of income. The 'accia' ending means 'bad' in
the sense of 'unhealthy': there used to be mosquitoes and malaria.
The eradication of the mosquito and the transformation of the
Eastern Plain into a rich agricultural region has sent Ghisonaccia
upward on a spiral of activity and prosperity.

The D 344 leaves Ghisonaccia for Ghisoni in a straight line NW for
27km through intensely cultivated flat farmlands and smallholdings, a countryside of vineyards, orchards and cereal crops. In
summer and autumn every other house seems to offer peaches,
apricots, grapes and vegetables for sale at the roadside. After St.
Antoine the D 344 turns due W and there is a sudden and dramatic
change in the landscape. The Fium Orbu (the 'blind river', 45km
long, rising at 2352m on Monte Renoso and reaching the E coast at
Calgarello SE of Ghisonaccia) forces its way through the canyon of
the Défilé de l'Inzecca. 2km upriver is the Défilé des Strette where
the river thunders and froths over giant boulders at the bottom of
the 300m deep ravine.

   Ghisoni (658m, 1019 inhab.) is set deep in a valley between the
heights of the Col de Sorba to the N and the Col de Verde to the S
and is surrounded by the forests of Sorba and Marmano. In 1985
vast tracts of forests in this part of Corsica were devastated by fire.
Ghisoni is in the Parc Naturel Régional de la Corse (see Rte 16) and
by taking the D 69 N over the Col de Sorba one reaches (19km)
Vivario on the N 193 Bastia–Ajaccio road, 30km S of Corte. Vivario

is also on the railway line between Bastia and Ajaccio.

From Ghisonaccia, across the Fiumorbu and S down the N 198 for 2km is Migliacciaru where a turning to the right, the D 145, leads up into the Fiumorbu by the valley of the Abatesco.

The FIUMORBU is a small region known for its turbulent history and the independent and recklessly brave nature of its people. 19km from Ghisonaccia is *Prunelli di Fiumorbo* (I Prunelle di Fiumorbu, 580m, 2339 inhab.), built on a rocky promontory giving, in clear weather, fantastic views of the Plain, the lagoons and the sea. At the highest point of the village stands the church of *Santa Maria Assunta* and a 20-minute walk below the village reaches the ruins of the church of *Saint-Jean-Baptiste* (6–7C) on a spur of rock overlooking the Plain and the sea. A nave with one door and no light apart from one tiny E window. A beautifully engraved lintel with the Cross, the Hand of God and the Dove. Moving and impressive, this small *piève* survived the Barbarian invasions and its stones have outlasted both the church built in the 11C to replace it and a nearby abbey. Nothing remains of either.

On the N 198 going S the next hamlet after Migliacciaru is yet another Casamozza. After crossing the Abatesco, 5km S, on the left, is the Étang de Palo, the smallest and most southerly lagoon on the E coast. Between the étang and the estuary of the River Travo is the military aerodrome of Solenzara (to which the public is not admitted). 2km beyond and a few 100m to the left is the *Marine de Solaro* which takes its name from the village of Solaro, built safely in the mountain foothills 8.5km to the W but keeping an outlet to the sea. 3.5km S on the S bank of the River Solenzara (rises 20km SW in the Punta de Taffanatu di Palin) is the small town of the same name, 102km S of Bastia, 2km N of Porto Vecchio and 67km N of Bonifacio.
Solenzara (300m, 1399 inhab.) is part of the commune of Sari di Porto Vecchio (8km inland by the D 68 leading N from Solenzara) and a good centre for a traditional seaside holiday, Solenzara has to the N a wide sandy beach shaded by eucalyptus trees planted optimistically in the 19C as an antidote to malaria and to the S of the town a rocky coastline begins. The Côte des Nacres (the Mother of Pearl Coast) takes its name from the large number of shells along the shore. There is a *port de plaisance* for 350 berths whose building was long delayed by violent storms which smashed tons of concrete. Holiday camps, caravan and camping sites, and a variety of hotels. Nothing of architectural interest, most of the building has been done recently and quickly, partly to house the families of the Zara Air Force base personnel and to meet the growth of tourism. Only 27km from Porto Vecchio, Solenzara is also only 30km by the D 268 from the Col de Bavella and some of the most dramatic Corsican mountain scenery.

9   From Solenzara to Porto Vecchio and Bonifacio

ROAD (N 198) 68km.—41km Porto Vecchio—27km Bonifacio.

Going S from Solenzara the N 198 stays very close to the shore and there are many good places for swimming reached from the road itself or from seaside hamlets. Access is easy but as there is little shade it is as well to look out for the patches of maritime pine and scrub to seaward of the road. 10km from Solenzara, *Les Logis de Favone*, holiday village and motel and 1km further S the *Marine de Favone* at the mouth of the river of the same name. A fine 800m beach. 15km beyond Solenzara the *anse* or cove of Tarco, at the mouth of the Tarco River. Here too is a long fine beach and 5km beyond is the Bocca di Parata (44m) a crest between the estuaries of the Rivers Conca and Cavu. Remains of Genoese tower out on the *Punta di Fautea*. From the Bocca the N 198 turns almost due WSW inland for 4.5km to Santa Lucia di Porto Vecchio, crossing the Cavu.

From here the D 168A goes right up the valley of the Cavu, a very worthwhile but tortuous (and not to be considered in wet weather) route through deserted mountains. The road eventually finds its way to the D 368 and up to Zonza. The D 168D going left out of Santa Lucia leads in 4km to the tiny port of *Pinarellu* and the tree-shaded beach around its bay.

11.5km beyond Santa Lucia watch out for the second turning left after crossing the River Osu. It is marked to Torre with the blue *monument historique* sign but it is easy to miss. The road leads to the hamlet of **Torre**, 8km N of Porto Vecchio, and then stops. This is the place from which the Bronze Age (c 1600 BC) Torréens (see Filitosa, Rte 2) were given their name. Go into the village and anyone will show you how to reach the site which appears to be over and above some back gardens, but is in fact easy to get to. The best-preserved and most complete of Torréen fortresses in Corsica, semi-circular and built up against a granite mass, it has retained some of its stone roofing slabs.

This is a region of Corsica particularly rich in archaeological sites and a few hundred metres further down the N 198 from Torre is the D 759 to the right which leads in 2.5km to a T-junction with the D 559. Turn left and immediately one is among scattered houses forming the hamlets of *Arraggio* (Araghju). Look out for, or better still, ask for the way to the site. The most I have found there is a roughly-painted sign on the side of a house saying 'Ruines'. A path crosses a stream and then the footpath, narrow and stony, winds up through the maquis. Wear tough shoes, feel energetic, and allow 30–40 minutes each way (longer if there has been rain).

The CASTELLU D'ARAGHJU is one of the most complete and largest of Torréen fortresses. Impressive in its cyclopean proportions, the great entrance gives access to the fortress and the ruins of the religious centre. Surrounding the fort is a circular wall, on average 2m thick and 4m high, with rooms built against it and with steps to a walkway from which there are extensive views over the Araghju to Porto Vecchio.

There are two alternative ways to return to the N 198 to Porto Vecchio. Either continue S along the D 559 to the junction with the D 368 Zonza–Porto Vecchio road, turn left and in 4.5km reach the N 198 and turn right into the N suburbs of Porto Vecchio. Or return by the D 759 to the N 198 and turn right.

At Sainte Trinité, 2km S of the turn-off to Arraggio, the D 168A leads left (2km) to *Golfo di Sogno* (big camping site and 1200m-long beach). Continue 1km further and turn right to *Cala Rossa*, pine trees and a tourist development. In 2.5km further E the road reaches *Punta San Ciprianu*. If one continues along the D 168A direct from La Trinité one reaches the 2.5km-long beach of San Ciprianu and yet a further 7km to the NNE one reaches Pinarellu (see alternative route from Santa Lucia di Porto Vecchio).

Porto Vecchio (Porti Vechju, 70m, 8200 inhab.) is 143km from Bastia with Solenzara 41km, Ajaccio 149km, Corte 121km and Bonifacio 27km distant.

Porto Vecchio

'The Old Port' of its name is apt because this safe harbour, at the end of a deep almost fjord-like gulf at the S end of a long, flat and mostly harbourless coastline, has attracted voyagers from distant antiquity up until the present day. The Torréens, of course, made their presence clear; the Romans whose *Portus Syracusanus* this may have been, the Etruscans, Barbary pirates and then, inevitably, the Genoese, all made use of the port. The Banque of Saint Georges established a fortress here in 1539 to complete the chain of defences around the island and it became their second most important fortress, after Bastia, on the E coast. In 1564 Sampiero Corso, needing a port but failing to take Ajaccio from the Genoese, turned his attention to Porto Vecchio which he succeeded in taking on 30 July 1564. A true politician, cynically finding allies where it suited his purpose, Sampiero made common cause with the corsairs against Genoa. The Genoese in their turn called in their ally, Spain, whose ships defeated the

corsairs and whose men, under Genoese command, took Porto Vecchio on 26
November 1564. Prosperous under the Genoese, the town fell later into a
decline, largely due to malaria.

DDT at the end of World War II virtually eradicated the anopheles mosquito
and Porto Vecchio quickly regained its prosperity. Export of cork from the oak
forests of the district has suffered from the competition of plastic but more than a
third of Corsican wine is exported from Porto Vecchio and the tourist industry
has grown rapidly, exploiting the superb sandy beaches. Other attractions are
the coves of pink rock, the *port de plaisance* next to the *port de commerce*, a
proliferation of hotels in the town and on the coast, mountains and forests 20km
away, Figari airport at 25km and a wealth of Torréen sites. Porto Vecchio's rapid
growth as a tourist centre in recent years has left its mark on the town in
undistinguished architecture and seemingly haphazard planning but the atmosphere is that of a pleasant, easy-going and friendly place. It is small enough to go
around on foot and indeed that is preferable, avoiding the one-way system and
parking difficulties.

One of the many striking rocks unearthed by Daniel Vidoni
when draining his land at San Giovanni, near Porto Vecchio

The old town and the fortifications have retained their original
character. Of the 15–16C *Genoese fortifications*, raised on outcrops of
rosy pink porphyry, five bastions have survived as well as the
Genoese Gate opening E, with a view of the Gulf of Porto Vecchio, the

port and the salt marshes (the only salt pans on the E coast of Corsica are here). The streets in this part of the town are narrow, often with steps, finely carved old doors and covered alleys. The parish church, plain and solidly built, with a square tower, dates from 1868.

From the centre of the town the road to the Marina and the commercial port (1km) goes downhill through olive groves. The quayside has nothing of note architecturally, it is mostly modern with a few shops, cafés and restaurants. One can walk beyond to the commercial port but, apart from looking out to the gulf or back inland to the mountains rising beyond the town, there is little of interest. The harbour is on the estuary of the River Stabiacciu (22km long, rising on the E face of the Punta di a Vacca Morta at 1314m).

A. Excursions from Porto Vecchio: the Coast

The beaches on the Gulf to the N of the town—Golfo di Sogno, Cala Rossa, San C_ipria_nu and Pinarellu—are described above. To the S the Gulf and the port are protected by the peninsula of Piccovaggia, a round tour of which (29km) takes in some of the best beaches in southern Corsica. Take the N 198 out of Porto Vecchio in the direction of Bonifacio. After 2km and crossing the Stabiacciu take the first turning to the left (it is almost opposite the turning to the right onto the D 853 to Sotta). This road follows the N shore of the peninsula to (7.5km) Piccovaggia from which a minor road (left) leads to the *Punta di a Chiappa*. This is the furthermost point E of the peninsula. From the foot of the lighthouse there is an incomparable view of the Gulf, to the Punta San Ciprianu on the N side of the Gulf and inland to the mountainous backdrop. On the S side of this point there is a large and well-equipped naturist centre. Return to Piccovaggia, 3km to the S. Continuing S across cork oak woods, there is a track 500m down to the sea and the beach of *Palombaggia* (Palombaja) backed by rosy-red rocks and with sandy dunes shaded by umbrella pines. The sand is white, the bathing safe, the water clear and of every shade of blue and green.

5km offshore are the *Iles Cerbicale*, an archipelago of half-a-dozen uninhabited islets (15km from Porto Vecchio). Five of them constitute *La Réserve Naturelle des Iles Cerbicale* (founded 3 March 1981) covering 36 hectares. Predominantly gneiss and schiste and a little granite, the islets formed part of the Corsican coast until 10,000 years ago. All information regarding flora and fauna and visiting (very limited) can be obtained from M. le Conservateur des Réserves, Mairie de Porto Vecchio, 20137 Porto-Vecchio.

From Palombaggia keep to the coastal road to the hamlet of Bocca di l'Oru, then right for 1km to the N 198. Turn right and 6km back to Porto Vecchio. Or turn left on the N 198 and after 1.5km turn left again and 600m to Golfo di Santa Giulia. Do not be bewildered as to how to get to the sea: there is a large Club Méditerranée complex with macadamed paths and streetlighting, but by going on to the end one can both park and walk down to a fine and sheltered sandy beach, crowded in high season.

B. Excursions from Porto Vecchio: the Mountains

Leave Porto Vecchio by the N 198 in the direction of Solenzara and, in the suburbs, take the first road left, the D 368, crossing in 4.5km the D 559 (Arraggio is 3km to the right). The thick woods of cork and evergreen oaks give way to maritime and Corsican pines as the road rises steadily through a landscape of giant granite masses, the Forest of l'Ospedale.

Sunday wild boar hunters (back to camera, a friend from Porto Vecchio who has just been given a joint of sanglier)

19km from Porto Vecchio, *l'Ospedale* (812m), despite the distance a hamlet in the commune of Porto Vecchio, and owing its name to the presence there of a hospital in Roman times. Views over the Gulf, N along the E coast, S to Bonifacio and beyond to the coast of Sardinia (weather permitting, of course). Just beyond the village, on the left, is the artificial lake made by damming the high waters of the Osu. This is the *Barrage de l'Ospedale* whose waters supply the Porto Vecchio area. 10km beyond the village one crosses the Bocca d'Ilarata (1008m). From the left of the road views over the valleys of the Rizzanese and the Ortolo rivers.

40km from Porto Vecchio is *Zonza* (784m, 1503 inhab.). Built in terraces above the valley of the Asinao, solid old granite houses and narrow streets make this a village of 'mountain' character and its position, high above the surrounding forests of Ospedale, Zonza and Bavella, justifies its reputation as a pleasant summer resort, while the forests create an industry to tend the Corsican pines. Zonza is at a mountain crossroads, one road coming up from l'Ospedale, the D 268 going NE to the Col de Bavella (see Rte 16) and S to Levie and Sartène, and the D 420 going W to Aullène and Petreto-Bicchisano where it joins the N 196 to Ajaccio.

Share a spring with a bandit!

From Zonza S by the D 268 it is 9km to **Levie** (Livia, 656m, 2500 inhab.) a large village strung out on a granite plateau, the Pianu de Levie, between the valleys of the Rizzanese and the Fiumicicoli. It is one of the most interesting archaeological centres of Corsica, the prehistoric artifacts discovered at sites on the Pianu being brought together in the *Archaeological Museum* of Levie (open 1 June–30 September every day, 9.00–12.00 and 14.00–18.00; rest of the year every day except Sunday and public holidays, 10.00–12.00 and 14.00–17.00). The collections, which extend from pre-neolithic times to the Iron Age and come from the excavations at Cucuruzzu, Curacciaghiu, Caleca and Campo Vecchio, are constantly being added to as fresh discoveries are made by the Institut Corse de Préhistoire. The museum, signposted, is in the main street in a large old house standing in its own grounds, a gift to the community which also houses the Mairie.

A local tradition maintains that Pope Sixtus V (1585–90) was born of parents who came from Levie. His name was Félix Peretti, a widespread family name hereabouts (a local schoolmaster, Jean Baptiste de Peretti, kindly acted as volunteer guide to the sites and also invited us to his parents' house). This Pope is said to have given the exceptional ivory crucifix to his parish church of *Saint Nicolas* (permission to view from the priest whose house is opposite the foot of the steps leading down to the Carbini road from the romanesque church). Possibly a 15C Florentine work, the anatomical detail and portrayal of physical suffering are of a rare beauty and perfection.

To reach the fortified Torréen complex of *Castellu de Cucuruzzu* take the D 268 S out of Levie, in the direction of Sainte Lucie de Tallano. At 3.5km there is a signpost to the site. Follow this road to the right and after 3.5km there is parking space and an easy 800m walk

15C ivory crucifix, Levie

up a shaded track to the site. Those wishing to visit Curacciaghiu and other archaeological sites on the Pianu di Levie, some of them involving walks and moderate climbs, are advised to ask for information at the Levie Museum. On the way, at 2km from the main road and to the right of the track there is a footpath leading to the *Caleca* site of a 1st millennium BC funeral chamber set inside three concentric stone circles. Excavations on the Levie Pianu have been going on since 1959 under the direction of Roger Grosjean.

The c 1400 BC **Castellu de Cucuruzzu**, like other Torréen fortified settlements, makes use of a rocky hilltop to incorporate the natural rock into the structure of the town. Entrance is by a roughly-formed stairway between two rocks, mounting up to and passing through a rampart within which were constructed casemates with narrow slits to keep watch on the countryside below. A walkway leads round to the E side and an open space or terrace on one side of which were raised the massive boulders of the central monument, backed by a gigantic rock wall. Entry is by two successive openings framed by massive lintels set on equally massive vertical rocks serving as pillars. The chamber itself is ingeniously vaulted with stones without, of course, the benefit of any kind of mortar. The summit of the monument can be reached from outside by a stairway of rocks and from there can be appreciated the strength of this position from which there are views for a great distance in every direction. The E extent of the rocky spur was occupied by a fortified Torréen village.

Castellu de Cucuruzzu, Bronze Age Torréen fortress

When the fortress and village were occupied dense forest surrounded the site, providing game. A torrent just below provided fish as well as water. The inhabitants cultivated cereals, charred grains of wheat were found during the excavations. The *castellu* was set on the hilltop so that it had sun throughout the day and in every season of the year.

From the parking place a track leads off and after about 300m there is a signpost to the Castellu de Capula and the Chapelle Lorenzu (about 20 minutes' walk). The site of the *Castellu de Capula* was in constant human occupation from the Bronze Age until the destruction of the medieval castle in 1259 after a long period of clan warfare. In the construction of the castle practical use was made of a dolmen (it can be seen protruding from the wall as one climbs the rock stairway to the remains of the castle). There is also a headless menhir with vestiges of a vertical sheathed sword held in front of the figure and the etching of a spine and ribs on the back still visible.

The *Chapel of San Lorenzu*, the product of pious but misguided zeal, has the ruins of an earlier chapel next to it. The original chapel was 13C romanesque and each 10 August, the feast of Saint Laurence, a pilgrimage was made to it from Levie and the other villages below. In 1916, when all able-bodied men were away at the Great War, the good *curé* of Levie noticed that the roof of the chapel was in bad repair. He consequently had the chapel demolished and some of its stones employed in the construction of a splendid new chapel which met with the disapproval of many of his warrior parishioners when they returned. The new chapel is very plain and inoffensive and the ruins of the old, rising just above the ground, add to the peaceful atmosphere under the boughs of the oaks.

While in this district, **Sainte Lucie di Tallano** (Santa Lucia di Tallà, 450m, 1500 inhab.), 8.5km to the SW on the D 268, can be visited. One of Corsica's loveliest villages, Sainte Lucie stands on a wooded hillside in a landscape rich in orchards and vineyards (it produces a notable wine). It had to be repopulated from the surrounding villages after its population was decimated by plague in 1348. This was della Rocca territory and Rinuccio della Rocca, a '...tempestuous Corsican warlord...a true prince of the Renaissance, a discriminating lover of the arts' (Dorothy Carrington: 'Granite Island'), endowed a Franciscan monastery at Sainte Lucie in 1492. Six years later he gave the monastery church a Crucifixion and a reredos of the Virgin and Child with Saints by the Master of Castel Sardo, a painter of probably Catalan origin, and his studio. Rinuccio also presented to the parish church of Sainte Lucie a 15C marble font in the shape of a hand and a marble bas-relief in Florentine style of an adolescent plump-faced Virgin and Child, dated MCCCC LXXXX VIIII at the top and flanked by the arms of 'Rinuccio de Rocha' at the bottom.

In a quarry due S of Sainte Lucie was worked the extremely rare rock (thought to be exclusive to Corsica until some was found in Finland) *diorite orbiculaire*. There is said to be none left and as the walk to the quarry is not easy most visitors can get an idea of what the rock is like from the piece set into the village war memorial. Marked like a panther skin, the orbs of the *diorite orbiculaire* are formed of concentric circles of white feldspar and black amphibole and can measure up to 6cm in diameter.

Return to Levie, retracing the route N up the D 268. From here an alternative way back to Porto Vecchio by a picturesque route is to leave the village by the D 59 which goes S.—8km on is *Carbini* (600m, 408 inhab.), with rows of lime trees along the road, and long low houses, many with elaborate and well-fashioned porches. The church of *San Giovanni Battista* was built in the first half of the 12C and is the former *piévanie*, or what remains because originally there were two churches, San Giovanni Battista and San Quilico of which only a bell tower still stands, very well restored in the late 19C by the Historical Monuments Service (perhaps at the instigation of Mérimée who wrote direct to the Minister about Carbini a mere 40 or so years earlier). Fine decorative arcading, particularly on the W front.

Carbini may exude peace and calm today but 600 years ago there was an outburt of heresy which was violently suppressed. The Giovannali sect was founded in Carbini c 1354, taking its name from the church. Franciscan in origin, it sought spiritual perfection, the sharing of worldly goods and family life and the equality of the sexes. Its members defied the feudal and ecclesiastical laws and their teaching spread in the east of Corsica. Pope Urban V, declaring them Satanists, mounted a Papal Crusade in 1362 and sent soldiers who hunted them down and massacred them, not only at Carbini but far away at Alesani in the Castagniccia. There are many fascinating and baffling sides to the whole story and links with similar movements in continental Europe. There is much to be discovered about this sect but it will not, I imagine, be in Carbini.

2km S from Carbini a footpath off to the left of the D 59 leads to some vestiges of the Torréen *Castellu de l'Accinto* in 1km and then to the Punta di a Vacca Morta. 7km beyond Carbini the road climbs sharply into the mountains between the scrubby mountain oaks to the Col de Bacinu.

On the Cagna plateau

To the right, 4km beyond the col, there is a rough track, which gets ever rougher, climbing up into the dramatic wilderness of the Montagne de Cagna. After about 6km there is a plateau with a few stone cabins and houses called *Bitalza* and a view E over to the Golfe de Porto Vecchio and S over the Bouches de Bonifacio to the Sardinian hills behind the port of Santa Teresa di Gallura. The twin summits of Capelu form a backdrop to Bitalza. Only sturdy and high-slung motors can negotiate this track without too much risk of fractured sumps but with provisions, rucksacks and stout footgear this is a good day's exploration. For dedicated walkers, well equipped and experienced in mountain travel, there are a dozen or so good itineraries in the Massif de Cagna, including the *Uomo di Cagna* (1217m), a sphere of rock 10m in diameter balanced on a narrow socle. It can be seen from most places in the southern plains and marks the S extremity of the central mountain ranges of Corsica. This Man of Cagna is most easily accessible from the village of Giannuccio at the end of the D 50 which leads N from the Sartène–Bonifacio road N 196 (see Michel Fabrikant: 'Guide des Montagnes Corses').

At the foot of the S slopes of the Cagna Massif the D 59 goes through the Tunnel d'Usciolu and after crossing another mountain ridge reaches (10km) Sotta, just before which take the left fork, the D 259, into the village. *Sotta* (130m, 1150 inhab.) recalls a mountain village in its fine granite houses yet is a village of the plain, set among fields and cattle pastures. 10km to Porto Vecchio by the D 853 and the N 198. At 4.5km is the village of *Ceccia* above which stands the 3rd millennium BC monument of *Tappa*. It can be difficult to find: do not go into the hamlet but watch out for a track through the vineyards to the right after the turning to the right to Cardetto. The track is almost opposite a small house standing on the road. Follow this straight, flat track as far as it goes. Immediately to the right is a maquis-covered high mound, a typical Torréen site. Ascent is relatively easy to the cyclopean walls and the central chamber they surround.

Sunday afternoon theological discussion at 1200m on the Uomo di Cagna mountain: left, a Porto Vecchio master-mason; right, the Abbé of Bonifacio

Porto Vecchio to Bonifacio is 27km by the N 198. Access to the sea and the beaches are described in the passages on the coastal environs of Porto Vecchio and Bonifacio respectively. The road crosses a desert region of a low plateau covered with maquis and dotted with cork oaks. At the·Bocca d'Aresia (68m) there is a view W to the Cagna Massif. 4km beyond the D 59 leads off to the right to join the D 859 road to Sotta (right) and Figari Airport (left). Closer to Bonifacio the landscape becomes less arid and desolate with areas of cultivation and olive groves. Approaching Bonifacio from the N brings home the extent of its geographical and geological isolation and explains much of the distinctive character and speech of the Bonafaciens or Bonifazinchi.

10 Le Cap Corse: From Bastia to Saint-Florent along the Coast Road

ROAD (D 80) 110km.—10km *Erbalunga.*—15.5km *Commune de Sisco* (to left of road).—28km *Sta. Severa* (and detour to W along the D 180).—61.5km *Pino.*—93.5km *Nonza.*

Bus tours of the Cap start from 1 Rue du Nouveau Port, Bastia.

CAP CORSE is not a cape but a peninsula, an extended index finger pointing to France from the clenched right fist, seen palmside, of Corsica.

The Cap is broadly that part of the island to the N of the D 81 road from Bastia on the Tyrrhenian coast in the E to Saint-Florent on the Mediterranean coast in the W via the Col de Teghime (541m), a distance of 23km. This winding road, where care is needed, is the divide between Cap Corse and the Nebbio (see Rte 13). Cap Corse itself is 40km long and 15km across at its widest point. Bastia in the S forms the divide between the Eastern Plain and, to the N, the mountainous spine of the peninsula which hugs the E coast, the continuation of the central mountain chain of the island. The highest point along the mountain chain of Cap Corse (800–1000m high) is Monte Stello (1307m).

The D 80 follows the coastline around the whole of the Cap Corse peninsula so the circuit may be made either clockwise or anti-clockwise, either from Saint-Florent or from Bastia. Starting from Bastia however, and following the sun in an anti-clockwise exploration, the variety of the Cap Corse landscape opens out more dramatically.

Leave Bastia from the NE corner of the Place St. Nicolas. This is the starting point of the D 80, the corniche road that follows the entire coastline of the Cap (translated in a French guide book as 'a cornish road with rocky coasts'). The road to the Cap is very clearly marked but remember, as always, not only that spelling undergoes changes but that road numbers also do and on many maps that are not bang up to date the D 80 appears under its maiden number N 198.

3km N of Bastia, *Pietranera* is a residential suburb of Bastia with villas tucked into the hillside on the left of the road and fitted into most of the available space above the sea on the right. 5.5km *Miomo*, a small fishing port with a mostly residential village clustered around it. There is pleasant bathing and a Genoese tower in a well-preserved state. 7.5km *Lavasina*, one of the hamlets forming the commune of

Brando. *Notre Dame des Grâces* (1677) is rough-cast in a pleasantly
faded pink but flanking it is an ugly thick-set campanile surmounted
by a Virgin in the worst 'plaster saint' style. Inside, above the
black-and-white marble altar, from a Pistoia monastery in Tuscany,
hangs a painting of the Virgin and Child (school of Perugino, 16C)
known as the Madonna of Lavasina (darkened with age). It is credited
with miraculous powers to protect the local fishermen. In an ex-voto
collection on the interior walls of the church stories, usually in the
vernacular, are told of sailors who were delivered from peril on the
sea. A confessional box in sculpted wood dates from 1680. The
pilgrimage on 8 September (Birth of the Holy Virgin) is attended by
large crowds, with a torchlight procession on the shore the night
before.

To the left of the D 80 lies the commune of BRANDO (Brandu) that
gives its name to a number of hamlets none of which, in Cap Corse
tradition, is actually called Brando. Take the D 54 to the left, just S of
the bridge over the Lavasina and before entering the village to which
the river gives its name. At 4km is *Pozzo*, the starting point for the
ascent of Monte Stello, at 1307m the highest mountain in Cap Corse.

The summit of *Monte Stello* can be reached by a stiffish climb, the round trip
taking 5 hours. Park the car in the Rue Napoléon, left of the church, and ahead is
the footpath through the maquis. The path passes two ruined buildings and
immediately after the second one the mountain ridge comes in sight. From the
summit there are views (according to weather, and the earlier in the day the
ascent is made the better) N to the tip of Cap Corse, E to the Golfe de Saint
Florent, SW to the Balagne and S and E to the mountains of Central Corsica and
down along the Eastern Plain. Check by telephone (36 04 96, recorded forecast)
before setting out.
   3km further on lies *Castello* with the church of *Sainte-Marie des Neiges* (Santa
Maria di e Nevi), c 9–10C, a single nave and oven-vaulted apse. N wall
incorporates earlier (6 or 7C) bas-relief animals, a boat, birds and rose designs. S
wall decorated with frescoes from 1386, 15C altarpiece of the Virgin and Child
on wood.—After a further 3km the D 54 reaches Erbalunga.

Back on the D 80 coastal road, 2.5km N of Lavasina and 10km from
Bastia is *Erbalunga* (1000 inhab.) a fishing hamlet in the commune of
Brando. A tongue of schist projects into the sea, protecting the tiny
port from the N wind. The houses appear to have been built
haphazardly, one against another at a variety of angles. Like a
miniature Manhattan, as much as possible has been fitted onto the
available rock and many of the buildings seem to rise out of the water.
A Genoese tower, the seaward side somewhat weather-worn, sits at
the tip of the promontory. It is not surprising that Erbalunga has for
long been a favourite with painters. It is the native village of the
forebears of Paul Valéry (1871–1945), the poet. The church of *St.
Erasme* is set on a terrace above the road from Bastia, from which the
procession of penitents called the *Cerca* (or the Search, the Quest),
sets out before 7 am on Good Friday. Walking a 7km route, the
penitents visit the churches and chapels of the Brando hamlets and
return at noon to Erbalunga. In the evening the torchlit procession of
cowled figures enact the *Granitola*—the Snail—winding and
tightening on itself. Possibly a pre-Christian fertility ceremony, it is
now, to be on the safe side, followed by other penitents who form the
sign of the cross.—5.5km further on is *Marine de Sisco* which takes its
name from the commune of Sisco comprised of 17 hamlets scattered
along the valley of the River Sisco.

To visit the Sisco churches take the D 32 which runs along the valley floor, climbing nearly 700m into the mountains. It eventually peters out into a track that reaches the hamlet of *Cortina Sutana* (3km) and the D 232 coming W from the Marine de Pietracorbara. The D 32 then turns due N to reach villages as far as Carbonnace where the D 32 runs NW towards the coast and the D 132 loops and twists its way down to the E coast at Porticciolo on the D 80, 10.5k N of Marine de Sisco. If it is planned to visit the Sisco hamlets by car allow plenty of time because the roads are narrow and winding. Walking is preferable, to take in the beauty of the hillsides on which chestnut trees and evergreen oaks rise above the thick growth of myrtle, heather, bramble and arbutus.

SAN MICHELE
Sisco

Up a footpath to the left of the D 32, 1km before the road ends (see above) is the little romanesque chapel of *San Michele* (1030m) standing on a plinth of rock from which there are outstanding views of the E coast of Cap Corse and the Tuscan islands. Pilgrimage is made here from the Sisco villages on 29 September. The parish church of SAINT-MARTIN, surrounded by oaks on its terrace overlooking the sea, houses relics transferred here from the local Convent of Sainte Catherine (Santa Catalina) in the 17C. Sailors, returning from Palestine in the 13C, are said to have promised the best of their cargo to the first church they reached should they be delivered from the storm. Once safe ashore they forgot their promise but were reminded by a second storm and took their treasures to Saint Catherine's Convent. Among them were a clod of the earth from which Adam was moulded, stones from Sinai, hairs from St. John the Baptist's cloak, a portion of the Virgin's coat and one of Enoch's fingers. The most striking relic is the so-called skull of St. John Chrysostom encased in a mask of hammered copper, silvered and gilded, said to have been made in the 13C in the Sisco valley, a metal-working centre in the Middle Ages. (Enquire at the Bastia Office du Tourisme for information and permission to view.)

Santa Catalina, Cap Corse

16.5km further on is SANTA CATALINA, the former convent of Sainte Catherine, now a church. 2km Beyond Sisco a statue of Saint Catherine stands on the left, high above the road, and a hairpin bend below it leads into the road up to Santa Catalina, the first sight of which is the massive fortified square tower beside the church. In front is a kind of rough lawn dominated by an ancient olive tree and set on the low walls surrounding the grass are large Ali Baba-style jars painted cream. There is more than a hint of the East and Islam in the jars and the shells and pottery dishes set around the semi-circular window of the W façade (modern glass depicting a crimson rising sun with a gold background and sunrays represented by radiating metal lines). To the right of the window is the date of the first restoration of the church: MCCCCXLIII (1443). Note the diamond and lozenge decoration over the two W doors. The queue of pilgrims to view the relief would have entered by one door and left by the other. Unfortunately this romanesque church is bare and in bad repair. On entering, to the left is a massive pillar that seems to support a roughly-made modern semi-circular gallery. There is a badly battered 17C altar with baroque barley-sugar columns. Plaster is falling off the walls. Elegant organ in bad condition by Mustel, Paris, no date, another organ in decrepit state against the S wall. A circular crypt (12C?) is reached by two stairs or 'tomboli', thought by Mme G. Moracchini-Mazel, the historian and great authority on Corsican romanesque architecture, to have been an attempt to reproduce the Holy Sepulchre at Jerusalem. It was here that the relics were kept which are now at Saint-Martin, and when one remembers that they were brought from Palestine it perhaps explains the numerous reminders of the East encountered here. The Convent is now a home for old people and is not open to the public.

20km from Bastia, and at the foot of the D 232 if returning from the Sisco detour, is *Marine de Pietracorbara* (Petracurbara). Just before a sharp bend to the right to follow the line of the bay is the *Torre dell'Aquila* (the Eagle Tower) to the left.—6km *Marine de Porticciolo* with just beyond it the D 132 that corkscrews its way inland through the Cagnano hamlets to join the D 32. 3km further is *Santa Severa* with its small port, the Marine de Luri, at the estuary of the River Luri. This fertile valley, filled with vineyards and citrus groves, is followed by the D 180, the principal road (apart from the D 80 further N) to cross Cap Corse, by which it is 16km to Pino.

From Santa Severa a detour can be made along the D 180 to Pino. 6km The Luri hamlet of *Piazza* (762 inhab.) with church of *Saint Pierre* (17C). Inside are pillars painted to resemble marble and walls decorated with blue, grey and light brown lozenges in geometric patterns. The wooden reredos holds a 15C painting representing the life of St. Peter. The background to the Quo Vadis scene incorporates valuable architectural details of the castles and fortified houses of the 15C lords of Cap Corse. There is a separate campanile of 1821 set, with the Luri commune building, in a large square with trees and the war memorial.

A road leads from the Col de Santa Lucia (marked) to the *Maison d'Enfants de Luri* (500m above the Luri valley) which has provided home and education for hundreds of children between the ages of 6 and 16, many of them brought here with health or family background problems. Much of their time is spent outdoors—planting trees, clearing mountain tracks and in running the museum where their archaeological finds are displayed, including thousands of pieces of pottery, necklaces and rings, which they identify, classify, often put together with great skill when possible. They and their director, the poet Jean Paul Sermonte, are justly proud to show visitors around the museum. Many of their digs have been around *Seneca's Tower* which stands 200m above the Col de Santa Lucia on a peak of the Ventiggiole (640m). Legend claims that Lucius Annaeus Seneca (c 4 BC–AD 65), exiled from Rome in 41–49 by the Emperor Claudius, dwelt here, although it would be more likely that he lived in one of the Roman colonies such as Mariana or Aléria. The tower is a 30-minute steady climb from the Maison d'Enfants by a steep footpath through cistus brush and low trees (fine views on a clear day, especially before noon, to the Tuscan islands and coast and to the E and W coasts of the Cap).

The school stands on the site of the Castel dei Motti, a watchtower guarding the Motti château (1246) which became a Capucin monastery, dedicated to St. Nicolas, in 1548. Since 1925 it has been the Maison d'Enfants. A notice outside the museum states 'This museum was founded on 20 November 1971 and was created by the children of the open air school of Luri 1970–71'.

At 34.5km from Bastia by way of Santa Severa on the D 80 is the *Marine de Meria*, a hamlet and sandy beach on the Luri estuary, 4km N of which is *Macinaggio*, now a small port for fishing boats but more important in the past. Paoli, returning from England, landed herę on 13 July 1790. On 10 March 1793 Napoleon Bonaparte came ashore and on 2 December 1869 the Empress Eugénie landed from 'l'Aigle' on her way back from Egypt where she had attended the opening of the Suez Canal.

By a footpath leading due N from Macinaggio, 3.5km and taking 2–2½ hours there and back, one reaches the chapel of *Santa Maria di a Chiappella*, on a bleak and bare stretch of coast, overlooking the tiny island of Finocchiarola. Romanesque, twin apses from 11C, restored in 18C. A Genoese tower close by, now in ruins, was built 1549. At the N extremity of Cap de Corse is the commune of *Rogliano* (Ruglianu, 530 inhab.).

In the mid 17C the commune was a stronghold of the powerful family da Mare and had a population of 4000–5000. The Romans had also a settlement here. From the 11C the da Mare were the masters of all they surveyed, and a good deal of land they could not see, until in 1553 Jacques da Mare broke with Genoa and supported Sampiero's revolt. Genoa had the da Mare château demolished and the site is called locally 'Castelacciu' (the bad château), while the nearby château of the Negroni family, old allies of the da Mare, is merely 'castellu'.

There are ruins of a Franciscan monastery nearby (on private property) and the 16C church of *St. Agnel* whose classical façade was restored and enlarged in the 18C. The 16C church of *St. Cosmo and St. Damien* was largely destroyed by fire in 1947. The nave was probably built in the 10C or earlier and its rectangular campanile was set at an angle to the façade.

From Macinaggio the main road, the D 80, turns W to cross the Cap peninsula by the Col St. Nicolas (300m). The first turning right after the col leads, on a very minor road by way of Granaggiolo and the D 253, to the N of Cap Corse and *Barcaggio*, 16km by very narrow roads. Barcaggio's fine sandy beach, where the Acqua Tignase reaches the sea, was guarded against invaders by the Genoese Angello Tower.

On the way to Centuri Port on the W coast of the Cap there is a turning marked to the *Moulin Mattei* (some way off the road and little to see) from which there are good views over the Tuscan sea to the islands of Capraja and Elba and N to the tip of Cap Corse and S down through the island towards the often snow-capped Monte Cinto, Corsica's highest mountain (2710m).

Centuri Port was set up in the 18C as a fishing port specialising in lobsters, and anchovies. Lobsters are still the mainstay of the port's commerce and a feature of local menus. Centuri is a centre for wet-suited submarine fishermen. Fishing and eating apart, Centuri is very attractive with its multi-coloured houses grouped around the little harbour. 4km to the E and seen from the road is the château of General Cipriani (1844–1918) built in the 19C in medieval style. Going S from Centuri Port the D 35 rejoins the D 80 at Pecorile.

At 58.5km from Bastia is *Pruno*, a spectacular bay enclosed by cliffs making it almost impossible to get down to the sea. At the village of *Morsiglia* (Mursiglia, 120 inhab.) the solid towers are a reminder that the inhabitants had repeatedly to take shelter from invaders. 3km further on, *Pino* (Pinu, 145m, 200 inhab.) is set in luxuriant vegetation. It has a pebbly beach, a baroque church, a Genoese tower and a Franciscan monastery dating from 1486. Olive trees, fig trees, chestnuts and planes flourish all around. In the chapel is a fresco and above the altar a painting of the Virgin flanked by St. Francis and St. Bernardino of Siena. A road to the right 8km

Centuri Port, Cap Corse

further on leads down to the Marine de Giottani and the Genoese tower of *Castelluccio*.

6km S and 82km from Bastia, *Marinca*, principal hamlet of the Canari commune, can be reached by a tortuous mountain road of 3km on the flank of Monte Cuccaro (832m). It is worth the effort of a slow drive because there is a splendid view from the Place du Clocher over the W coast of the Cap. The church of *Santa Maria Assunta* is late 12C Pisan. There are schist tiles of a striking green but ignore the 18C addition of a window to the façade, one of a number of misguided architectural 'improvements'. But look at the cornices and the curious human and animal faces. The parish church of *Saint François* was formerly a Franciscan monastery chapel. On the left as one goes in is St. Michael subduing the dragon and weighing human souls. In the sacristy there is a figure of Christ dressed as a penitent.

4km S of the Marinca turn-off is one of the most terrifying sights in the whole of Corsica: the abandoned asbestos mine, begun in 1948 and closed in 1966 but leaving screes and dunes of sterile grey dust and rusting metal. Fortunately it does not spread far and 2km further on the tiny beach of light green pebbles at the bay of the *Marine d'Albo* is watched over by the customary Genoese tower and it is Corsica back to normal again.

   Nonza (152m, 210 inhab.) is 14km further S and 93.5km from Bastia. St. Julie, who was born in Nonza or Carthage, was crucified for her Christian faith on the orders of the Roman Prefect Barbarus. Her body was taken to Brescia in Italy in 734 at the time of the threat of a Saracen invasion. There is a pilgrimage on 22 May to Nonza and the fountain of St. Julie is approached by 164 steps from the road to Pino. From the fountain there is a good view of the village and the Genoese tower (which can be reached from the centre of the village), and views of the Cap Corse coast down to Saint-Florent, of the Balagne and the massif of Monte Cinto. In the church of *Sainte Julie*, above a polychromatic marble altar of 1694, is a painting of the crucifixion of the saint in 303.

Genoese tower, Nonza, Cap Corse

After the cession of Corsica by Genoa to France by the Treaty of Versailles of 15 May 1768 those Corsicans who supported Paoli resisted the French forces. General de Grandmaison set siege to Nonza but his 1200 soldiers were unable to take the Genoese tower which kept up a constant musket fire and bombardment from the solitary cannon. Grandmaison parleyed with the stubborn Corsican defence and agreed to accord full military honours and a safe passage through the French lines of survivors wishing to rejoin Paoli on surrender. The terms were accepted but one old limping man called Jacques Casella came out as the French presented arms. By an ingenious system of cables he had kept up a continuous fire and gave the impression that the tower was defended by a large force. The French were full of admiration and the promise of safe conduct to Paoli was honoured. 'The defence force of Nonza tower was me alone', Casella said.

The D 80 closely follows the coast, giving extensive views of the Golfe de Saint Florent and over to the Désert des Agriates. At the Estuary of the Fium'Albino the road turns SE towards the commune de Patrimonio, renowned for its wine, and joins the D 81 which returns to the coast at Saint-Florent.

11 La Casinca

To the S of Bastia and to the NE of the Castagniccia, lying between the lower valley of the Golo to the N and the lower valley of the Fium'Alto to the S, is this tiny (8330 hectares) and virtually self-contained region called the **Casinca**. To the W the Monte Sant'Angelo rises to 1218m and to the E is the coastal plain. This is the most densely populated region of Corsica and now, with the eastern seaboard drained and the mosquito vanquished, it is also the most fertile area, producing cereals, citrus fruits, vines and tobacco with, on the terraces inland to the W, groves of olive and chestnut trees.

From Bastia take the N 193 S for 20km and at Casamozza cross the Golo and follow the N 198 towards Aléria. Either take the second turning to the right, the D 10, which leads to the Casinca village of Olmo, or take the third turning right, the D 237, to Loreto-di-Casinca.

36km from Bastia, in the heart of the Casinca, is *Loreto-di-Casinca* (Loretu di Casinca, 630m, 525 inhab.), a village on the chestnut-covered lower slopes of Monte Sant'Angelo. There is a car park in the Piana, the town square bordered by plane trees. Go on foot to the end of the main street flanked by houses of green schist, to where the church and a campanile stand on a terrace from which there is a view of the whole of the Casinca as well as the Biguglia lagoon, Bastia and the E coast from Erbalunga in the N to the estuary of the Fium'Alto in the S, the isles of Elba, Pianosa and Monte Cristo, and, in fine weather, the coast of Tuscany.

There is a footpath to the summit of *Monte Sant'Angelo* from Loreto-di-Casinca. Leaving the village by the D 6 in the direction of Silvareccio, take the first track leading off to the right. 90 minutes to the summit (1218m) and 45 minutes back to Loreto. Splendid panorama from the top.

From Loreto-di-Casinca there is also a delightful walk through the chestnut woods to Olmo. Again, take the D 6, but going towards Vescovato. In less than 2km a narrow road, marked, goes off to the left to *Olmo* (Olmu, 540m, 502 inhab.), an amphitheatre village on the right bank of the Golo.

Take the D 6 S in the direction of Silvareccio to the junction with the D 237 (which continues W to the Bocca di Sant'Agostino, 670m, the mountain pass connecting the Casinca with the Castigniccia). Turn right and continue S along the D 237 and after 4km turn left and follow the D 206 to *Penta di Casinca* (A Penta di Casinca, 400m, 1101 inhab.). The village consists of a single street of tall grey schist houses strung out along a rocky spur, with the heights of Monte Sant'Angelo to the W and to the E a view out to the eastern coastal plain and the Biguglia lagoon. Just outside the village is a cemetery and the road to it passes under an aqueduct. Engraved on the arch is 'Oghie a me' (today it is my turn) and on the other side mourners returning from the funeral read 'dumane a te' (tomorrow it will be yours).

Fork left immediately on leaving the village, then left again, and after 1km turn right onto the D 6 to *Castellare di Casinca* (580 inhab.), another typical Casinca village built on a spur of rock looking out to sea. Follow the road 2km to the junction with the N 198, turn left in the direction of Bastia, and after 3km take the second turning on the left, the D 37, reaching in 2km *Venzolasca* (U Venzulasca, 35m, 1100 inhab.), another village of a single street of tall houses built along a ridge between two valleys. Fork right after leaving the village to the W.

2.5km along the D 237 is **Vescovato** (U Viscuvatu, 140m, 2030 inhab.), the capital of the Casinca which now gives its name to the commune. The name means 'bishopric' and from 1269 to 1570 it was the seat of the bishops of Mariana, being healthier and more easily defended than Mariana itself which had suffered the depredations of both mosquitoes and the Moors. After 1570 the bishops of Mariana took up residence in Bastia.

Carved door panel in the Casinca

Cars may be left close to the main square which overlooks the coastal plain and has a fine fountain presided over by an eagle. Ask at the Mairie for the key to the former cathedral church of *San Martino*, originally a chapel, enlarged in the 15C by the Bishops of Mariana. The greatest treasure of the church is the white marble *tabernacle* sculpted by a Genoese artist in 1441. It portrays the Resurrection and the sleeping Roman soldiers lying against the tomb, elbows propped on their knees and with plump childish faces, are a triumph of the expression of martial boredom. The left hand of the soldier on the right is long-fingered and elegant. Either the sculptor wished to express something about the nature of these dormant guards or his own pleasure in forming the hand got the better of him.

Vescovato, by Edward Lear

There are several historical figures, famous both inside and outside Corsica, who were natives of, or at one time lived in, Vescovato. Among them is Anton Pietro Filippini whose house displays his arms and a 1575 inscription. His 'Historia di Corsica', an invaluable source book on the island, was published in 1594. In the house in which was born the patriot Andrea Colonna-Ceccaldi (who organised resistance to Genoa in the 18C) Joachim Murat, named King of Naples in 1808 by Napoleon, stayed in 1815 before his expedition to Calabria where he was taken prisoner by the restored Bourbons and shot. Luce or Louis de Casabianca (1752–98), also born here, commanded the French flagship 'l'Orient' at the Battle of Aboukir on 10 August 1798. His 12-year-old son Jacques was beside him and when Luce was killed Jacques, obeying his father's orders not to abandon ship, refused to leave when 'l'Orient' caught fire. He was blown up with the ship, an heroic end that brought poetic inspiration to Felicia Hemans who immortalised him in 'The boy stood on the burning deck'. Mirabeau (1749–91) was stationed here for a short time while a serving soldier and a couple of centuries earlier it was in Vescovato that Henri II of France, who had been persuaded by the Corsican patriot Sampiero Corso to take the island from the Genoese, had a public declaration made that Corsica was henceforth incorporated into the Kingdom of France and could no more be abandoned than the crown itself. Two years later Henri II, with cynical treachery, handed Corsica back to Genoa.

The D 237 leads back from Vescovato in 4.5km to the N 198 and, turning left to Casamozza one can return to Bastia, 20km on the N 193.

12 La Castagniccia

The **Castagniccia** (Haute Corse) is a high-lying region of hills and mountains of medium height (800–1700m) in NE Corsica, bounded to the N by the valley of the River Golo, to the S by the valley of the River Tavignano, to the W by Monte San Petrone and its outliers, and separated from the Tyrrhenian Sea by the Casinca region to the NE and the Eastern Plain. The district takes its name from the *Castanea sativa*, the sweet chestnut of the *Fagaceae* family of trees. Familiar to Northerners as the nut roasted in the fire in winter and sold in city streets or as *marrons glacés* and chestnut stuffing, it once formed the staple diet of mountain people when ground into flour. The wood of the tree was used for carpentry, cabinet making, as stakes to support vines and as firewood. Both wood and fruit were used in barter with other regions to obtain oil, soft fruit and cereals. Those chestnuts not gathered for milling sustain the large troupes of semi-wild pigs so often encountered throughout the district, usually just around a bend in the road. The importance of the chestnut has declined with the development of communications that ensure a regular supply of wheat flour. The chestnut plantations which man had developed in place of the indigenous oak woods have lost their pre-eminent importance in the local economy and the trees themselves have been both neglected and afflicted with 'the ink disease'. Although to the eye of the visitor the Castagniccia in spring and summer is one vast billowing ocean of green, and of gold and russet in autumn, a closer inspection reveals the stark skeletons of dead trees.

The people of the Castagniccia have always been hard-working: they have not relied exclusively on the chestnut crop. The traditional occupations still flourish, although on nothing like the scale that they did in the past and even up to this century. Among them are potteries, woodcarving and pipe-making, the forging of arms and agricultural implements from ore brought from the island of Elba, leatherwork and the making of shoes. The villages of this high country were built on elevations so that the inhabitants could see out across the chestnut forests and if necessary defend themselves against attack. The settlements in this once most densely-populated region of Corsica are liberally dotted about the tree-covered countryside.

The approaches to the Castagniccia are easy but the roads in the interior of the region are still for the most part winding and narrow so that time must be allowed and care taken.

Approaching the Castagniccia from Bastia take the N 193 S for 20km and turn right to follow the N 193 at Casamozza where the N 198 continues S towards Aléria. The N 193 and the railway follow the course of the River Golo, a picturesque and varied route. There are a number of narrow turnings off to the left that lead into the Castagniccia but much time can be wasted in the intricacies of minor roads and it is very easy to get lost. It is preferable to continue to (46km) Ponte Leccia. Take the first road left just before reaching the Golo and the Genoese bridge, the D 71, which runs along the S slopes of the Serra Debbione, a twisting lonely road with scarcely a building alongside but with fine views W to the red pinnacles of Popolasca and SW to the Rotondo range of mountains.

14.5km from Ponte Leccia is **Morosaglia** (Merusaglia, 800m, 1015 inhab.), birthplace of Corsica's most illustrious patriot and statesman, Pasquale or Pascal Paoli, born on 6 April 1725. He was the youngest son of Hyacinthe Paoli (1690–1768; sounding less of a spring flower with his name in its original Corsican form of Giacinto), who had been a minister of King Theodore I, the first and last foreign king of Corsica. Theodor von Neuhof had landed at Aléria on 12 March 1736, was crowned constitutional monarch in April and by November of the same year was on his way out of his kingdom by taking boat at

Solenzara. The Genoese appealed to the French to help them control the still-rebellious Corsicans. This suited the French who defeated the rebels and stayed in Corsica until 1741. Many Corsican patriots left the island, including Hyacinthe Paoli who took his youngest son with him to Naples. Pasquale Paoli's return as an adult to Corsica as General of the Nation and his two periods of exile in England belong to another part of this book (see Historical Introduction).

The solid and quite modest house where Paoli was born is beyond the main village street, to the left of the road. It is now converted in part into a *museum* (open 9.00–12.00 and 15.00–18.00 every day). The ground floor is a chapel with a family vault where Paoli's remains were interred when they were brought in 1889 from St. Pancras old cemetery, London, where he had been buried in 1807. (There is a bust of Paoli in Westminster Abbey but, contrary to popular belief, he was never buried there.) The first floor, including the room where he was born, displays proclamations, the resolutions of the Corsican Parliament of his time, and engravings of the many portraits made of him by Reynolds, Gérard, Lawrence and others.

Paoli was baptised in the church of *Santa Reparata*, a 5–10-minute walk up and above the main street of the village. Ask the way to it because the track winds up between the town's back gardens. This single-nave church of romanesque origin, with many later modifications, is set, as so often in Corsica, on a spur of rock overlooking the village. The sculpted pair of interlaced and tail-consuming serpents are probably three to four centuries earlier than the date of 1550 seen above the W door, having been saved from an earlier building to be set into the wall. The Stations of the Cross are by an unknown late 18C local painter, *naïf* in style like those at Carcheto. The man who stands on a ladder to hand down the body of Christ from the Cross holds one end of the shroud in his left hand but, his right hand supporting Christ's arm, he holds the other end of the shroud between his teeth so that the body shall remain wrapped in decency before the eyes of the women. The Cross is held upright by two wooden stakes, the tops burred over when they were hammered into the ground, a detail so familiar to the painter that he did not even think about it.

The school at Morosaglia, the *Pascal Paoli School*, cannot be missed because its name is painted boldly on the walls. It was the former Rostino monastery, a meeting place in the first half of the 18C of a *consulta* dedicated to the liberation of Corsica from Genoese domination. Clemente Paoli, older brother of Pasquale and much overshadowed by him, was a tough and effective Corsican resistance fighter against all foreign assailants who, having retired from politics, died in the Couvent de Rostino in 1793.

At 4km from Morosaglia the Col de Prato (985m) is the highest point on the D 71 as it crosses the mountain spine of the Castagniccia. Just E and beyond the Col there is, in clear weather, an extensive panorama of the Castagniccia and over the coastal plain to the Tyrrhenian Sea. Between the Col and Piedicroce there are four left turnings to the E leading to the villages of the Fium'Alto valley and to the scattered mountain villages towards the valley of the Golo. These are better visited from Piedicroce and are described below.

At 18km beyond the Col de Prato is *Campana* (A Campana, 746m, 95 inhab.). The church of *St. André* is reached on foot; ask for the key in the village. It contains an Adoration des Bergers attributed to

Zurbarán (1598–1664) or to one of his pupils (see paintings in the National Gallery, London, and in Cordoba).

Campana sits on the side of *Monte San Petrone* (1767m). To climb the mountain follow the road right to Campodonico and take the path leading to the right from the hamlet (about 6 hours there and back). From the summit there is a panoramic view of the chestnut forests, the Eastern Plain up to Cap Corse in the N and, to the W, the central mountain chain. 3km from Campana are the ruins of the *Orezza monastery*.

Of Franciscan foundation, the monastery became a centre of Corsican patrotism and resistance to foreigners: principally the Genoese but later the French as well. During the years of the first major Corsican insurrection, 1730–34, the mountain rebels came down to the plains and attacked the centres of Genoese government in the Eastern Plain. Among the leaders were Andrea Ceccaldi of Vescovato, Luigi Giafferi of Talasani and Gio. Francesco Lusinchi of Zivaco.

Consultes (*consulta* in Corsican) were established to decide the course that the rebellion should take. Initially the assemblies had their seat in Corte but in March 1730 an assembly held at the St. François monastery at Orezza gave ecclesiastical blessing to the rising against Genoa. In 1735 the *consulte* at Orezza proclaimed Corsica independent but the following half century saw the seven-month wonder of King Theodore, interventions by the French, British and Sardinians and the Generalship of Pasquale Paoli from 1755–69, when he retired to England. Paoli returned to Corsica on 17 July 1790 and at the Orezza Assembly in September of that year he was elected Commander-in-Chief of the Corsican National Guards and later Président du Conseil Général du Départ-ement de la Corse. So Orezza played a large part in Corsican history but today there is little to see except the ruins of the monastery invaded by brambles and, on occasion, cows who wander off the road. The building was destroyed not by the Genoese or the French but by Corsica's last invaders, the Germans, who blew it up during their retreat in 1943.

1km to the S on the D 71 is *Piedicroce* (Pedicroce, literally 'at the foot of the Cross', 636m, 250 inhab.). A large village in the centre of the Castagniccia, it is built on a 150m-high terrace on the SE slopes of Monte San Petrone, overlooking the natural amphitheatre of the Orezza, which gives its name to Corsica's most famous mineral water and is the place where the Fium'Alto rises. There is an extensive view from the terrace of the church of *Saints Peter and Paul* which is large, with a baroque façade of 1761 and a square tower. It has the oldest ORGAN in Corsica, built at the beginning of the 17C and recently restored to magnificent appearance and tone. A 16C painting on wood depicts the Virgin and Child flanked by two angel musicians.

There are two roads out of Piedicroce. The D 506 runs due N until it reaches the Fium'Alto where it turns due E to follow the valley towards the coast, joining the N 198 at (23.5km) Folelli. The first turn off to the right from the D 506 as one leaves Piedicroce leads to the *Orezza source*. There is a neglected courtyard in front of a building which looks as if it had been designed as a small château or manor house, many of its windows now broken. In the centre of the courtyard, its ornamental fountain now gone, is the spring water bubbling out of the iron-reddened ground. There is a sad air of general dilapidation, which is surprising as one finds bottled Orezza water in every café and restaurant in the island. A cascade of broken glass glitters its way down into the Fium'Alto ravine like greenish snow, bottles which did not survive recycling.

The D 71 leaves Piedicroce to the E and in under 2km goes through the hamlet of *Pie d'Orezza* (Ped'Orezza, 637m, 68 inhab.). Way up on the mountainside, hanging over it, is Campodonico. 3.5km *Carcheto-Brustico* (Carchetu Brusticu, 630m, 108 inhab.) where the baroque parish church of *Sainte Marguerite*, its façade intricately decorated, contains two striking, although sharply contrasting, works of art. The delicately sculpted alabaster statuette of the Virgin and Child, with crown and sceptre, is probably 18C Italian. The Stations of the Cross, dated 1 June 1790, are the work of a local painter who, as at Morosaglia and in other Corsican churches, depicted local costume, tools and habits. In the Crucifixion a curly-haired chubby child holds out the basket of nails and a hammer to one of the two men nailing Christ to the cross and, as the body is placed in the tomb, the painter included four women mourners or *voceratrices* wearing 18C Corsican clothes. Turning from the sacred to the horrific, one can still see the ivy-covered remains of a Carcheto house that belonged to a notorious bandit of the beginning of this century called François-Marie Castelli, one of whose victims lay dying for 18 hours on 6 May 1912 with nobody daring to go to her aid.

After a further 3km the D 71 crosses from the higher valley of the Fium'Alto to the valley of the Alesani by the Bocca di Arcarota (819m). There is a good view of the surrounding chestnut-covered coun-tryside and over to the sea in the E and the mountains to the W. 11km *Valle d'Alesani* (E Valle d'Alisgiani, 620m, 501 inhab.), a collection of hamlets in the chestnut forests on the left bank of the Alesani River.

The history of the valley of the Alesani and its people is to some extent a microcosm of the history of Corsica: that of invasion and resistance. Among the invaders, repelled with varying degrees of success or endured under repressive regimes, were Greeks, Romans, Vandals, Ligurians, Byzantines, North African and Turkish pirates, and at various periods the forces of Aragon, Pisa, Genoa, France, Italy and Germany. The bizarre episode of King Theodore of Corsica also closely touched the valley. It was at the Franciscan monastery of Alesani, which had long been a centre of resistance against the Genoese, that Theodore was crowned King of Corsica on 15 April 1736. The Westphalian Baron Theodor von Neuhof (1694–1756), a professional rogue and adventurer with some personal knowledge of the courts of Europe and their ways (and of debtors' prisons), after meeting Corsican exiles in Italy convinced some 'Greek and Jewish merchants in Tunis whom he had somehow inspired with confidence in its success' (Carrington: 'Granite Island') to finance his attempt. He landed at Aléria in March 1736 with money, guns, ammunition and dressed in flamboyant clothes. While the church bells rang from the tower of the Alesani monastery and the crowd sang, a laurel wreath was placed on his head while he swore to be loyal to the constitution. By November Neuhof was discredited and penniless and fled from the island. His luck had run out and after further unsuccessful exploits he died in poverty in London in 1756 where there is a memorial to him, placed by Horace Walpole, just above that to Hazlitt, in the churchyard of Saint Anne's church, Soho.

The *monastery of Alesani* is 5km along the D 17 leading out of the village of Valle d'Alesani to the right. The church contains a Virgin and Child painted on wood, c 1450, known as *La Vierge à la Cerise* because the Virgin holds a cherry to the Infant's mouth. Ascribed to the Sienese artist Sano di Pietro, it is painted in the style of earlier centuries which typified much of his work (see Moracchini and Carrington: 'Trésors Oubliés des Églises de Corse').

At (12km) *Sant Andrea di Cotone* (408m) the road leaves the valley of the Alesani and runs along the flank of the mountains overlooking the Eastern Plain.

A minor road, the D 517, goes S and crosses the Alesani Dam but there is no right of way for motor traffic. I have walked it without being challenged and the view over the Barrage de l'Alesani and over the Eastern Plain to the sea is very impressive. Time and possible right-of-way difficulties make it a dubiously worthwhile walking detour.

4km from Sant Andrea di Cotone the D 71 reaches **Cervioni** (326m, 1600 inhab.). From the village square, which has a low wall on the E side, there is a splendid view over the Eastern Plain and the sea. Up and above the village on the slopes of Monte Castello (1109m) and all around there are chestnut groves, terraces of olive trees, and vines. The former cathedral church of *Sainte Marie and Saint Erasme* (c 1580) was built at the instigation of Alexandre Sauli, Bishop of Aléria, who made Cervione the seat of his diocese. Sauli was canonised in 1904 and wall paintings on either side of the entrance depict his progress to Cervione on a white horse and his magisterial expulsion, by the force of faith, of the Barbary pirates. There are choir stalls and frescoes. The *Bishop's Palace* opposite was Neuhof's first residence as king-designate of Corsica on his way to coronation at the Alesani monastery, and is now a *museum* concentrating on local archaeology and the traditional Corsican way of life in the mountains. It displays a large collection of locks and keys, including that said to belong to the lock-up 'cantarno' built by Paoli in 1760. The museum also shows pans for roasting chestnuts, blacksmiths' tools and knives made locally. Cervione has a local radio station which broadcasts in Corsican throughout the day and night. (Other Corsican broadcasting stations are in Ajaccio, Calvi and Bastia.) The names of streets, squares, public buildings and wall plaques commemorating notable citizens are inscribed in Corsican.

The *statue of La Madonna* is 1½ hours' walk there and back by a rough path leading out of Cervione to the WSW (the best way to find the path is to ask in the village). This 16C white marble statue of the Virgin was found by sailors on the shore at Prunete after a Genoese ship on its way to Cordova with Florentine works of art was wrecked. The statue is life-size and stands in the *Chapelle de Notre Dame de Scobiccia* to which there is an annual pilgrimage on 15 August when Mass is celebrated there at dawn.—Fine view over the Eastern Plain to the Tuscan islands.

To visit the *Chapelle Santa Cristina* leave Cervioni to the N by the D 71 and drive to the village of *Valle di Campoloro* (500m). The key to the chapel is at the Mairie: ask there for directions to the narrow track to the chapel, about 30 minutes' walk there and back (some of the distance can be covered, with care, by car). The walls of the small twin-apsed chapel (15C) are covered with frescoes dated 1473, unfortunately indifferently restored at some time in the past. Christ in Majesty is depicted in each apse. On the N wall a dark-complexioned monk who may be the *donateur* of the frescoes or the artist who painted them. Despite the retouching and the effects of damp and neglect during the centuries the frescoes are remarkable for their lively colours and the characterisation in the faces. From Valle di Campoloro it is 5.5km on the D 71 to the N 198, the main road along the E coast.

From Valle di Campoloro N the D 33 is a corniche overlooking the Eastern Plain. 4km from the Valle is *San-Nicolao* (Santu Niculaiu, 250m, 1031 inhab.), a remote village set among olive groves, chestnut woods and orchards on the E rim of the Castagniccia overlooking the Eastern Plain from its mountainside balcony. The 17C baroque church with an imposing bell tower was built on the site of an older romanesque church.

From San Nicolao the D 34 turns E towards the N 198 and Moriani Plage (5km). The D 330 winds N 10.5km to *Talasani*, birthplace of Luigi Giafferi (1680–1745), a great fighter for Corsican freedom who beat the Genoese at the battle of Furiani.—10km further is *Folelli*, at the junction of the D 330 and the N 198, just N of the Fium'Alto.

The heart of the Castagniccia: Along the D 515

The D 515 wends its tortuous and picturesque way N, starting from the Col San Cristofano, 7km N of Piedicroce on the D 71.—3km *Croce* (A Croce) where there is a private MUSEUM devoted to the way of life in the Castagniccia in the past (open on Saturday and Sunday afternoons). The founder and proprietor gives a graphic and fascinating explanation of how the people lived. The ground floor of a typical house of the region was reserved for domestic animals and at night the ladder was pulled up to the first floor where the family lived. In the museum are sieves for removing the outer skin of the chestnuts which were then baked and sieved again until the second skin came away, after which they were carried to the miller who took 20 per cent of the resultant flour as his payment.

Because chestnuts are particularly rich in vitamins it was possible to live for long periods through hard winters or during troubled times almost exclusively on bread made from chestnut flour to which, as it is sweetish, salt was added. Baskets were carried to hold the chestnuts and three-pronged long forks to pull them off the branches. Preparation, peeling, baking and milling took place during November or the beginning of December, according to the weather and state of the crop. Now people eat wheaten bread and the falling off in demand for chestnuts has meant the neglect of the trees: one sees as many dead chestnut trees as one saw dead elms in Britain during the Dutch Elm scourge. Chestnut cultivation and industry began to decline in the 1920s and 1930s and was not much revived during the Second World War despite severe food shortages. Chestnuts now feed the half-wild pigs and the wood is still used, though less than in the past, to make articles of furniture from cradles to coffins. It would appear from the study of fossils that the sweet chestnut, roughly the same tree as today, was growing in Corsica some 25 million years ago.

5km from Croce, *La Porta* (A Porta, 520m, 518 inhab.) has had its share of turbulence and endured battles against Romans, Vandals, Arabs and Genoese. The church of *Saint-Jean-Baptiste* was designed by a Milanese architect and built in 1648. It has a façade (1707) painted in ocre and white and has been added to since. The organ, built in the Italian style in 1780 by a monk at Rogliano in Cap Corse, was placed in the organ loft in 1800. It was restored by Jacques Chailley, a Paris music teacher, his son and villagers during vacations in 1963–65 and concerts are now held there in summer. The church contains a polychromatic ceiling and pulpit, grey trompe l'oeil decoration (1886), a 17C Christ painted on wood and an 18C painting of the Beheading of St. John the Baptist. The *campanile* built in 1720 is considered the finest baroque bell tower in the whole of Corsica.

La Porta is the birthplace of two brothers who are among France's most famous soldiers: Comte Horace (1772–1851) and Tiburce Sebastiani (1786–1871). Horace served with distinction during the Spanish and Russian campaigns and went on to become Deputé for Corsica and first Navy Minister and then Foreign Minister under Louis-Philippe; he was subsequently French ambassador to London in 1835–40. Very handsome, he was nicknamed 'le Cupidon de l'Empire'. This First Empire cupid was obviously much more than just a pretty face and ended up a Marshal of France. His brother reached the rank of general during Napoleon's campaigns. Born before the Revolution, he lived to see the Franco-Prussian war.

The oil press or *franghju* at La Porta has been recently restored after many years of idleness and brought back into service in the Government's attempt to stimulate a revival in olive production.

8km N of La Porta is the *Col de Sant'Antone* (687m). It was in the monastery here, now in ruins, that Pasquale Paoli was elected General of the Nation (Capu Generale) on 13 July 1755 by the Casabianca Assembly. Follow the D 51 to the left from the Col de Sant'Antone, reaching in 9km *Campile*. In this village was made the long thin knife which gave its Italian name to the world. The *vendetta* (from Latin *vindicta*, vengeance) has a blade decorated with scrolls and flourishes and the Italian words '*Che la mia ferita sia mortale*' or in Corsican '*Chi a mio terita sia murtale*' ('May my wound prove fatal'). The use of *vendetta* in the sense of a family feud, usually hereditary, has been extended to mean any kind of relentless and 'vindictive' campaign between one group and another.

It is 2km to the hamlet of *Canaghia* which used to be known until the beginning of the present century for a particular kind of pottery rendered very heat-resistant by mixing asbestos with the clay. The potters were women who moulded their pots by hand without a wheel. From Canaghia it is 5km NE to the hamlet of Barchetta and on the N 193 by the River Golo, 28.5km to Bastia and 17.5km to Ponte Leccia.

13   Le Nebbio and Saint-Florent

The **Nebbio** (Nebbiu) is a clearly-defined geographical area, easily reached from Bastia in the E and from Saint-Florent in the W.

It is a fertile region, partly plain, partly hills and valleys, irrigated by the River Aliso (rising at 1508m on Monte Grimaseto, 20km long) and its tributaries which run into the Golfe de Saint Florent on the N limits of the Nebbio. The region is framed to the S and E by the mountainous ridges that run from the Col de Teghime to the Col di Tenda, and to the W by the Tenda massif (the watershed of the River Aliso which runs into the Golfe de Saint Florent and the River Ostriconi which flows W to reach the sea at the S limit of the Désert des Agriates). For visitors whose time is limited a circular tour of the Nebbio is one of the most rewarding in the island.

Leave Bastia by the D 81 (still marked as N 199 on some maps) going due N from the Palais de Justice to loop around and set off towards the Col de Teghime (10km) and Saint-Florent (23km). From this road there are extended views over the Étang de Biguglia and the sea. 10km *Col de Teghime* (548m) where there is a monument to those who fought and those who died in the battles for Liberation 1–2 October 1943. In clear weather fine views to the Étang de Biguglia, the Eastern Plain and over the Tyrrhenian Sea to the Isles of Elba and Capraja and to the W the Nebbio, Golfe de Saint Florent and the Désert des Agriates. To the left the D 38 runs from the Col to the village of Oletta (8.5km).

7km along the D 81 *Patrimonio* (Patrimoniu, 516 inhab.), one of the best-known Corsican names because of the famous wines from this district, the first in Corsica to be designated *appellation controlée*. An oft-repeated story, probably apocryphal, is that a bishop, touring the region and celebrating the virtues of the Corsican race said 'Among you there are no traitors except one, your wine is treacherous'; he had obviously sampled it on the episcopal visit. 1km further the Bocca di San Bernardino (76m) where the D 80 goes N and to the right up the W coast of Cap Corse and the D 81 continues SW to (23km) Saint-Florent.

A. Saint-Florent

Saint-Florent (San Fiurenzu, 1355 inhab.) is a popular holiday resort with excellent hotels and restaurants, the latter situated both along the harbour and around the Place des Portes, the principal square of the old town. The harbour itself has been dredged and is well organised for the many sailing boats using it. The citadel, massive and well-preserved, is today the HQ of the gendarmerie.

Saint-Florent

The Roman town was 1km inland from the present port, where the Cathedral of the Nebbio now stands. When the Genoese in 1440 built their citadel on the shore of the Gulf a new town grew up around it and the site chosen by the Romans was abandoned. Until the 18C Saint-Florent was the seat of the Bishop of Nebbio and of the Genoese governor of the province. Built on the marshy estuary of the Aliso, malaria was a constant menace. The strategic importance of Saint-Florent was fought over by Corsicans, Genoese and French during the war of 1553–69 and again during the struggles for independence of 1729–69. Between the mosquito and human assailants Saint-Florent fell into decay and even the attempts to revive the port during the Second Empire did not help much because the harbour silted up but work on it during the past 30 years has kept it clear for sailing boats.

It was from Saint-Florent on 14 October 1795 that Paoli boarded an English frigate for Livorno and thence to London, never to return. A large crowd of supporters came to see him off and Sir Gilbert Elliot ordained that Paoli, as Governor of Corsica, should receive full military honours on his departure. However, the end of Elliot's Corsican career was also imminent; only 11 months later he followed Paoli to England. On 15 June 1794 a decision had been taken at Corte to put the island under the protection of King George III and Sir Gilbert Elliot was named Viceroy of Corsica over Paoli. But in November 1796 Bonaparte's Army of Italy took the island in the name of the French republic and Corsica has remained French ever since.

The most exciting and interesting aspect of Saint-Florent is the Cathedral of the Nebbio, perhaps in part because of the way in which it is approached by an unpromising narrow road leading out of the main part of the village (where anyone will give you directions). This becomes a suburban road bordered by small villas and bungalows and then, suddenly, to the left of the road on a slight rise, is the church of **Santa Maria Assunta**, the Cathedral of the Nebbio, starkly beautiful on its sward of rough grass, with a farmyard to one side and vineyards stretching below. The first time I saw it it was encased orthopaedically in splints and could not be visited. The second time all the restoration had been completed and there it was, its honey-coloured walls expertly restored and free of scaffolding.

Saint-Florent, Cathedral of the Nebbio

The Cathedral of Santa Maria Assunta was built by the Pisans in the first quarter of the 12C as was La Canonica, the church of Santa Maria-Assunta, the former cathedral of the diocese of Mariana close to Bastia (see Rte 8), which it resembles. These two cathedrals are outstanding examples of romanesque architecture in Corsica. Built of fine-grained pale limestone, the Nebbio cathedral's W front is elegant

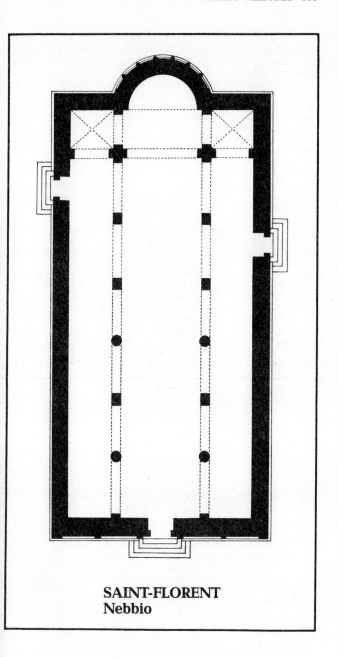

SAINT-FLORENT
Nebbio

and dignified with semi-circular blind arcades arranged in two tiers, five rising from ground level and the three top ones reaching almost to the pitch of the roof, leaving room in the small triangle at the top for a slender Greek cross. The lintel and pillars are decorated at intervals in relief resembling shells engraved with concentric lines. The decorated capitals of the graceful pilasters show, on the left, a four-legged creature in high relief and, on the right, a pair of intertwined snakes. The beast is lion-like with its mane and long tail and yet, the closer one looks, it becomes apparent that the animal is more fantastic than leonine. The cathedral had at one time a campanile, demolished in the 19C.

Enter the church by the door in the S wall. (The key may be borrowed from the Syndicat d'Initiative on the first floor of the Mairie, on the Bastia road, open 10.00–12.00 and 15.00–18.00 on weekdays. Passport or identity card and a small sum of money are held until the key is returned.) Inside, a nave and two aisles divided by pillars whose capitals are decorated with shells, foliage, fabulous animals and serpents, a ram, and abstract designs. In the vaulted apse is a statue of the Virgin and Child in white marble (given by Jean-Jérôme Doria in 1691), placed above the gilded wooden statue of Saint Flor, a Roman soldier martyred for his Christian faith in the 3C. To the right of the entrance door is a glass case in which are exhibited the mummified remains of Saint Flor (not Saint Florent) taken from the Roman catacombs and sent to the Bishop of the Nebbio by Pope Clement XIV in 1771. In size and height the body would seem to be that of a youth of 14–18 years old, possibly of North African origin, dressed in the 18C conception of a Roman soldier's outfit: a highly unsuitable kind of battle-dress made mostly of fine chain mail. There is something most touching about this small figure, dressed as it were by the theatre wardrobe.

In the nave (left) is the tomb of General Antoine Gentili (1745–98) who, when young, had been a supporter of Paoli in the fight for Corsican independence, but deserted him and became his rival when Paoli called on England for help. Bonaparte made him general commanding a division and he took part in the liberation of Corsica from the British in 1796. One of the most notable bishops of the Nebbio was Monsignor Giustiniani, whose description of Corsica in 1531 is a valuable source-book. He was a Hebraic scholar at the Collège de France in the reign of François I.

B. Nebbio villages

A circular tour of the Nebbio can be made from Saint-Florent by taking the D 81 road across the Aliso in the direction of Calvi. For 4km this road passes along the S edge of the Désert des Agriates (see Rte 4) until the turning to the left and S on to the D 62, a narrow and winding road through pastures giving way to olive groves. At 10km along the D 62, *Santo Pietro di Tenda* (Santu Petru di Tenda, 360m, 565 inhab.). The houses of this village are stretched out along the flank of the Tenda ridge above the Aliso valley. Two separate baroque churches (one is in fact a chapel), are joined in a single façade by a square campanile of peach-coloured stone built between the two, and an archway. The campanile has a square-faced clock which looks as if it were enlarged from a digital watch. When I was there it was not working and gave the wrong time and behind the church the old and elegant round face of an earlier clock was telling centuries-old time to the nettles. The church of *Saint Jean* (open to visitors) has the chapel of the *Sainte-Croix Fraternity* next door to it. The interior walls of the church are painted in trompe l'oeil marble and there is an 18C Descent from the Cross of which an old man said that he remembered it being taken down 50–70 years ago to be 'revivified'. Despite that it is still very dark and needs expert cleaning. A stage has been built in front of the altar: 'some idea of some Pope to bring the Mass to the people', commented the same informant (presumably referring to Pope Paul VI who presided over the Vatican II reforms). The marble altar-rail has been amputated at each end to make way for this new concept of the Holy table and either side has been panelled in plywood. The result is an aesthetic disaster.

Menhir, enclosed with companion cherry tree, Pieve

The road from Santo Pietro to (7.5km) *Pieve* (450m, 108 inhab.) is a typical mountain route with water cascading down from the rocks on to the surface of the road. In front of the church, which has been largely cement-rendered and has a campanile of green and buff stone built in drystone style, are two menhirs (always described as standing side by side). One remains upright, standing in a kind of iron playpen with a cherry tree beside it, but the other (in 1986) was broken and lying flat on the ground. Wandering around this scattered village I saw in the garden of a small house what looked like a very good menhir, placed there like a garden gnome. Close-to it looked original or like a very good fake.

2.5km from Pieve is *Rapale* (383m, 200 inhab.). The striking church has a square tower and pyramidal roof with, to the right of the main door, a plaque 'A la memoire de Lapina Robert tué par les Italiens 26 août 1943'. From the war memorial one learns that in 1914–18 11 villagers were killed and 1939–45 12 soldiers and two civilians—another example of Corsica's sacrifice in France's wars.

San Michele di Muratu

5km from Rapale after forking right onto the D 162, the church of **San Michele de Murato** (San Michele di Muratu) stands at a T-junction about 1km from the village of *Murato* (Muratu, 497m, 840 inhab.). Standing on a green level by itself, theatrical in its splendid isolation and somewhat elevated from the surrounding countryside, San Michele is one of the outstanding churches of Corsica. It defies adequate description because it has to be experienced in person and anyone who visits Corsica should make every effort to see it. It is as unique an experience as seeing the Taj Mahal, the Tower of London or the Golden Gate Bridge for the first time: the coloured postcards fall aside and one is left in admiration before the reality.

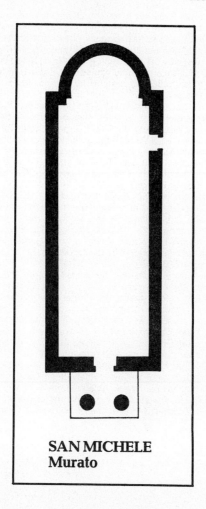

SAN MICHELE
Murato

The most striking aspect of this church is the combination of colours in the stone of which it is built. Madame Geneviève Moracchini-Mazel says in her invaluable book 'Corse Romane' that '... the master masons used for this church a dark green stone from the bed of the nearby Bevinco River, a kind of serpentine marble with a close, compact grain, easy to work and offering great possibilities to sculptors'. San Michele exhibits the most imaginative polychromatic use of stone in the walls of the church. With the predominant green-and-white blocks of serpentine are mixed pink and yellow stones.

San Michele is less interesting inside but there are remains of a fresco of the Annunciation (possibly 12–15C) on the arch of the apse.

The whereabouts of the key to the church has varied during the years I have been there but its safe keeping remains in spirit at least with the curé of Murato who, like so many priests in Corsica, the rest of France and the UK, has too many parishes. On my last visit the key was in the care of a charming lady in a house about 300m down the D 162 from the church, on the right. I would suggest enquiring at the house nearest to the church where the key is obtainable at present.

5km from Murato is the *Bocca di San Stefano* on the D 82. From this 349m-high pass there is a view left over the valley of the Aliso, the Golfe de Saint-Florent and the Désert des Agriates. Take the D 82 going N towards Oletta. At under 2km the village of *Olmeta di Tuda* (300m, 277 inhab.) with many tall elm trees and a fine 17C Sacrifice of Abraham. A château was built here by Marshal Horace Sebastiani (1772–1851), elder brother of Tiburce Sebastiani (1786–1871), both of whom were born at La Porta (see Rte 12).

3km further on, *Oletta* (250m, 1030 inhab.), whose houses are spread out over the hillside overlooking the valley of the Guadello which has the richest land in the Nebbio and is noted for its Roquefort-style cheese. The 18C church of *St. André* is on the site of an older church of which a relic, a very early and primitive bas relief of the Creation, is incorporated in the façade of the present church. There is a triptych painted on wood (1534) of the Virgin giving the breast to the child Jesus flanked by Saints Reparata and André.

From Oletta the D 38 runs N to the Col de Teghime (541m), a distance of 8.5km, and meets the Bastia–Saint-Florent D 81 road. Alternatively, returning S by the D 82 to Bocca di San Stefano, continue along the D 82 as it turns left and E towards the N 193 and the Eastern Plain. This road follows the course of the Bevinco River through the gorge called the Défilé de Lancone. A twisting, truly mountain route with views over precipices to the course of the Bevinco. When the canyon through which the road passes opens out there are broad views of the lower valley and estuary of the Bevinco, the Biguglia lagoon and the sea. At 22km from Saint-Florent the D 82 joins the N 193 at *Casatora*, a hamlet of the commune of Biguglia (2056 inhab.). Turn left and N on the N 193 to reach Bastia.

III CENTRAL CORSICA

14 Corte

Corte (Corti, 486m, 6200 inhab.) is sous préfecture of the Haute Corse.

Set geographically a little to the N of the very centre of Corsica, Corte is the only major town that is not a sea port (although not on the coast itself Sartène has its port in Propriano). The town stands at the confluence of the rivers Restonica (rises Lac de Melo, 1711m, flows 15km E to join the Tavignano) and Tavignano (rises Lac de Nino, 1743m, and flows E 80km, taking in the waters of the Vecchio, Corsigliese and Tagnone and reaching the sea at Aléria).

Corte

Historically as well as geographically Corte is at the heart of Corsica and the spirit of independence. From the earliest times there was always a settlement here and by the 11C Corte was a fortress town. It was conquered by the Genoese in the 13C, later taken by the Moors, who called it Mascara, and then occupied in the name of the King of Aragon by Vincentello d'Istria after he had defeated the Genoese at Morosaglia. He had the citadel built between 1419 and 1425 but in 1434 he was caught by the Genoese and literally lost his head to them. The Banque de Saint Georges took over the town in 1459; the Corsican Sampiero took it for France in 1553; it was retaken by the Genoese and then by the Corsicans themselves who lost it again in 1564. Corte thus see-sawed back and forth until in November 1755 Pasquale Paoli, the Corsican leader, had Corte named the capital of Corsica. The new constitution of Corsica, way ahead of its time, was voted by the new government convened at Corte, where Paoli also founded a university. Paoli's requests for French recognition and protection of Corsica were rejected, and when his army was defeated by the French at Ponte Nuovo, France proclaimed the island to be French on 15 August 1769, the very day on which Napoleon Bonaparte was born. Constitution, university and an independent Corsica were no more.

Corte has never been capital of Corsica again but in 1981 it recovered its status of a university town. After lengthy discussion it was decided that the new Università di Corsica should direct its studies towards defining Corsica's role in the modern world and assisting it to play an active part. Among its main objectives are the study of the Corsican language and literature and establishing and obtaining just recognition of Corsican culture. Arts, science, law and economics are read here by some 500 undergraduates, in addition to the special Corsican studies. There is also the Institut d'Hélio-énergétique for the study of solar power.

The older part of the town is built on a hill that rises abruptly from the river plain and on top of the hill is a cliff-sided gigantic rock on which stands the citadel. It is a town to be explored on foot (car-parks are clearly marked and cars can also be left towards the top end of the main street, the Cours Paoli, near the Post Office).

Approaching Corte along the N 193 from Bastia one enters the town by the Cours Paoli. On the left is the wide tree-lined Place du Duc de Padoue (the duke was Napoleon's general Arrighi de Casanova; 1778–1853). Less than one third of the way down this becomes the Avenue De Gaulle, a cul de sac with trees and flowers in the middle. From the entrance to the Place one can look down the Cours Paoli, over much of newer Corte to the left and up to the old town set on the rock above the Place Paoli where the Cours ends. There is not much in the newer town of architectural interest but the Cours is a pleasant, unpretentious street of shops selling clothes, fruit, shotguns, books, spectacles, local produce, etc. The Place Paoli is of modest proportions and on market days it is packed with stalls, overlooked by the grave eyes of Paoli, raised in bronze by public subscription in 1854, and surrounded by modest cafés and shops. In fact, there is nothing of the tourist trap about Corte.

From behind the statue of the 'Father of the Nation' the Rue Scoliscia leads sharply up over cobbles, aided now and then by flights of shallow steps, to the Place Gaffori, the Ville Haute and the Citadelle. Here is a bronze statue (1901) in memory of General Gian'Pietro Gaffori (1704–53).

This Corte doctor of medicine was named head of state when a constitution was adopted in October 1752, to take effect when the French troops left Corsica. In 1750 the Gaffori mansion, behind the statue, was besieged by the Genoese. The general was away but his wife Faustina persuaded those who talked of surrender to hold out by brandishing a lighted torch over an open barrel of gunpowder. Gaffori arrived and the siege was lifted. This scene is depicted in bas-relief on the pedestal of the statue of Gaffori who was assassinated on 3 October 1753 in an ambush laid by members of a rival Corsican family and Gaffori's own brother, in the pay of Genoa.

The Gaffori house is still marked by the bullets fired during the struggle for independence. Facing it on the square is the _Eglise de l'Annonciation_, built in 1450 but much altered in the 17C, including the façade. Of most interest inside are a finely carved pulpit and early 18C vestry furniture from the (no-longer extant) Franciscan monastery at Corte. A small marble statue of the Virgin is dated 1613.

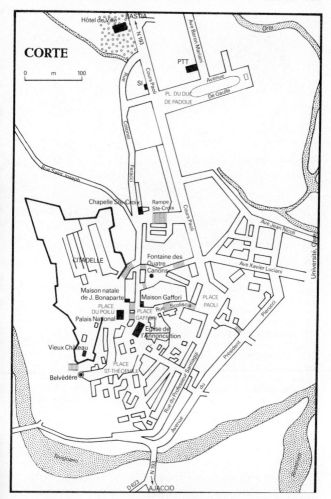

The *Palais National* (Palazzu Nazionale), reached by a stairway going up through an archway from the Place Gaffori, was from 1755–69 the seat of the Corsican independent government. It has been restored in recent years and since October 1982 it houses, fittingly, the Institut d'Études Corses of the University.

The Citadel was built by Vincentello d'Istria, the King of Aragon's viceroy in 1420, and the barracks were added in the time of Louis XV. Since 1962 the citadel has been occupied by the Foreign Legion and is not open to the public. Opposite the gateway to the citadel is No. 1 Place du Poilu, the ancestral house of the Arrighi de Casanova family, in which Napoleon's father Charles lived in 1768 and where in the

Corte, by Edward Lear

same year Napoleon's brother Joseph, later King of Spain (1808–13), was born.

Follow the ramp along the Citadel wall to the *Belvédère* from which there is a breathtaking view and where one gets the best impression of the fortress set on top of its rock. Below, the Tavignano and the Restonica rivers emerge from their respective gorges to join and in the distance rise the mountain peaks of the great central ranges. Look at the oldest (15C) part of the fortress on the edge of the precipice that falls a sheer 100m to the Tavignano below: it was from here that Corsican prisoners, including members of the Gaffori family, managed to escape. One can still get down to the Tavignano, though somewhat more easily and without fear of pursuit, by a stairway and a steep path that leads to a footbridge over the river at a favourite bathing spot.

A. Excursions from Corte: Gorges du Tavignano (on foot)

The Tavignano expedition is for walkers only, experienced and well-equipped with large-scale maps, ample food and a good idea of how much and what they want to do. The route starts in the centre of town. Climb up the steps of the Rampe Sainte Croix leading off the Cours Paoli, follow the Rue Saint Joseph which begins opposite the Chapelle Sainte Croix (cars can be left on an open space at the end of this street), and it is here that the track begins, way-marked in yellow and following the left bank W. 30 minutes' walk reaches the beginning of the gorge and in 2½ hours the footbridge to the path leading to the Lac de Nino (see Rte 15). The path to the right leads to the Bocca à l'Arinella and winds up the great left hand wall of the gorge. 4 hours from Corte is the Fontaine d'Argent whose silver water gushes out of the rock beside a gigantic Corsican pine. From here on the path goes through the Corsican pine and beech Forêt de Melo until it comes out on the stony grazing grounds of a plateau. In 6–7 hours from Corte the Bocca de l'Arinella (1592m) is reached, on the ridge dividing the valleys of the Tavignano and the Golo (see Rte 15). Views over the Niolo and the two valleys and to Rotondo and the outliers of the massif. From here the choice is between returning to Corte or carrying on along downward paths to Calacuccia (about 2 hours) or to the Calacuccia dam (about 1½ hours). For those who do not want to undertake the whole journey all sections of it are picturesque and rewarding but in my opinion the starting point of Corte is preferable to that of Calacuccia, and if you like to have the sun behind you as you walk I suggest that a very early morning start from Corte is ideal.

B. Excursions from Corte: Gorges de la Restonica (on foot)

The Restonica Gorge and the Melo and Capitello Lakes offer an equally pleasant but less arduous choice of walks. Leave Corte by the Ajaccio road, crossing the bridge over the Tavignano and just over the river take the D 623 to the right, where there is the Parc Régional Information Centre and the folkcraft Casa di l'Artigiani. A motor road goes up the valley for 15km but can be a bit rough at the upper end, particularly in early spring or when there has been heavy rain. The river runs over tumbled rocks and the valley sides are dotted with chestnut trees that soon give way to maritime pines of a kind peculiar to Corsica. The top edges of the ravine are often jagged and spiky, with pines between the rocky turrets. Beyond the Tragone bridge the valley narrows and closes in to form a true gorge and the road clings closer to the river which can be reached at certain points where pools, ideal for bathing, have formed. The road, by this time a fairly bumpy track, dusty too when it is dry, comes to an end at the Bergeries de Grotelle (1375m), a traditional halt for the shepherds taking their flocks up to the higher pastures and the Lac de Melo.

For those who do not want to come as far as this there are two footpaths that can be explored in part or in their entire length. The first, to the right 500m before reaching the Tragone bridge, goes to the Tavignano valley and the footpath leading back to Corte. Allow a good 2 hours up to the Col de Cappellaccia (1600m) and an hour down the path which forks right and to the NE to reach the Tavignano.

From the Bergeries de Grotelle there is a pleasant walk to the Melo and Capitello lakes. From the bergeries, where cars can be left, follow the visible track up to the right which levels out and crosses pastures on the banks of the Restonica. To the right is the long ridge of the Capu a Chiostru (2295m) and to the left, across the pastures of the upper Restonica, is the great massif of the Rotondo. As one draws closer to the giant wall of rock that holds the *Lac de Melo* a choice of route presents itself. Either go straight ahead, climbing up through scrub on potholed paths and then clamber up the rocks direct to the top, like climbing to the edge of a giant rock saucepan, or follow the cairns to the left through the alders, cross the river and take the easier way up on the left side of the lake. When there has been rain the smooth rocks on the frontal approach are very slippery. 3 hours there and back.

To get to the Lac de Capitello take the path along the N shore of Melo, at the far end of which the path forks (that to the left goes S to the Bocca a la Soglia (2052m) and joins in 2 hours the GR 20). Follow the right fork from where in 50 minutes, after taking another fork to the SW, one reaches the *Lac de Capitello* (1930m). At 200m higher than Melo, set in a deep bowl (maximum depth 40m) carved out of the granite in the Ice Age, Capitello's waters are very cold on the sunniest summer day and usually covered with ice for more than half of the year. Above the lake tower the E cornices of Capu a i Sorbi. Going due S along the E bank of the lake leads to the GR 20. Allow a good 4 hours there and back to the Bergeries de Grotelle.

C. Excursions from Corte: Monte Rotondo (on foot)

Monte Rotondo (2622m) is a mountaineering expedition presenting only medium difficulties for the experienced walker but it is a round trip of about 10 active hours and it is essential to be well-equipped with footwear, change of warm clothing, waterproofs and, it goes without saying, the right maps and a compass. But those who have studied the map and made their plans will know all this. What is optional but preferable is to reach the summit at sunrise for the benefit of the spectacular view of most of Corsica and the N of Sardinia. In order to do this, the previous night, or some of it, must be spent either at the Bergeries de Timozzo or camping in the lee of rocks close to the Lac d'Oriente (see below).

Leave Corte by the D 623 'Gorges de la Restonica' road (see above) and travel 11.8km, crossing the Pont de Tragone. About 800m beyond the bridge take the path to the left up the course of the Timozzo stream, following the mule track that winds up through trees on the left bank of the ravine in which the stream flows. In just under 2 hours the Bergeries of Timozzo are reached (1520m), a group of typical Corsican drystone huts set in a rock-strewn combe, just off the main track but clearly visible from the approach. From the bergeries the track continues up the course of the Timozzo but if the bergeries are bypassed the route continues through alders and at around 1600m rejoins the Timozzo torrent at a waterfall. At about 90 minutes beyond the bergeries one reaches the Triggone spring (1920m) in an alder-covered depression which is a possible camping site. The path continues on the right bank of the stream and, where the going levels out somewhat, crosses to the left bank. In about 40 minutes from Triggone the path reaches the grassy plateau of the *Lac d'Oriente* (Lavu de l'Oriente, 2061m). Michel Fabrikant in his comprehensive and invaluable 'Guide des Montagnes Corses' (see Bibliography), in which he details seven Rotondo climbs, comments 'some maintain that this name is a deformation of "Lac d'Argento" which is not unlikely because there is nothing "eastern" about the lake'. Silver it certainly is, not deep and with bog on some parts of the shore. The N face of Rotondo is immediately to the S with a col to the right of the summit called the Collet du Rotondo. Camp may be made here in the

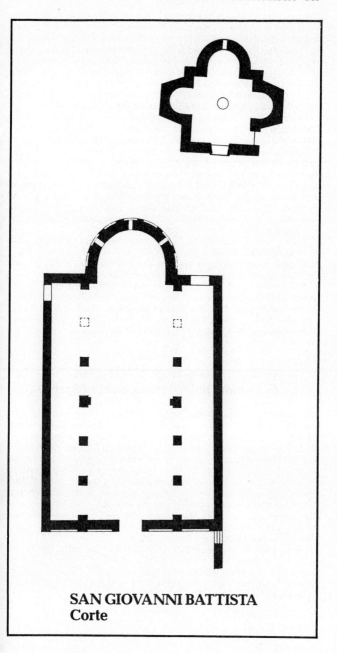

SAN GIOVANNI BATTISTA
Corte

shelter of the rocks around the lake (see above) in order to make an early start the following morning. If setting off in the dark a powerful torch is essential for picking out the rather infrequent cairns marking the path. Head almost due S for the cliffs straight ahead and a path to the right climbs to the Col de Rio Secco (75 minutes from the Lac d'Oriente). A massive block of rock barring the way is scrambled around by the S face and from there a climb of a few dozen metres reaches the summit of *Rotondo* (2622m). Views N to Monte Cinto and around the other points of the compass to the sea and Sardinia.

There are two alternatives to returning by the route just described. The first is to carry on along the track until descending due E from Rotondo, passing S of the tiny Lac de Pozzolo (2350m). The track turns NNE and shortly afterwards follows the course of a narrow stream. In 3½ hours the Bergeries de Spiscie (1650m, pronounced *spiché*, meaning waterfalls) are reached and in a further 75 minutes the bergeries de Rivisecco (1270m) at the confluence of two streams which form the Rivisecco stream. The track follows the stream closely to its meeting with the Restonica where, turning right and E, the Restonica is eventually crossed by the Pont de Rivisecco leading on to the D 623 road to Corte (c 6½ hours from Rotondo).

The second route lies to the S of the summit of Monte Rotondo, past the *Lac du Monte Rotondo* (2321m). (Although this name is easiest for identification, the lake appears on maps, according to date of edition, as either Lac de Betaniella or, most recently, as Lavu Bellebone.) This is the largest of the Corsican lakes, set in a glacier-gouged basin surrounded by jagged peaks. The path passes to the E of the lake and in 90 minutes reaches the Refuge de Pietra Piana (Pétra Piana, 1842m), close to the GR 20 along which it is 10–11 hours SE to Vizzavona and 10–11 hours NW to the Col de Vergio.

D. Excursions from Corte: San Giovanni Battista and Santa Mariona

Two churches within walking distance of Corte are worth visiting. *San Giovanni Battista* is a church and baptistery. Leave Corte by the N 200 road to Aléria. A little under 2km beyond the railway bridge take the second turning to the right, narrow and rather rough but it can be driven over, and just beyond the railway line (800m) and on the right is the ruined church. Probably 9C and one of the oldest churches in Corsica, the fabric has been extensively pillaged up until and including this century. Slabs of the rock facing were incorporated into buildings in the neighbourhood and the altar steps and benches and the square pillars of the three naves have all vanished. The two buildings, church and baptistry, were set side by side and may have been raised on the site of a Roman village.

Santa Mariona church is 1km N of Corte, to the left of the N 193 road, just beyond the cemetery. A Pisan church, it has twin apses at the E end, one of only three such plans in Corsica. Although it now stands in ruins among the olive groves, enough remains to get an idea of its former glory.

15 Le Niolo: from Corte to Porto via Evisa

ROAD (D 84) 86km.—27km Calacuccia.—49.5km Station de
Vergio.—63km Evisa.

The **Niolo** (Niolu) district is a basin of the upper Golo (Golu), the most
important river of Corsica (84km long, reaching the E coast to the S of
La Canonica and Bastia-Poretta Airport).

This plateau region, 800–1000m high and 15km long by 10km wide,
is surrounded by mountains. To the S these range up to 2000m in
height (Punta Artica and Monte Tozzu), and to the N up to 2500m
(Monte Cinto, Punta Minuta and Paglia Orba).

The most inaccessible region of all Corsica until the building of the
D 84 road at the end of the last century, Le Niolo is also the most
independent in spirit. Its people always opposed invaders from the
lands below, Genoese and French alike: a hopeless revolt against the
French in 1774 was put down with a remorseless and crushing
campaign of scorched earth, burned villages, torture and hangings.
The inhabitants, some of whom are ruddy-complexioned, blond or
sandy-haired and blue-eyed, and above average height for the island,
may (as they often choose to believe) be descendants of an earlier race
in Corsica, perhaps those who built the megaliths. Distinguishing
physical characteristics have been preserved down the centuries by
the isolation of the region and prolonged intermarrying.

The Niolins relied for a living on their flocks of sheep and goats and travelled to
the high pastures in the surrounding mountains for the summer, staying in stone
huts close to their animals. From early September to the end of May there was
the flock-migration—transhumance—to the W shore by the Fango valley or to
the E shore pastures on the plain by the Scala di Santa Regina. The raising of
sheep and goats is still the major occupation, on a smaller scale than in the past
but much helped by the Roquefort cheese industry. The Niolo forests of Corsican
pines are an important source of employment and income. Work, followed by
tourism, came to the region after the building in 1968 of the Calacuccia dam and
artificial lake on the river Golo for the irrigation of the Eastern Plain and
provision of electric power and water to the E seaboard and Bastia. Tourist
attractions include fishing, sailing, mountaineering, walking, pony-trekking,
exploring the 8km circumference of the lake and even skiing, 25km W of
Calacuccia at the Station de Vergio (see below).

From Corte to the capital of the Niolo, Calacuccia, is 27km. Leave
Corte by the N 193 going N in the direction of Bastia. Just outside the
town, and immediately after the bridge over the River Orta, turn left
onto the D 18 which goes up the Orta valley for 12km to Ponte Castirla
(344m). Here take the D 84 road to the left and 5.5km further on to the
E the road enters the *Scala di Santa Regina* (the Queen of Heaven's
Ladder), the only means of communication with Corte and the E until
the building of the road in 1889, originally a mule track hacked out of
the granite and rising by stages. The almost purple cliffs rise sheer
from the Golo torrent in the depths of the gorge and the road clings
and winds its way above it, towered over by vertical cliffs on the right
of the road. It is claustrophobically impressive as an approach to the
Niolo and explains the region's long and almost total isolation from
the rest of the island. Some idea of what this original route was like
may be had from getting out at the Ponte di l'Accia over the Ruda
stream which joins the Golo here and walking 150m up a track on the

left bank of the stream to an old bridge, the Ponte Sottano.

   Calacuccia (830m, 1350 inhab.), at the NE corner of the reservoir or lake, is a commune comprised of four hamlets close together in the chestnut groves of the plateau. In the 18C parish church of *Saints Pierre et Paul* is a striking wooden 17C *Christ on the Cross*. It is unusual because of the way in which the sculptor, in this isolated region and ignorant of conventional artistic methods, obtained his effects through the exaggeration of the facial features, muscles and bones, to convey physical torture. Many old and solid stone houses, one dated 1560. On the outskirts, to the right of the D 84, is the *Franciscan monastery* (1600) set among the chestnut trees and with a dolmen close by.

The D 218 which goes around the lake (8km) leaves Calacuccia as the village is entered by the D 84 from Corte. 3km W along the S shore is *Casamaccioli* (Casamacciuli, 868m, 501 inhab.), not actually on the lakeside but slightly to the S, surrounded by chestnut trees and at the foot of the wooded ridge that seals the Niolo to the S. View of the Cinto massif to the NW. *La Nativité*, the parish church, has a wooden figure of Saint Roch, a plague saint popular in Corsica from the end of the 16C. The Niolin who carved the saint made him a Corsican man of the mountains, with his staff and his little dog, and his purposeful stride and startled expression perhaps derived from his awareness of the bubonic lesion on his thigh. The 15C wooden statue of the Virgin is carried in procession from the church on 8 September (Nativity of the Virgin) across the ground where the Fair of la Santa du Niolo is held for three days. The procession of cowled penitents forms the Granitola, the snail-like spiral form common to many Corsican religious gatherings (see Erbalunga, Rte 10). On the afternoon of the first day the mountain shepherds gather at the fair to compete with one another in poetic improvisation and oratory.

It was at Calacuccia that Prosper Mérimée noted down an outstanding *voceru*, a traditional Corsican telling of a violent death demanding vengeance (see Introduction). It was composed, in the same loose sense of 'composition' applied to all folk songs and ballads, around the story of Maria Felice. When her brother, a priest, was murdered, Maria composed at his funeral a *voceru* of lament and a call for vengeance. The shepherd to whom she was betrothed, instead of seeking out the killer, left with his flock for the winter pastures close to the Golfe de Galéria. Beset by premonition, the young man eventually returned home only to find Maria's funeral in progress, in the classic tradition of all such stories. She had died of despair at her brother's death and of shame at her fiancé's failure to conform to the pattern of vendetta. He committed suicide on her grave.

The D 84 can be re-joined by taking the D 218 out of Casamaccioli due E (3km). Completing the round trip by returning E along the D 84, 3.5km to the W of Calacuccia is the village of *Albertacce* (867m, 825 inhab.). It has a small archaeological museum (open every day July and August, Saturdays and Sundays June and September; small entrance fee). Founded by the archaeologist Lucien Acquaviva, it contains exhibits from megalithic times to the Roman period.

A. Mountain walks from Calacuccia: Monte Cinto

Monte Cinto, at 2710m, is the highest mountain in Corsica. Leave Calacuccia by the D 218 which branches N from the D 84 just W of the town. After 3km fork right on to the D 18 to reach, 2.5km further, Lozzi. (On foot and by the shortcuts which are marked allow 30 minutes.) From Lozzi to Cinto is a climb of 7½ hours. Allow 5 hours for coming down the same way or 4 hours down to Haut Asco (see Rte 16 and the section on the GR 20 long-distance path). It is *essential* to seek information and advice locally on conditions on this and all high mountain paths, on how to dress suitably, what to carry for eating and sleeping, the whereabouts of bergeries or similar overnight shelters and the best times to travel for physical comfort and maximum visibility. Corsicans are proud of their country and want visitors to share it with the minimum risk of danger or discomfort but personal ability must depend on each traveller's own assessment. Tackling Cinto can be tough going.

B. Le Lac de Nino

The *Lac de Nino* (1743m) is the source of the River Tavignano (80km long, with the Restonica, Vecchio, Corsigliese and Tagnone joining it as tributaries before it reaches the E coast at Aléria) and is a relatively easy and rewarding walk from Calacuccia. Take the D 84 W towards the Col de Vergio for 14km to the Chiarasghiu fountain (Funtana di u Chiarasghiu, 1129m). Just beyond the bridge take the path to the left which goes in the direction of the GR 20, leading S in 45 minutes to the *Bocca di San Petru* (1446m, Col de Saint Pierre on some maps); statue of the saint and chapel. Stay on the GR 20 going SE from here for 1 hour to the Bocca Redda (Bocca a Reta, 1883m). This was the old mule track which followed the ridge of San Tomaghiu and of which there are traces where the stones underfoot are set in a form of paving. The track reaches the edge of the lake in 45 minutes. The *Lac de Nino* is about 500m by 350m, well-stocked with trout and the land around the edges spongy and scored with runnels of water, rather like a Scottish peat hag but not so boggy and easier walking.

There are two alternative ways down. That leading to the Maison Forestière de Popaja (or Popagghia) on the D 84 takes 85 minutes. Climb W from the lake to reach in a few minutes the Bocca di Stazzona (1762m) a great rocky shelf (legend says a herd of the devil's cattle turned to stone by Saint Martin) between Monte Tozzo (2007m) and la Punta Artica (2327m). A steep ravine path takes one through the forest of the Valdo Niellu (the Dark Forest), the largest and one of the most beautiful of Corsica's forests. Some of the Corsican pines are hundreds of years old and 40–50m high; in the higher reaches there are beech and birch.

The second route is to Calacuccia, about 6 hours' walk. Take the path from the NE corner of the lake, or the GR 20 from the S shore (the tracks converge) and follow the track to the left way-marked in yellow, and not the red-and-white markings of the GR 20. It is a walk of 1 hour to the Ceppu bergerie where there is a spring. Leave on the left the iron cross where the bandit Cappa was caught and shot. Walking for half an hour brings you to the footpath which follows the left bank of the Tavignano. This steadily climbs above the valley and the beech trees of the Corte-Campotile Forest, crossing a boulder-strewn plateau and the Dinadelli stream, followed by easier walking across pastures to (2 hours) the Canalelli spring. 15 minutes' further walking brings one to the Bocca Capizolu. Two footpaths on either side of this col lead down, in about 1 hour, to Casamaccioli but, if heading for Calacuccia, leave these paths on the left and take a path just below the ridge going E for a few hundred metres to the Bocca a l'Arinella (1592m). From here onwards the way is clearly marked and it is 2 hours down to the dam and a further 10 minutes to Calacuccia village.

An 8½-hour walk through picturesque country may be taken by going up to the Bocca a l'Arinella and then following the course of the Tavignano through its gorges to Corte.

C. Other walks from Calacuccia

There is a tour of the Valdo Niellu Forest; to the Guagnerola (1837m) and Capronale (1370m) cols; to the valleys of the Tula and Viro rivers; to Capu Tafonatu (2343m), the Pierced Mountain through which the infuriated Satan hurled a broken ploughshare in the same annoying incident in which his oxen were turned to stone (see above, Bocca di Stazzona). The starting points for these and for other expeditions of varying ruggedness are on, or easily reached from, the D 84: the Maison Forestière de Popaja (12km from Calacuccia), the Maison Ciattarinu (19km), the Maison Cantonnière de Frascaghiu (9.5km), and a number of stages on the GR 20 (see Rte 16).

At 22.5km on the D 84 from Calacuccia is the *Station de Vergio* (Verghiu, Vergiu, 1404m), 60m lower and 1.5km down the D 84 from the col. Hotel Castel de Vergio (two teleskis, ski equipment hire) is the highest hotel in Corsica. Vergio is 18.7km from the W coast, 80km from Ajaccio and 100km from Bastia. It is a centre for alpine and cross-country skiing from December–April (depending on snow conditions) and in summer for expeditions in the surrounding mountains and the forests of Valdu Niellu and Aïtone; the GR 20 is within 2km of the Station de Ski.

From the Station the D 84 crosses the GR 20 and describes a tight horseshoe (the Fer à Cheval) before reaching the *Col de Vergio* (Verghiu or Vergiu, 1464m), the highest mountain pass in Corsica that one can drive over (sometimes blocked by snow in winter and early spring, warning signs 'Col ouvert' or 'Col fermé' well in advance on the D 84 approaches on either side). 200m before the actual summit, on either side and a few metres off the road, are wide views of the surrounding peaks and mountain ranges and the valleys of the Porto to the W and the Golo to the E. A well-trodden 80m path leading up NW from the col brings the pierced Tafonatu summit into view. *Capo a la Cuccula* (Capu à Cuccula, 2049m) is a 2½-hour there-and-back medium easy walk from the col. From the Cricche ridge can be seen Tafonatu to the N, Cinto to the NE, the Niolo basin ENE, the Rotondo massif to the E and SE, and the Golfe de Porto and the Mediterranean to the W.

The D 84 for the next 10km goes through the magnificent *Forest of Aïtone* with giant Corsican pines, larch, beech and holm oak. Some fine specimens of Corsican pine around two centuries old and 50m high may be seen around the Maison Forestière d'Aïtone, 7.5km from the Col de Vergio.

A fairly easy expedition begins on a track behind the Maison Forestière leading to the Bocca di Salto (1350m), 1 hour, on to the Bocca de Cocavera (1833m), 3 hours, and beyond to the Bocca di Capronale (1370m), 5 hours, whence one may make a 5-hour descent to the D 84 at Maison de Ciattarinu. Whether the shorter or longer expedition is undertaken, this is one of the grandest and most beautiful Corsican forest regions.

Edward Lear's impression of Evisa

The 5km to Evisa are through chestnut woods which also surround **Evisa** itself (850m, 750 inhab.). 36km from Calacuccia and out of the Niolo region which ends at the Col de Vergio, 23km from Porto, and situated between the Aïtone Forest and the Spelunca Gorges, Evisa has frequently been called the Pearl of Corsica. It is a very attractive place, its houses ranged steeply and tightly on the rocky spur that separates the Porto and Aïtone rivers. All around are the chestnut plantations and the darker green of the Corsican pines and firs, broken up on occasion by beech groves, a backdrop which is in turn backed by the encircling mountain chains and peaks, broken only to the SW where the valleys lead to the sea. The closeness of both sea and mountains make Evisa a pleasant holiday centre in all seasons, without the disadvantage of being in a crowded area. There are a half-dozen hotels and a *village de vacances* called the Paesolu d'Aïtone. Apart from sea-bathing and skiing, Evisa is one of the best centres in Corsica for mountain-walking with a variety to suit all capabilities, ranging from easy strolls of an hour to 5–6-hour long-distance mountain walks which, in order to avoid having to return by the same route, could be improved by the two-car arrangement if a group is walking.

To reach the *Aïtone mill and waterfall* take the D 84 in the direction of the Col de Vergio to just beyond the right-hand turn to Vico. Then follow the first forest track to the left, 2 hours there and back.

Similarly, to reach the *Belvédère* take the D 84 for 3km in the direction of Col de Vergio. A forest path to the left winds up among the pines to the Belvédère (975m), a spur of rock jutting out over the Aïtone river with a view of tumbling red rocks and a glimpse of the sea beyond. 2 hours there and back.

Walks to the *Bocca di Salto, Bocca di Cocavera* and *Bocca di Capronale* are described above in the inverse direction.

The *Spelunca Gorge and Ota* is a walk which, taking 3 hours each way, may be better organised by having a car at Ota for the return journey. Take the D 84 in the direction of Porto. At the end of the wall around the cemetery take a footpath going down on the right towards the Aïtone ravine and then along the precipice, at the foot of which the river flows. The path corkscrews downwards to the confluence of the Aïtone and Tavulella. Cross over by the Genoese Zaglia bridge, the half-way point of the walk, after which the *cirque* and gorge of Spelunca begin. *L'Antre*, the lair, den or cavern, is an amphitheatre surrounded by steep red pinnacled rocks; this dramatic landscape can be seen from the Evisa–Porto road. Follow the track along the left bank of the river through the gorge, an old mule track with traces of rough steps that were set in the moer difficult places for the pack animals. An hour's walk ends at the D 124 road, from which the D 84 is reached by turning left, 12.5km from Evisa. By carrying on along the track for another half hour the *two bridges of Ota* are reached, a double bridge across the Onca and the Aïtone which come together here to form the River Porto. From here there is the choice of continuing to Ota along the right bank or taking the path downstream that leads to the remains of the Genoese bridge of Pianella and joins up with the Evisa road.

Ota (335m, 605 inhab.), reached from the D 84 at 12.5km from Evisa, is the chief settlement of the commune to which it gives its name and to which Porto belongs. It is set in an amphitheatre at the foot of Capo d'Ota (1220m). The soil of this basin is fertile and there are olive and chestnut groves and vineyards, while vegetables and cereals are also cultivated. A local characteristic of the solid houses is the external staircase. Ota is full of stairways in the streets too and there are several very good restaurants, worth bearing in mind should you be staying in Porto in the high season and prepared to drive 5.5km up to the cooler air and extensive views (see Rte 6).

16 Le Parc Naturel Régional de la Corse: from Ponte Leccia to Bocognano

ROAD (N 193) 62km.—24km Corte.—34km Venaco.—44km Vivario.

The Parc Naturel consists of 200,000 hectares and lies diagonally, like a sash, across the island from the NW coast S of Calvi to the Forest of l'Ospedale in the SE, just to the N of Porto-Vecchio.

The Parc incorporates 80km of coastline and most of the great central Corsican mountain chain. In width it varies from 10–30km and is 120km long, the most northerly point being the Bocca di San Colombano, 6km to the E of Belgodère, and the most southerly point the Montagne de Cagna.

The Parc was established on 2 February 1971 and the intention went beyond the designation of an area of outstanding beauty. The aim was to revitalise this area whose economy had always been principally pastoral but which had declined for a variety of reasons including the drift to the towns with the depopulation of the mountains and the transformation of traditional Eastern Plain winter pastures into vineyards and farms. In order to feed their flocks in autumn the shepherds resorted to burning the maquis in summer and bringing their sheep and goats to feed on the resulting new growth as they came down from the mountains. The bergeries fell into ruin and a way of life was rapidly dying. The aim was to reverse this trend and bring life and livelihood to the mountains. First of all some 200 bergeries were rebuilt to give shepherds shelter during the transhumance; communications with other parts of the island were improved, ending the historical isolation from the towns and people of the coast; and a reorganisation of the selling of produce was undertaken. In addition to this revitalisation of pastoral economy the region's tourist potential was realised (until then tourism had been confined to the coast). The need to reconcile this with the traditional way of life was dealt with in the most sensible way. A force of guides, mostly young men from the villages and used to the hard mountain life, was recruited to explain to the local people the aims of the Parc and to dispel their fears of tourists marching across crops and scaring animals. On the other side, those who came as tourists had to be made aware of the mutual respect necessary to avoid friction, as well as being provided with mountain shelters, information and rescue facilities. Ski centres were built, the GR 20 long-distance path through the Parc mapped and way-marked and pamphlets and books were written and published on flora, fauna, geology and archaeology. The fact that the people who live there go about their affairs in the normal way dispels any hint of artificial preservation or of an open-air museum.

An Association des Amis du Parc exists, founded in 1972 (BP 417, 20184 Ajaccio). One of the main objectives of the Parc and its staff is, of course, the conservation of Corsican flora and fauna, particularly of endangered species such as the *mouflon* which had been hunted almost to extinction. This wild sheep (*Ovis musimon*), about the same size as the domestic animal, with magnificently horned rams, is brownish-grey with a dark dorsal streak and in agility resembles the chamois. It used to be fairly common in Spain but is now extinct there and lives only in Corsica and Sardinia. The *mouflon* is strictly protected in Corsica as are the *gypaete* (*Gypaetus barbatus*), the bearded vulture or lammergeyer, and the 'royal' eagles and kites and the fish buzzard.

It is important to remember that this is a Parc Naturel founded on the initiative of the people who live and make their living here and not a Parc National established by law and administered by the Government. Unauthorised camping, *le camping sauvage*, is strictly forbidden, principally because of the danger of fire: Corsica has been ravaged by forest fires. Camping is allowed on the GR 20, in the Restonica Valley and at the Col de Bavella or when permission is granted by the landowner. Ask at Mairies or Maisons Forestières where possible, otherwise at the most likely-looking house near to where one wishes to camp.

If walking in the mountains it is advisable to take the two Institut Geographique National (IGN) 1:50,000 Itineraires Pedestres maps 'No. 20 Corse Nord: de Calvi a Vizzavona' and 'No. 23 Corse Sud: de

Vizzavona à la Montagne de Cagna'. The volume to use in the series 'Topo-Guide des Sentiers de Grande Randonnée' is the 'Sentier de la Corse de Calenzana à Conca GR 20' and the maps recommended are the IGN Blue Series, sheets 4149/E, 4150/E, 4251/E, 4251/O, 4253/E, 4253/O, 4254/E (E = East and O = Ouest). If no extended mountain walking is intended the IGN 1:100,000 Cartes Touristiques Nos 73 and 74, Corse Nord and Corse Sud, are perfectly adequate.

Books: (see also Bibliography):

The Parc Naturel Régional de la Corse Guides: Serie 'Itineraires';

Civilisations perdues en Alta Rocca;

Oiseaux de Corse;

Plantes et Fleurs recontrées;

Poissons de Corse;

Roches et Paysages de la Corse.

These subsidised and low-price books, profusely illustrated with photographs and diagrams, fit easily into pockets and rucksacks. Layout of illustrations and text makes minimal demand on knowledge of French.

Fabrikant, Michel. *Guide des Montagnes Corses* (Didier et Richard, Grenoble, 1982).

De Paese a Paese: de Village en Village. Pamphlets, with maps printed on the inside, giving details of walks, how to get there, where to stay etc. for a number of districts. Among them: 'Le Venacais', 'Le Bozio', 'Strada Tra Mare E Monte: de Galéria à Cargèse' (set of six leaflets) and 'Le Taravo'.

All the above are available in bookshops, the Parc Naturel offices and information centres. In case of difficulty or for further information write to l'Association des Amis du Parc, BP 417, 20184 Ajaccio Cedex.

The organisation Muntagne Corse in Liberta aims to make the Corsican mountains known to visitors and to bring together tourists and the people who live in the mountains. It arranges walking tours for people of all ages with such themes as Mountain Ecology, Rock Climbing, Entomology and the Under 20s in the Mountains. For information, including prices, contact: Muntagne Corse in Liberta, Parc Bilello, Imm. Girolata, Avenue Napoleon III, 20000 Ajaccio. For information may be obtained from the following: Le Comité Régional de Tourisme, 38 Cours Napoleon, BP 162, 20178 Ajaccio Cedex (tel (95) 21.55.31 and 32); for Haute Corse, l'Office du Tourisme, 35 Boulevard Paoli, 20200 Bastia (tel (95) 31.12.04); for Corse du Sud, le Syndicat d'Initiative, Hôtel de Ville, Place Foch, 20000 Ajaccio (tel (95) 21.40.87).

The GR 20: Sentier de la Corse de Calenzana à Conca. Le Comité National des Sentiers de Grande Randonnée of La Fédération Française de la Randonnée Pédestre has been responsible for planning and organising long-distance paths in France, known as the GRs, of which the Corsican path is GR 20. It is roughly 200km long and runs from Calenzana close to Calvi in the NW of the island to Conca to the N of Porto-Vecchio in the SE. Since 1977 it has been completely *balisé* (way-marked) in the distinctive GR stripes of white above red, on boulders, rock faces, tree trunks, walls and on specially erected posts and cairns when necessary. The GR can generally be travelled between mid June and the beginning of November according to the weather and how long the spring snow lingers. Remember that the greatest number of walkers on it come between 14 July and 1 September and during those six weeks the Parc Naturel refuges, of which there are 11, tend to be full unless one arrives in mid- or late afternoon. This also applies to the small hotels and pensions in the villages that can be reached from the path.

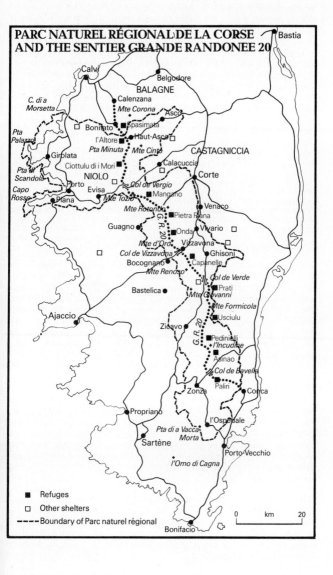

**PARC NATUREL RÉGIONAL DE LA CORSE
AND THE SENTIER GRANDE RANDONEE 20**

Bastia

Calvi

Belgodore

BALAGNE

Calenzana

Mte Corona

Asco

Bonifato   Spasimata

l'Altore   Haut-Asco

Pta Minuta   *Mte Cinto*   CASTAGNICCIA

Girolata

Ciottulu di i Mori

NIOLO   Calacuccia

Corte

Porto   Evisa   *Col de Vergio*

Mte Tozzo   Mangano

Plana

Mte Rotondo   Venaco

Pietra Piana

Guagno   Onda   Vivario

Mte d'Oro   Vizzavona

Col de Vizzavona   Ghisoni

Bocognano   Capanelle

Mte Renoso   *Col de Verde*

Prati

Bastelica   *Mte Giovanni*

Mte Formicola

Ajaccio   Usciulu

Zicavo   Pedinielli

l'Incudine

Asinao

Col de Bavella

Zonza   Paliri

Proprianо   Conca

l'Ospedale

*Pta di a Vacca
Morta*

Sartène

Porto-Vecchio

l'Omo di Cagna

C. di a
Morsetta

Pta
Palazzu

Pta di
Scandola

Capo
Rosso

G.R. 20

G.R. 20

■ Refuges

□ Other shelters

-----Boundary of Parc naturel régional

0   km   20

Bonifacio

A reasonable time to allow for the whole of the GR 20 is 2–3 weeks, nearer 3 when going down to villages for food is allowed for. The path may be joined or left at a number of *bretelles*, connecting side paths way-marked with a single yellow stripe, or at those points where the GR 20 crosses roads, for example near the Col de Vergio, close to Vizzavona, the Col de Verde and the Col de Bavella. The only point where the GR 20 passes close to the railway is at the Gare de Vizzavona where there are fairly frequent trains to and from Ajaccio, Bastia, Corte, Calvi, l'Ile Rousse and many places in between such as Venaco, Vivario, Bocognano or Ponte Leccia, which may serve as bases for mountain expeditions. Vizzavona is the half-way point and the N part of the GR 20 is higher and harder than the S half. The 'Topo-Guide' to the GR 20 is essential as a guide to where and how to go, what to expect, equipment and maps to be carried (see above). It can be bought in bookshops, newsagents and shops and information offices of the Parc Naturel.

Much of the Parc Naturel may be visited and seen from the roads which run through, across and in and out of it, many of which feature in other sections of this Guide. Bearing in mind that the spine of the island is the mountain chain that also runs roughly down the centre of the Parc, the motor roads either lie along the valleys or are carved into the mountainside. The following is an itinerary from which much of the Parc in all its beauty and grandeur may be seen. Most of this route is followed closely by the railway from Bastia to Ajaccio which is also an excellent way of experiencing the Parc without driving or walking. Areas of the Parc excluded from this tour, for instance the W coast and the S, are covered in other sections of this Guide.

Leaving Bastia by the N 193 it is 20km S to Casamozza, then follow the N 193 W along the valley of the Golo (as does the railway). Another 18km brings one to *Ponte Nuovo* (Ponte Novu, 167m) it owes its name to the five-arched bridge built by the Genoese. It was here that the Corsicans under Paoli were defeated and massacred by the French on 8 May 1769, an event which put a temporary stop to the campaign for Corsican independence and drove Paoli to seek refuge in England (he left Corsica on 13 June 1769). Commemorative stone at the end of the bridge.

The next Genoese bridge, in better order, is 8km further at *Ponte Leccia*, a large village at one of Corsica's principal crossroads. Here the N 193 turns S and carries on down the valley of the Golo; the N 197 goes N by a valley route, chiefly close to the rivers Navaccia and San Colombano and the route of the railway, and eventually reaches the coast 7km to the E of l'Ile Rousse; the D 71 travels E to Morosaglia and the heart of the Castagniccia. The railway forks at Ponte Leccia too, one branch following the N 197 N until it reaches the coast, continuing to l'Ile Rousse and Calvi as 'Le Tramway de la Balagne', the other staying close to the N 193 on its way S to Corte, Vizzavona and eventually Ajaccio.

The valley of the Asco is a comparatively short trip from Ponte Leccia (33km, returning by the same road) through magnificent scenery to one of the main centres of the Parc Naturel. Take the N 197 N for 2km then turn left on to the D 47 into the valley of the River Asco (35km long, rising at the Bocca Stranciacone, 1987m, and joining the Golo close to Ponte Leccia).

At 7.5km from Ponte Leccia a road to the right, the D 47 (the road to Asco becomes the D 147), reaches in 3km the village of *Moltifao* (Moltifau, 662 inhab.) built on the heights separating the valleys of the Asco and the Tartagine. Known for the quality of its honey, in this district beehives are set everywhere on the terraces of fruit and olive trees. The parish church of the *Annunciation* has a fragment of a 15C interpretation of God the Father, re-used in a piece of sacristy furniture, and there is a complete wooden retable of 1545, the Crowning of the Virgin. 3km N of Moltifao is *Castifao* (Castifau, 506m, 436 inhab.), also renowned for its honey (*fau* means honeycomb) and built above the Tartagine in mounting stages, with tall solemn houses in narrow stepped streets. There was a Franciscan monastery here, now only a few ruins left, and to the SW are the ruins of the Chapelle de Saint Augustin (San Agostino).

At 9km from Ponte Leccia, Les Gorges de l'Asco begin with mountains towering 1000m on either side. The road winds above the river whose right bank is rocky and arid while the left bank is scattered with clumps of juniper. 9.5km further is *Asco* (Ascu, 620m, 380 inhab.), a true mountain village, its austere tall houses, outside stairs and covered passageways all reflecting the isolation in which the villagers lived until the road was brought there in 1937. The settlement is said to be of Ligurian origin and the present village to date from the 11C. Because of its isolation and the enforced self-sufficiency of its people a specific form of local government grew up among them, in which much of the essential village work was organised on a community basis and decisions were taken and disputes settled by *sages* or *paceri*, presiding over assemblies of elders and widows. On the W outskirts of Asco a road to the S leads to the bank of the Asco by a single-arch Genoese bridge.

The D 147 carries on up the valley of the Asco which from here on has the name of the Stranciancone, soon entering the Corsican pines of the *Carozzica forest* (which has suffered severely from fire) which rises to 1900m and the bare rock of the high mountains.

Haut Asco (1450m), at the end of the D 147 and 11km from Asco, was Corsica's first winter sports centre, set up when the road, with the help of the Foreign Legion, was extended to the plateau of Stagnu in 1964. Monte Cinto lies to the S, Capo Stranciacone to the W and La Mufrella to the NW with a *bretelle* to the GR 20. (There is a hotel-restaurant, open December–April for skiing but depending to some extent on the quantity and state of the snow, with two ski-lifts and a number of chalets. For those looking for downhill skiing, this is a departure point for the high ski route of Corsica. The hotel is open during the summer for mountaineering and mountain walking.)

Monte Cinto (2706m) is a 6-hour walk up from Haut Asco and 4¼ hours down. From Haut Asco take the path going due S, way-marked in red and with numerous cairns. The route leads first through trees until the valley of the Tighiettu stream which is crossed by a footbridge. The path goes up by a narrow gorge to Capu Borba (2207m), reached about 4 hours after leaving Haut Asco. From the col take the path climbing up to the left which follows glacial debris or moraine, and at the ridge take the facing slope leading to the summit (2710m), the highest point of Corsica. When the weather is good, and it is clearer in spring and winter than in summer and clearest of all at dawn in whatever season, the panorama is superb. One can see to the S the mountains of Rotondo, D'Oro and Renoso with beyond them the peaks of the Sartenais and Sardinia, to the N Calvi and the sea, to the SW the gulfs of Ajaccio, Porto and Sagone, and to the NE the Isle of Elba. For those who are touring on foot the way down from Cinto to Calacuccia is by the SE face and the Bergeries de Biccarello and Lozzi. Allow 5–5½ hours for the descent.

There is also a walk from Asco to Calacuccia via the *Bocca di Serra Piana* (allow 8–9 hours). The path goes by way of the bergeries of

Misaldi, Pinnera and, beyond the Bocca di Serra Piana (1846m), Menta and Caracuto and the village of Corscia.

At 6½–7-hour walk from Asco, **Monte Padro** (Padru, 2393m) gives a fine view over to the NW and l'Ile Rousse and S to Cinto. The path begins 200m beyond a small bridge 1.5km W from Asco along the Haut Asco road. Look carefully for it as there is no signpost or waymark. This leads in 3 hours to the Bergeries d'Intrata. From here take the left bank of the stream leading to the right through the trees and then climb the scree to the right. In 3½ hours from Intrata one reaches the summit of Padro which forms the NE pillar of the Cinto massif.

There are other mountain walks of varying severity and length of time from both Asco and Haut Asco but one that should be mentioned here is that to the *cirque and forest of Bonifato*, a walk of about 8½–9 hours, by way of La Mufrella (the *mouflonne*). Leave Haut Asco heading W for the trees and the path way-marked in two yellow stripes (this is a *bretelle* of the GR 20) to the Breche de Stagnu (1985m); about 2 hours' walking. The Breche de Stagnu is c 300m N of the Bocca Culaghia or Culaja where the track joins the red-and-white way-marked GR 20. The GR 20 has an offshoot here which leads to the summit of *La Mufrella* (2148m), fine view in clear weather. By following the main GR 20 one passes by the foot of the mountain where in a glacial combe there is the tiny *Lac de la Mufrella*, with alders scattered around its shore. The mountain and lake are well-named: I have both heard and seen mouflon rattling across the mountainside scree. From the lake it is 2 hours to the Parc Régional refuge at Spasimata (1190m), surrounded by Corsican pines, a spring, and ruins of an old stone hut. The Forest of Bonifato suffered severely from fire in 1982 and there are detours down to Calenzana (275m), for which allow 7 hours.

Travelling S from Ponte Leccia the N 193 continues to follow the Golo valley for 9km to *Francardo* (226m), a timber-processing centre for the tree trunks brought from the Valdo-Niello forest. The D 84 leads off to the right for the Golo gorges and the Scala di Santa Regina (see Rte 15), Evisa, Porto and the W coast.

2km further on at Caporalino a turning to the left, the D 818, leads to *Omessa* in just under 2km where the *chapel of the Annunciation* has a fine marble Virgin and Child (mid 15C?). The curly hair of the Infant and the bird he holds recall the work of Donatello and later Florentine sculptors. The church of *St. André*, with its tall graceful campanile, has some good Italian paintings.

17km Col de San Quilico (559m) between the catchments of the Golo and the Tavignano; 500m beyond the D 41 leaves (left) for the villages of the Castagniccia (see Rte 12). Corte is 24km from Ponte Leccia (see Rte 14) and from Corte it is 8.5km to *Santo Pietro di Venaco* (San Petru di Venacu, 860m, 322 inhab.). This is a pleasant summer resort popular with town-dwellers from Ajaccio and Bastia (it is linked to both by the railway) as is *Venaco* 1.5km S (Venacu, 565m, 1501 inhab.) set in the middle of Corsica with Ajaccio 80km and Bastia 82km distant. There are two churches. The parish church of *Saint Michel* is baroque with a trompe l'oeil ceiling painting of Abraham and Isaac threatened by a giant sword against a Corsican landscape. The church of *Saint Antoine* in the hamlet of Lugo, contiguous with Venaco, has some striking modern stained-glass windows and sta-tions of the Cross in black-and-white mosaic, work by a local artist

(1960). The war memorial near to the church of Saint Michel is a typical reminder of how much Corsican blood was shed for France in the Great War of 1914–18. There are 77 Venacais, the dead from one average-sized village.

This is a countryside of chestnut groves, very well watered by streams, with some vineyards, orchards, meadows and pastures. The main occupation is the raising of sheep, goats and cattle. One of the many good local cheeses is le Venaco, made from ewes' milk. The district, like the inhabitants of Venaco, is called le Venacais and it offers a variety of attractions to the tourist including trout fishing in the Vecchio and other rivers and walking 'da paese a paese' (from village to village), walking that is no more demanding than fell or dale rambling and offers great variety in landscape and villages.

A good centre for a holiday in the Venacais is the hotel complex of *E Caselle* (the little houses) in a loop of the river Vecchio, 6km from Venaco. There are huts built of big stones and with efficient plumbing, most of them hidden among trees, and a central hotel building with swimming pool, tennis and riding facilities and a menu specialising in Corsican dishes, all set in a spacious park above the tumbling Vecchio (there are paths down to the river). E Caselle was created by Jean Pagni, a native of Venaco, who tired of Paris after five years at the Sorbonne, returned and decided to build a country hotel. He started by using his own hands and taking the bulk of his material, stones and sand, from the river. Everyone thought he was mad but the result is a triumph of good taste, imagination and determination.

The Altiani bridge

Within the Venacais it is easy to drive to the hill villages or to plan gentle walks that for the most part follow ancient trackways or mule paths. At 3.5km from E Caselle the Vecchio, flowing E, joins the Tavignano and near the confluence the latter is crossed by the *Altiani bridge*, a fine stone bridge built by the Genoese and widened this century. Locally it is called the 'Laricio bridge' because just before it was finished a great Laricio or Corsican pine trunk was driven against it by flood waters and nearly wrecked it. At the end of the bridge, on the left bank, is the little chapel of *San Giovanni Battista* (10C or even earlier) which has recently been cleaned out and lovingly restored after having been used as a bergerie for a long time.

Going S from Venaco, 10km down the N 193 is Vivario, 44km from Ponte Leccia. *Vivario* (Vivariu, 650m, 800 inhab.) is surrounded by the forests of Vizzavona, Cervello and Sorba. The ruins standing on a hill overlooking the station, with the romantic name of Arabie Petrée, are those of one of a line of forts built by the Genoese to 'pacify' the interior.

There are two routes to the E coast from Vivario, both of them taking time and both providing magnificent experience of the Parc. The D 343, the most northerly route, passes through *Vezzani* (785m, 700 inhab.), on the NE outskirts of the Forest of Sorba, where there is a long-established copper mine. From October to November the Corsican pine cones are gathered and dried out in Vivario on a kind of malting floor to separate the pine nuts which are then packed and sent to the mainland. The road from Vezzani joins the D 344 at the E end of the Défilé de l'Inzecca and continues towards Ghisonaccia and Aléria.

The D 69 leaves Vivario by the SSE and passes by the Col de Sorba (1311m), where there are magnificent views, to *Ghisoni* (658m, 950 inhab.; see Rte 9). Here the D 344 branches off to the E, passing through the Défilé des Strette and the Défilé de l'Inzecca to meet the road from Vezzani and continue to the E coast.

Taking the D 69 due S from Ghisoni the road runs parallel to the Fiumorbu to the E, beyond which lie the twin peaks of Christe Eleison (1260m) and Kyrie Eleison (1535m), so named when members of the proscribed sect of the Giovannali (see Rte 9) were burned alive after being captured during the Papal crusade against them in 1362. An old priest defied the bishop to say a Mass for the dying and at the first words of the Kyrie Eleison a white dove flew in a circle above the burning martyrs.

The Col de Verde (1289m), 17km from Ghisoni, is the pass that joins the valleys of the Fiumorbo and the Taravo and is surrounded by beech groves. 22km S of the Col de Verde is *Zicavo* (Zicavu, 727m, 773 inhab.), set among chestnut and beech-covered mountains. This is a centre for cross-country skiing and for climbing Monte Incudine (Corsican for anvil, the shape of a rock on the ridge).

Monte Incudine (2136m) was a much longer expedition from Zicavo in the past than it is today, now that improved roadways have made it easier to get to a closer starting point. Take the D 69 going S towards Bocca di a Vaccia and Aullène. Watch out for a rough forest track going left at 9.5km from Zicavo, the D 428 which crosses the beech woods of the Bosco di u Corscione (the Fôret Dominiale de Corscione), climbing through a mountain landscape where there are occasional fine views of the Taravo valley glimpsed between the trees. After 7km there is a track to the right leading to the *Chapelle de Saint Pierre* (San Petru, 1360m), a small, simple building. There is a primitive sheltering place nearby which is suitable for camping (but take all the usual precautions). A few hundred metres before the chapel track the main path leads to the right towards l'Incudine, the summit of which is reached in 4½ hours. Some may choose to leave their vehicles here or near this point. It depends very much on the toughness of the car and height off the ground. From here on for the 5km to the Bergerie de Cavallara it is rough going with boulders on the track and streams to be forded, but the route is negotiable by Land Rovers, jeeps and similar sturdy vehicles. All cars must be left, in any case, at the Bergerie de Cavallara from which point the forest track goes down into the valley where one picks up the red-and-white waymarks of the GR 20. Follow the GR 20 by the footbridge across the Casamintellu stream and then up its right bank through beech forests to a wide clearing and the Refuge de Pediniellu (1620m), a typical Parc refuge, this one has room for 24. From here it is 2 hours' walking following the GR 20 way-markings to the summit of Monte Incudine which is marked by a cross. View to the S of the jagged Aiguilles de Bavella, with Monte Renoso to the N, and the sea to the W and E.

The Forest of Bavella, by Edward Lear

From here SW to *Quenza*, starting along the GR 20, is about 5 hours. Instead of crossing the Col de Bavella however fork off to the right 2½ hours from the peak of l'Incudine, down the track past the Bergeries de Saparello and to the Zonza–Quenza D 420 road. 3 hours from the summit of the mountain, taking this route, there is the refuge of Asinao (1600m) which has room for 28.

From Vivario, 44km S of Ponte Leccia, the N 193 continues SSW, in 2km passes the Col de la Serra (804m) and soon enters the *Forest of Vizzavona*. One of the largest and most beautiful Corsican forests, it is relieved of coniferous monotony by the mixture of beech with Corsican pine. A fork to the right, 4km beyond the Col de la Serra, loops down through the trees to the *Gare de Vizzavona*. Apart from the station there is little there except some retired but interesting rolling stock and a few tree-surrounded houses of generous 19C proportions and style which were once hotels when Vizzavona-Gare (920m) was a popular summer mountain resort with those useful direct links by rail with Ajaccio and Bastia. There are still small hotels and summer visitors and it is above all a very important centre for both forest walks and mountaineering.

A starting point common to a number of expeditions is the hamlet of *La Foce*, a kind of rural suburb of Vizzavona, 2.5km S on the N 193. From La Foce, and the GR 20 which crosses the N 193 just above the village at the Maison Forestière de Vizzavona, paths which are mostly way-marked lead to: *les Cascades des Anglais* (these small waterfalls can be very small in a dry summer; the origin of the name is still a mystery); the ruined Genoese *Fort de Vizzavona*; *le chemin des Deux Ponts*; *La Madonuccia* (stones which suggest a statue of Our Lady, with fine views of the Gravona valley, the S face of Monte d'Oro and Sant'Elisio). All these walks are easy, taking no more than 2–3 hours and offering a variety of forest and mountain scenery. There is little point in giving details of itineraries as information and advice is willingly given by local people who are also very helpful when one considers planning expeditions to three of Corsica's principal mountains which can be reached from Vizzavona.

A. Monte Rotondo

Monte Rotondo (2822m) is the highest and furthest of the three local mountains. Allow 6 hours or so each way whether following the valley of the Manganello or that of the Verghello. Both valleys can be reached from the N 193 going N towards Corte, the first by turning left to Canaglia and driving as far as the Maison Forestière de Busso. Leave the car here and walk on for 4km past the hamlet of Canaglia to the Tolla waterfall where the GR 20 is joined, just before the Bergeries de Tolla (shelter possible here at most times). Follow the GR 20 to the Bergeries de Gialgo and then to the Refuge de Petra Piana where the GR 20 is left for the path going due N to the lake and the summit of Rotondo.

The Verghello valley route is reached by turning left at the Pont du Vecchio further N along the N 193 and following the track around the Bergeries de Puzzatello to a point just below the Solibello Bergerie, beyond which there is a parking place. From here it is about 5 hours' walk to Rotondo, taking 1½ hours to the Bocca Tripoli from which, in 2 hours, the Bergeries de Muraccioli are reached, where there is shelter for the night or in bad weather. Usually the bergeries are occupied in late spring and summer by shepherds and members of their families *en transhumance*. They are helpful about camping there but remember that they are earning their living and should be shown respect and courtesy by those passing through. Just under 2 hours from the bergeries the Lac du Monte Rotondo is reached. (For description of the lake and mountain, and ascent from the Restonica valley see Rte 14.)

B. Monte Renoso

There are three ways to the summit of Monte Renoso from Vizzavona. Renoso (2352m) occupies the region that lies between the Cols de Vizzavona and de Verde and the climb from the Ghisoni side is now made much easier by being able to drive to the ski station at the Bergeries de Capanelle.

From Vizzavona it takes 8½ hours to reach Renoso by the GR 20 route that begins near the Maison Forestière de Vizzavona, following clear and well-marked forest paths to the Bocca Palmente (1645m), a walk of about 2¾ hours. At the Capanelle ski station follow a track which is cairn-marked from the top of the ski-lift W to a stony plateau (about 2.25km) and turning S ascend to the summit. This is about 3 hours from Capanelle.

There are two other ways to climb Monte Renoso, one by the valley of the Gravona (5 hours) and the other by the Punta di l'Oriente (2112m; 6 hours). Seek local advice as to which of the three routes, according to prevailing weather and season, is recommended. From the summit there is a panoramic view of the whole of southern Corsica, to the sea on both W and E coasts and to the Straits of Bonifacio and Sardinia. Below to the N lies the *Lac de Bastiani* or Bastani (2090m) flanked on either side by a tiny lochan. For most of the year there are *neves* (blocks of crystalline ice and snow welded together by alternating frost and sun) around the shores but the trout and char survive happily.

C. Monte d'Oro

Michel Fabrikant, that great authority on Corsican mountains, says that the name Monte d'Oro is a form of the old Celtic root from which are derived many names applied to water such as 'torrent', Durance and Dordogne, Monte d'Oro being the source of torrents and rivers in this region. There are several routes from Vizzavona to Monte d'Oro (2389m) and, if so inclined, a round trip may be made.

One climb of 10–11 hours starts from the hamlet of La Foce. Take the Agnone road, the one that leads to the Cascade des Anglais, and park when the road comes to an end, where the GR 20 passes. Follow the GR 20 to the Bergeries de Tortetto (1364m) which are just to the S of the GR 20 among the beeches (2 hours to here), cross the Agnone by the ford·and leaving the GR 20, climb the pebbly slopes to the Col du Porc (Bocca di Porco, 2159m) by a track to the right. Another hour's climb brings one to the summit of Monte d'Oro with a view (if it is clear or sufficiently early in the morning) of Cinto and Rotondo to the N, Renoso and Sardinia to the S, to the E the sea and the Tuscan Isles, and to the W the white buildings of Ajaccio and the sea beyond. Allow about 4 hours for the return to Vizzavona by the yellow way-marked route around the N shoulder of Monte d'Oro. In the first hour on the way down there is a tiny grassy plateau surrounded by steep escarpments and just above it the houses of Vizzavona can be seen through a gap in the rocks. This path is more a natural stairway and is aptly named La Scala. After 2 hours, and nearly half-way down, with the most difficult descent done, one reaches the Bergeries de Puzzatelli (1526m). They appeared to be no longer in use when I last saw them but can provide shelter. The path continues to be clearly marked in yellow through the Corsican pine forest, traversing the Ghilareto ravine (1080m) and crossing the Tineta stream by a ford. From thence over the Agnone by bridge, and over one more bridge back into Vizzavona and the road to the railway station.

The *Col de Vizzavona* (1163m), 3km S along the N 193 beyond the turning to the village of Vizzavona, is a plateau connecting the valleys of the Tavignano and the Gravona (rises in the Vizzavona massif, 44km long, reaches the W coast in the Golfe d'Ajaccio). From here it is

9km to **Bocognano** (Bucugnanu, 700m, 650 inhab.), a group of
hamlets scattered through the chestnut forests that surround the main
village, which is worth a visit. Next to the post office in the one-sided
main street is a tree-shaded terrace with benches from where one can
look out over the woodlands to Monte d'Oro, and a fountain.
Breath-taking and majestic, it is built of large stones, like an up-ended
cobbled street. It dates from 1883 and must have been constructed
entirely out of civic pride because Bocognano's popularity as a
summer retreat from Ajaccio had not then been established.

Bocognano possesses a bandit story as decorative as the fountain. In the early
19C a shepherd called Bonelli, who was known by the name of Bellacoscia
(beautiful thighs), lived in the valley of Pentica with three common-law wives,
sisters by whom he had eighteen children. Two of his sons, Antoine and
Jacques, became bandits in 1848 after Antoine shot the mayor, and thenceforth
the brothers ruled as undisputed masters of the Pentica gorge. Again and again
the gendarmerie tried to capture them and in 1888 the Minister of War even
authorised an expedition against the Bonelli bandits. They nevertheless eluded
the law and remained free to entertain in their maquis hide-out aristocrats in
search of a thrill, including German princesses and Prince Roland Bonaparte as
well as writers like Pierre Loti, no doubt in search of copy. On 25 June 1892
Antoine, four times *in absentia* condemned to death for murder, gave himself up
and was put on trial in Bastia where he was acquitted 'to a thunder of applause',
dying in his bed at Bocognano at around 100 years old in 1912. Jacques stayed in
the maquis until he died of pneumonia in 1897 and was buried by companions in
a temporarily-dammed river bed to comply with his wish that no man should
walk over his grave.
    Anyone in Bocagnano will tell you how to get to the old Bonelli stamping
ground in the grim gorge of Pentica, but only undertake it for the exercise
because it is more than 3 hours' walk and the houses and site have been long
abandoned.

Follow the N 193 W, closely accompanied by the railway. 9km from
Bocognano, and just beyond a bridge, a path leads left and a
10-minute walk brings one to the ruins of a medieval tower, 100m
beyond which is a bronze age *statue-menhir*, standing at the limit of
the Parc Naturel. It is 30km from here to Ajaccio.

INDEX

The intention of the index is to lead the reader to a description or reference as quickly as possible. Corsican language and spelling do not present a major problem. For example, a mountain pass in French is the term familiar to English-speaking readers, *col*. Both *col* and the Corsican *bocca* appear on maps so they are listed here under both headings. *Lavu* appears less frequently so lakes are listed here under French *lacs* and *bergeries*, mountain sheepfolds doubling as shelters appear under that heading. Mountains with the prefix Monte are listed thus, those without, e.g. La Mufrella, Paglia Orba, appear under their names. Rivers, islands and capes are listed under their names together with gorges, valleys etc. bearing the generic name.

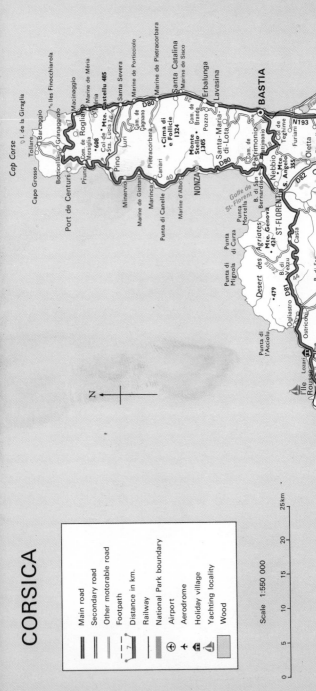

CORSICA

| Main road |
| Secondary road |
| Other motorable road |
| Footpath |
| Distance in km. |
| Railway |
| National Park boundary |
| Airport |
| Aerodrome |
| Holiday village |
| Yachting locality |
| Wood |

Scale 1:550 000

0   5   10   15   20   25km

N

Cap Corse

I. de la Giraglia

Cap Grosso

Capo Grosso

Tollare

Barcaggio

Boticella

Granaggiolo

Port de Centuri

Prunu

Com. de Rogliano

Morsiglia

Macinaggio

Marine de Méria

Meria

•608   Col de Mte.
Sta. Lucia ** Castellu 485

Santa Severa

Pino

Minervio

Marine de Giottani

Luri

Com. de
Capano

Marine de Porticiolo

Marine de Pietracorbara

Santa Catalina

Marine de Sisco

Pietracorbara

Canari

•Cima di
e Follicie
1324

Erbalunga

Com. de
Brando

Lavasina

Punta di Canelle

Marino

Monte
Stello •
1305

Pozzo

82

BASTIA

Marine d'Albo

NONZA

Santa-Maria-
di-Lota

Com. de
Teghime

Col de
Teghime

N193

Furiani

D80

40

D80

Golfe de
St-Florent

Patrimonio

Nebbio

Mte.
S. Angelo • 355

D82

Biguglia

Oletta

Olmeta

Punta di
Mortella

B. di San
Bernardino

ST-FLORENT

Santo-Pietra-
di-Tenda

Rapale

Punta di Curza

Desert des
Agriates

Mte. Genova•
421

Casta

Punta di
Mignola

•479

B. di
Vezzu

D81

B. di San
Pancraziu

Osricchione   Urtaca

Novavalle

Punta di
l'Acciolu

Ogliastro

Ostricone

44

Algodere

Lozari

Sta.-Reparata-
di-Balagna

I'Ile
Rousse

Monticello

Algajola

Marine de
Sant'Ambrogio

1976

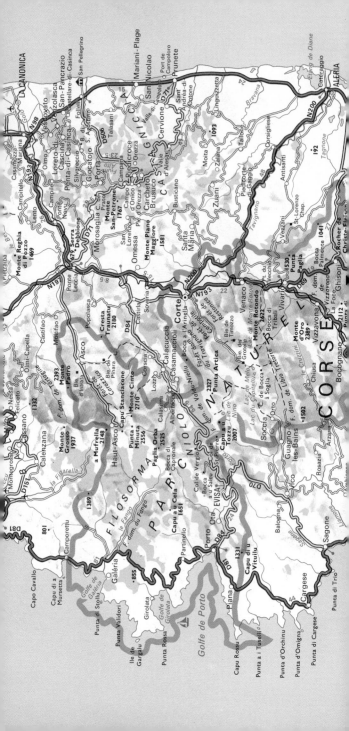